The Informal Media Economy

The Informal
Media Economy

Ramon Lobato and Julian Thomas

polity

First published in 2015 by Polity Press

Polity Press
65 Bridge Street
Cambridge CB2 1UR, UK

Polity Press
350 Main Street
Malden, MA 02148, USA

ISBN-13: 978-0-7456-7031-7
ISBN-13: 978-0-7456-7032-4(pb)

A catalogue record for this book is available from the British Library.

Library of Congress Cataloging-in-Publication Data

Lobato, Ramon.
    The informal media economy / Ramon Lobato, Julian Thomas.
      pages cm.
    Includes bibliographical references and index.
    ISBN 978-0-7456-7031-7 (hardback) – ISBN 978-0-7456-7032-4
(paperback)   1. Mass media–Technological innovations.   2. Mass media and technology.   I. Thomas, Julian.   II. Title.
    P96.T42L63 2015
    302.23–dc23
                              2014036746

Typeset in 10.5/12 Sabon
by Toppan Best-set Premedia Limited
Printed and bound in Great Britain by Clays Ltd, St Ives PLC

For further information on Polity, visit our website: politybooks.com

Contents

Preface

The Informal Media Economy is the culmination of research projects that we have individually and collaboratively pursued for a number of years. In earlier books, we studied the contours of informal media distribution and consumption and the historical background of formalization in cinema and print markets. In this book, we turn to the question of interactions: how the various elements of the media landscape come together and pull apart.

Many of the ideas in this book emerged out of our research on piracy – its history in digital and pre-digital environments, its logics and effects, and the public controversies that shape discussion around this topic. We found piracy, as a changing legal and extra-legal category that indexes a set of cultural-economic claims, to be a fascinating platform for research into media industries. In part, this book is intended as a corrective to today's partisan and unnecessarily antagonistic 'piracy debate', in which media industry problems (revenues, rights, business models) are discussed parochially without reference to wider issues in economy and society. Our basic aim in this book is to build a bridge between that media-specific discussion and a relevant, but disconnected, field of inquiry that bears very directly on those issues – social science research on informal economies.

Many people have helped us along the way. Heartfelt thanks are due to Alexandra Heller-Nicholas for her expert editing and research, and for her deep knowledge of the fringes of media culture. We are indebted to James Meese, Juan-Diego Sanin and Leah Tang for research assistance, and to Tom O'Regan, Megan Richardson, Patrick Vonderau, Stuart Cunningham, Leah Tang and Jock Given, who offered invaluable feedback on chapters. Thanks to all at the Swinburne Institute for Social Research, especially Grace Lee, Ellie Rennie and Scott Ewing, and to our colleagues in Swinburne's Department of Media and Communication and the ARC Centre of Excellence for Creative Industries and Innovation (including Stuart Cunningham, Jean Burgess, Ben Goldsmith, Michael Keane, Vijay Anand Selvarajan and Elaine Zhao), and to others who have helped along the way, including Esther Milne, Rosana Pinheiro-Machado, Ken Muise, Kath Wilson, Gerard Goggin, Eva Hemmungs-Wirtén, Barry Carr and Kathrin Schmeider. Finally, we thank the team at Polity who have worked on the book – especially Andrea Drugan, Elen Griffiths and Joe Devanny – and two anonymous readers for their helpful feedback.

The research underpinning this book was funded by a Discovery grant from the Australia Research Council (DP110101455). Our colleagues Stuart Cunningham and Dan Hunter have been wonderful collaborators on this project, and we wish to thank them for many stimulating conversations. We also acknowledge the generous participation of Joe Karaganis, Ravi Sundaram, Kathy Bowrey and other participants in our Piracy and Informal Economies Workshop, held at Swinburne in March 2011, and the Australian Academy of the Humanities for funding the event.

Some ideas in this book have been tried out in earlier publications: 'Histories of user-generated content: Between formal and informal economies' (co-authored with Dan Hunter), *International Journal of Communication* vol. 5 (2011): 899–914, reprinted in the edited collection *Amateur Media: Social, Cultural and Legal Perspectives* (Routledge, 2012, with D. Hunter and M. Richardson); 'The business of anti-piracy: New zones of enforcement and enterprise in the copyright wars', *International Journal of Communication* vol. 6 (2012): 606–625; 'Informal media economies', *Television and New Media* vol. 13.5 (2012): 1–4; and 'The fine line between the media business and piracy', *Inside Story*, 2 April 2012.

Introduction

This book is about informal media: flows of communication, information and entertainment in unregulated spaces. It is about the people who work in these spaces, from hackers and pirates to smugglers and street vendors, and the diverse media systems they create. It is also, importantly, a book about media companies and the strategies they use in their dealings with these people. As we wrote the book, we realized that the most important aspect of informal media might not be its exotic, shadowy existence in a parallel world, but its presence – sometimes unnoticed – in the most mainstream parts of the media industries, and in the most mundane and everyday media experiences. Consequently, we have become fascinated by the question of how formal and informal media systems interact. This book is the result of our research and experiments in this area.

Consider the example of iTunes, Apple's digital media player, which is firmly at the centre of our digital media retail and entertainment industries. Since its release in 2000, iTunes has become an integral part of the media economy – and our lives – in ways that few could have predicted. iTunes version 1.0 was a music player and library for our burgeoning MP3 collections. Extending the features of early freeware players, it provided randomized party soundtracks and office distraction for millions of people worldwide. Subsequent versions introduced additional features, like iPod synching, playlists, MP3 disc-burning and cross-fading. In 2003, iTunes morphed into a music store, offering a vast emporium of digital music for sale in track or album format and then, in 2005, TV episodes and movies. With the release of the iPhone in 2007, iTunes went mobile, joining us for the commute to work and the gym workout. By now, a generation of consumers was happily ensconced in the Apple economy, downloading tracks at 99 cents each, watching *Desperate Housewives* on their iPhones, and buying iTunes gift cards. Fast-forward to today, and iTunes – with its sibling, the App Store – is the premier global portal for digital content, channelling billions of dollars' worth of music, movies and software to consumers around the world.

The legend of Apple and its founder Steve Jobs has been told on many occasions, but there are aspects of iTunes' history that diverge from the usual tales of visionary innovation, suggesting different, less familiar narratives about how media industries work. We are referring, among other things, to Apple's deep reliance on – and exceptional application of – non-professional systems of media production and distribution. A great deal of the technological innovation behind Apple products, and commercial media software in general, has an unofficial pre-history of bedroom tinkering and experimentation. The basic architecture of iTunes, with its visualizers, plug-ins, metadata downloads, and playlists, came from a predecessor program, Soundjam, acquired by Apple in 2000; this, in turn was inspired by programs like the freeware MP3 player Winamp, created by three US college students in the late 1990s. The legacy of free software can still be seen today in the iTunes user interface. Similarly, the Compact Disk Database (CDDB) – now known as Gracenote – that allows iTunes to identify ripped tracks also began as an amateur, crowd-sourced effort. Apple's rise from computer manufacturer to media and communications behemoth is premised on these borrowings, deals and interactions.

Scratch the surface of iTunes and you will find many other connections to what we call informal media. Consider your own iTunes library: you probably have a rag-tag collection of audio files acquired from different places, possibly in a range of different formats (MP3, AAC, FLAC). They might have been imported from CD, copied from a hard drive or memory stick, downloaded as podcasts, or purchased from digital music stores or directly from artists. Depending on how you feel about intellectual property, you may also have a storehouse of pirated tracks that have been downloaded from BitTorrent, one-click hosting sites and MP3 blogs, or audio-ripped from YouTube. Each of these objects has its own circulatory history, and the slick iTunes interface does its best to flatten the differences between them. But there is no denying that the popularity of iTunes was premised on unauthorized sharing: in the beginning, the main reason people needed iTunes to play their MP3 files was because they had collected them using Napster, Limewire and Gnutella.

The iTunes library. Photo credit: Djenan Kozic (CC BY-ND license, 2007)

Apple and other media companies seek to reduce and contain the scope of informal activity through proprietary media formats, licensed protocols, closed media environments and digital rights management technologies, and they are often criticized on this score. But as the iTunes case shows, they also incorporate and exploit many non-commercial technologies, and they rely on consumer habits formed through informal media production and exchange. There is both a fundamental tension and – of greater interest to this book – a certain kind of *interdependency* between formal and informal media. Free software cultures helped build the technical foundations of iTunes. The MP3 file sharing craze provided the consumer competencies needed for Apple's success in music retailing. Hackers continue to redefine the platform, reverse-engineering AirPlay and Apple's strict media sharing protocols.

This is not an isolated example of interdependency between formal and informal media. Companies like Facebook rely almost entirely on users for their 'content'; software markets overflow with apps designed by non-professionals; and game developers outsource their research and development to unpaid volunteers. If we look closely, we can see interdependency in older media as well – in broadcasting, publishing, telecommunications and various other well-established media forms of the modern age. In *The Informal Media Economy* we discuss many of these historical examples. We consider unauthorized retransmissions of broadcasting, from the local, wired, redistribution network radio of the 1930s to the early cable television systems. We look at instances of informal enterprise in print culture, from parallel importing of books to unlicensed printing. We explore the way intellectual property law has shaped and responded to ground-level practices of piracy and trademark violation since the eighteenth century. So informality is not only or merely a digital phenomenon, although the technical, cultural and commercial disruptions associated with the internet have made it very visible, putting activities such as file sharing, unauthorized distribution and copying at the centre of contemporary media policy. Nor is this history a simple Western narrative of media and economic development. The informal media economy is a creature of trade and travel: it works across borders and cultures, and can tell us a great deal about other times and places.

If we wish to understand contemporary media, it is often useful to look for answers in other, less familiar parts of the economy. The history of media that we explore here is a story of firms, corporations, governments and institutions, but it is also a story of pirates, smugglers, hackers, fans and parallel importers. This means that a wide-angled view of media industry evolution is needed to make sense of current problems. To understand the challenges that the internet presents for the book trade, for example, we need also to understand the history of parallel book importing and textbook photocopying; to understand contemporary music retailing, we should know something about the history of street vending, piracy and free software development; and to understand mobile telecommunications, it is helpful to be familiar with phone unlocking businesses, reconditioners and grey importers.

Disentangling the intertwined histories of formal and informal media poses an interesting challenge for scholars of cultural industries. It also provides opportunities to rethink familiar narratives of industry change. A new wave of media scholarship is taking up this challenge, producing alternative vocabularies for industry analysis (Caldwell 2008; Holt and Perren 2009; Mayer, Banks and Caldwell 2009; Szczepanik and Vonderau 2013) and riveting histories of informal systems (Johns 2009; Sterne 2012; Brunton 2013). Such work does not comprise a consistent, coherent corpus – it represents a remarkable spectrum of ideas and disciplines. But we feel that there is a conversation that can be continued, and some useful connections to be made across the disciplines. *The Informal Media Economy* aims to get this conversation under way.

A Different Approach to Media Economy

Our general argument can be summed up as follows. Today's media landscape is characterized by a deep interdependency between formal and informal economies. Formal economies are industrially regulated. Informal economies operate without, or in partial articulation with, regulatory oversight. Neither zone can be fully understood without considering the other. Media history is a story of *interactions* between and across the formal and informal zones. These zones can be separated only for the purposes of analysis; in practice, they are engaged in constant cross-fertilization. As with a Rubik's cube, changes in one area of the media landscape produce realignments in unexpected places. In this book, we offer a series of explanatory concepts and examples to illustrate these interactions, showing how they can be analysed in a way that connects with longstanding concerns of media and cultural studies.

For simplicity, 'media' is used throughout this book to evoke a wide range of historically distinct, but now connected, consumer markets in communication, information and entertainment, from personal computing to recorded music. 'Media economy' is used in a similarly expansive way, to refer not just to media companies and the commodities they produce, but also the vast web of non-industrial activity (including non-market, domestic and criminal activity) around them. The media economy has both formal and informal elements, which are interconnected, as we saw in the iTunes example above; it encompasses the home, the street, online marketplaces, Bit-Torrent, Pirate Bay and VLC Player, as well as Sony, CBS and Apple.

It will perhaps be obvious by now that this book is not a work of conventional media economics. Although we are concerned with media economies, especially informal ones, we are not economists; we have come to this task as media scholars trained in critical analysis and cultural history, with an interest in economic structure and organization. *The Informal Media Economy* is our attempt to engage economic research from the outside, in a tangential but hopefully productive way, around issues of common concern – namely, the ongoing structural mutations in our media landscape and what this means for the way people communicate, work, consume and play.

Why study media economies at all? The topic may seem technical, even dry, but in our view it is a vital issue for social and cultural inquiry. After all, systems of communication shape our understanding of the world and help us define who we are, as individuals and communities. They are central to 'capital-P' politics and are deeply bound up with the subjective lifeworlds of the everyday. Media economies – as systems that organize this communicative capacity – are gateways for power, politics and pleasure. Defined in this way, the study of media economy has an inherently critical potential and is not simply a matter of forecasting trends, evaluating effectiveness of

particular policies, or tinkering with the levers of industry. Our attention throughout, then, is with the production, distribution and consumption of media services, goods and commodities. Although issues
of policy and politics arise throughout, we do not focus on the politics
of media texts and communities; nor do we cover underground or
resistant media systems, such as alternative publishing, activist media
or *samizdat* networks.

Media economies are important, and the way they are organized
and regulated has social consequences. So far, so good. But how
exactly should we go about studying them? *The Informal Media
Economy* is a synthetic book, which draws on – and modestly extends
– a range of theories and approaches. We like to think of this book
as a kind of 'add-on' for media industry research frameworks, like a
web browser extension or a Photoshop plug-in. It does not replace
established approaches, but it does augment them, extending their
capacity to communicate with each other in useful ways and allowing
them to see and respond to a wider array of phenomena. Attending
to informal processes, actors and systems permits a certain kind of
structural analysis, a certain kind of media sociology, a certain kind
of economic theorizing, and so on. In many cases, simply expanding
the definition of media industries to include informal agents brings a
new set of interactions and analytic possibilities into view.

In this sense, our approach can be distinguished from several
established traditions of eceonomic research on mass media – including political economy of communications, Frankfurt School culture
industry critique, neoclassical media economics and regulatory analysis. Typically focusing on consolidated and nationally regulated
sectors (publishing, film, TV, radio, telecommunications) and major
media players (whether public institutions like the BBC or corporate
behemoths like News Corporation), scholars working in these fields
have raised awareness of problems that matter deeply to citizens of
all nations – issues of competition and concentration among media
corporations, market domination, labour practices, and regulatory
failure. The political economy of communications tradition, which
stretches back to the pioneering work of Harold Innis in the 1950s
and Dallas Smythe in the 1960s and 1970s, and finds contemporary
expression in the work of eminent scholars including Janet Wasko,
Dwayne Winseck and Robert McChesney, has been a natural home
for much of this research.

Political economy, despite its acrimonious relationship with neoclassical media economics, shares a similar epistemology in that
it focuses on the 'institutions, subsidies, market structures, firms,
support mechanisms, and labor practices that define a media or

communication system', and the government policies that enable or restrain media industries (McChesney 2013: 64). Such an agenda has been forged against a twentieth-century backdrop of mass-media institutions, corporate takeovers, and structural concentration. The emergence of the internet, and the powerful new media and communications businesses that dominate it, has inspired renewed attention to the corporate sector and the problems that bedevil it, including vertical integration, monopoly and policy capture by elites – issues that seem ever more relevant in the 'winner takes all' economy of online services, apps and social networking. This orientation also reflects the norms of a particular tradition of positive analysis, in the sense that political economists tend to focus on large, publicly listed firms whose activities can be scrutinized in line with established social science and economic methods.

We are strongly influenced by both economics and political economy, and we do not intend this book as a critique of one or another tradition. Such critiques have appeared before and do not need to be made again. Let us instead make an uncontroversial claim about the limits of structural analysis. Most established ways of studying media economy take a top-down approach; they are not always equipped to deal with the more fast-moving and ephemeral aspects of our media landscape – the kind of phenomena we are interested in here. They also struggle to address a series of far-reaching changes that together have made the twentieth-century morphology of the media almost unrecognizable: the emergence of broadband and the mobile internet as new platforms for entertainment and information, for example, or the prospect of the end of the telephone system as a regulated, universally accessible communications network. As our opening story about iTunes demonstrated, a lot of significant and dynamic activity in global media happens at the edges of, or entirely outside, formal businesses and public institutions. We need to keep these edges in mind if we wish to understand how the media are changing today.

The Informal Economy: Uses and Abuses

So far, we have explained our take on media, and on media economy. Now let's consider the other, more mysterious word in our title: *informal*. The informal economy is an analytic concept that refers to a range of activities and processes occurring outside the official, authorized spaces of the economy. A challenging and contentious idea, the informal economy has generated a four-decade-long argument in social science, while curiously remaining disconnected from media studies. In this book, we want to make the case that an understanding of informal economy dynamics can greatly enrich how we think about contemporary media industries, but first we need to consider what this term means and where it has come from.

A basic definition of the informal economy would be something along the lines of 'the sum of economic activity occurring beyond the view of the state'. This includes activities like unregistered employment, domestic homework, street trade, non-market production and backyard tinkering. Most experts follow this general definition, although definitions vary from study to study. For example, some analysts include criminal activities in the informal economy, while others do not. This slipperiness is part of the character of informality. As Manuel Castells and Alejandro Portes (1989: 11) note, the informal economy is probably best understood as 'a common-sense notion whose moving social boundaries cannot be captured by a strict definition without closing the debate prematurely'.

These moving social boundaries can be seen in the range of normative claims made about the informal economy. Many commentators argue that informality is a threat to modern governance, portending the erosion of the hard-won gains of the regulating state. From this point of view, the informal economy is all about tax evasion, corruption, organized crime, under-the-table employment, unsafe workplaces and exploitation. But the informal economy is about desire as well as danger. Some ideas about informality have a utopian character, whether in the form of a romantic longing for a pre-modern, trust-based, face-to-face society; a quicksilver 'new economy' freed from the shackles of over-regulation; or a laissez-faire dream of unfettered individual entrepreneurialism.

Research on the informal economy began in the postwar years, and reflects the sociopolitical realities of postwar reconstruction, which involved a fresh wave of organizational reform in political processes, education systems, consumption patterns, regulatory architectures and technological research and development. The modern social sciences were a central part of this process. Sociology and economics took as their primary object of analysis the paradigmatic publics produced by the institutions of the formal economy: industrial workforces, consumer markets, urban populations and broadcast audiences. Their methodologies were shaped by the governmental needs of the modern state.

Against this backdrop of strong formalization and positive social science, a specific strand of economic research on informal activities began to emerge, first in anthropology and development studies,

An informal marketplace in Ghana. Image: Hiroo Yamagata
(CC BY-SA licence, 2005)

before migrating into public policy and administration. In the 1970s researchers began to speak of an informal economy, by which they meant activities, institutions and markets outside regular industry and beyond the purview of the state. This was a way of describing and theorizing residual economic activities that had never gone away – for example, loansharking and informal credit systems, or street vendors in developing nations – but which seemed esoteric from the point of view of postwar economics precisely because they existed outside the world of census data, GDP and state bureaucracy. A particular area of concern for international agencies, national governments and non-governmental organizations (NGOs) was informal employment, which was seen to be flourishing in the newly independent, fragile cities of the postcolonial world. Institutional research on this topic began to flourish.

While precursors to the informal economy concept can be found throughout the history of economics (Polanyi 1944; Gerry 1987), the term came to public attention in the 1970s mostly through the work of the British anthropologist Keith Hart. Hart, a specialist in West African cities, was interested in grassroots exchange and production, in how people actually made a living on a day-to-day basis. In his fieldwork in Ghana, he documented a patchwork of off-the-books activities – moonlighting, unregistered construction work, small-scale agriculture, and other kinds of unofficial (occasionally illegal) self-employment. This notion of the informal economy as a substratum of unregistered but productive economic activity struck a chord with development economists and featured heavily in International Labour Organization reports throughout the 1970s. Studies were commissioned in developing nations with the aim of measuring, tracking and harnessing informal economic activity, with a view to reintegrating this activity into the national economy.

By the 1980s the 'informal economy' was a widely recognized – albeit left-field – concept in social science, generating lively debate across a number of fields. In urban research, studies of informal housing and slums had appeared (Bromley 1979). In sociology, prominent scholars including Manuel Castells and Alejandro Portes (1989), Saskia Sassen (1988) and Stuart Henry (1981) were exploring informality in the first world, extending the discourse to include unregistered income-producing activities in rich nations. Friedrich Schneider and other economists were trying to measure the size of the informal economy as a proportion of GDP in different parts of the world. The institutional economist Elinor Ostrom, later a Nobel Prize winner, also worked widely in this area (Guha-Khasnobis, Kanbur and Ostrom 2006).

With time, the political complexion of informal economy research changed. As Hart (2009) argues, while the idea was first used as a shorthand for European economists struggling to understand the economic structures of third world nations and to assimilate this reality into their own worldviews, in the 1980s the idea began to acquire a new flavour as informalization became an official policy doctrine. Economic liberalization of the Reagan and Thatcher years – characterized by privatization of state assets, downsizing of public workforces and the winding-back of tariffs and subsidies – shifted the economic policy pendulum away from the active Keynesian state towards liberalization. Commitment to structure was giving way to an obsession with flexibility. Four decades on, after the global financial crisis and the long Western recession, the pendulum may perhaps be swinging the other way, as many countries make tentative moves to re-regulate areas of the economy previously characterized by laissez-faire sentiment (especially speculative finance), address the challenge of transnational tax evasion and bring more economic activity into view of the state.

Looking back at this long debate over the informal economy, we can make a few observations about the idea and its enduring impact on the way we think about economic life. First, in the wake of this wave of research and policy debate, there has been a general shift in socioeconomic thought towards a more relational conceptualization of 'the economy'. Once it was established that the informal economy was real, and that it was growing in many nations, people began to ask how it interacted with the formal economy. Early studies in the structuralist vein posited a fundamental separation between formal and informal economies, which were often equated with developed and peasant economies – witness Milton Santos's 1979 book, *The Shared Space: The Two Circuits of the Urban Economy in Underdeveloped Countries*, the cover of which memorably juxtaposed a peasant market and a modern factory. But over time this viewpoint was replaced by a more dynamic model of how formal and informal economies are connected, which stressed the mutually constitutive interactions between different parts of the economy. It came to be accepted that the formal and the informal are connected in complex ways: developments in one part of the economy typically have knock-on effects elsewhere. Castells and Portes (1989) describe this as the 'variable geometry' of formal–informal relations. Current research develops this line of thinking, emphasizing *interactions* rather than separation.

A second consequence of informal economies research has been a productive *diversification* of the terms, concepts and vocabularies used to describe economic life. In the wake of the informal economy debates and associated developments – including the poststructuralist turn in economic sociology and geography, and the take-up of feminist economic methodologies – there are now many competing models and metaphors for economic inquiry, all aiming to capture dimensions of economic life not visible in the discipline's traditional language. To name a few, we have Hart's informal economy model, the 'alternative economic spaces' of Leyshon, Lee and Williams (2003), the 'plural economies' of Laville (2010) and Gibson-Graham's 'diverse economies' (2006). Slightly further afield, in the Bourdieuslan tradition of cultural economy, new forms of 'capital' – 'cultural capital', 'social capital' and 'symbolic capital', for example – have become major objects of study. The result is a rich analytical vocabulary for conceptualizing economic processes in ways that expand the toolkit of neoclassical economics – a shift that owes much to the informal economy debates. Diversifying our concepts in this way enables creative thinking about economic life that does not rest with apparently settled concepts ('rational choice', 'GDP', 'utility') but tailors its concepts to suit actually existing economies while also inventing new epistemologies and languages. In their call for a renewal of economic theory in social science, Julie Graham and Katherine Gibson argued for a vision of 'diverse economies' in which value is 'liberally distributed rather than sequestered in certain activities and denied to others, and economic dynamics [are seen] as proliferating rather than reducible to a set of governing laws and mechanical logics' (Gibson-Graham 2006: 60). The kind of media industry theory we offer here owes a great debt to this strand of heterodox thinking.

In summary, the informal economy should be understood as a contested idea rooted in developmental theory, in postcolonial social science and in the postwar expansion of the state. The very idea of the informal as the space outside the formal, organized economy only makes sense within the context of a modernizing optic, committed to a certain 'path of development'. Many nations are at a point in history where informality is noticeable as a policy issue precisely because more of the economy is formal than ever before. As Saskia Sassen notes, 'The national is still the realm where formalization and institutionalization have all reached their highest level of development, though they rarely reach the most enlightened forms we conceive' (2008: 1). In such situations the informal economy inevitably has a whiff of exoticism, which may be dangerously seductive. Yet the idea is a very useful one, because it dissolves established categories and reconstitutes them in interesting ways. Informality is essentially about the unmeasurable, the uncertain and the unsettled; it's about rapid change, transformation, and things we don't fully, and may never, know. The power of the idea was an invitation for researchers to view ostensibly stable objects of knowledge from the perspective of this uncertainty.

What is the relevance of all this to media industry studies? Two lessons from this literature inform the arguments in this book. The first is about economic plurality. Transposing the pluralist framework of the informal economy into media industry research allows us to analyse media industries in a more multidimensional way, bringing into view not just the usual suspects (firms, consumers, governments), but also a wide range of other informal actors, from fansubbers and freeware developers to hackers and tinkerers, driven by both economic and non-economic motivations. Media industry research can learn a lot from this kind of thinking. Just as the concept of an informal economy denaturalizes the taken-for-granted notion of 'the economy' by revealing its fundamental but concealed elements, the idea gives us new ways to define, debate and analyse media industries.

A second lesson is about interdependence: the way informal economies shape formal economies, and vice versa. At its best, research on the informal economy goes beyond breathless description and dutiful documentation of minor practices to reveal something more interesting: the tango of mutual influence between formal and informal worlds. This is something media industry studies has often struggled with, torn between the top-heavy rigidities of political economy and institutional analysis, on the one hand, and, on the other, the bottom-up orientation of fan studies and cultural studies. It has usually been difficult to reconcile these planes of analysis in a satisfactory way. Throughout this book we aim to show how the volatile arrangement of formal and informal elements within media industries are continually changing, and how different parts of the whole are connected. We try not to privilege either top-down or bottom-up views but seek to move between planes of analysis and across different spaces of production (workplaces, studios, bedrooms), distribution (stores, street markets, digital shopfronts) and consumption (homes, phones, desktops), in different parts of the world, to give a sense of this variability.

Chapter by Chapter

This book is divided into seven chapters. The first chapter explains key concepts and our overall approach. Each subsequent chapter explores a current problem or debate in media studies, public policy and social science. Our approach in these chapters is to use an informal economies perspective to reconsider and extend these debates. Some chapters deal with regulatory issues; others consider more subjective experiences. Each topic has been chosen because it is contentious, fast-changing and poorly understood, and because it connects with another areas of scholarship that are relevant to the informal economies literature, such as economic geography or labour economics. The chapters engage with a select group of issues – they show some of the possibilities of our approach, but they do not cover everything. We are well aware of how much we have not addressed. One day we would like to write a second volume for this book which would cover a set of further issues we've not had space to deal with here. For the moment, we hope this present array of topics gives a useful guide to the potential applications and scope of the informal economy 'add-on'.

Chapter 1, 'Formal and Informal Media', sets out our approach to media industries analysis using, for the sake of consistency, the example of television. We introduce the idea of a spectrum of formality in the media economy, explain how elements of media industries are differentially positioned along it and show how actors migrate across this spectrum over time. Examples are drawn from broadcast and digital video industries in nations from India to Britain. The chapter also establishes a lexicon for the economic interactions that concern us throughout the book. We identify *functions* that informal activities perform within formal markets (gap-filling, incubating, outsourcing, taste-testing, priming and educating), *effects* that these activities can have on formal markets (from substitution to market extension and reconfiguration) and *controls* (from restriction to promotion). Finally, we illustrate these with examples of the BBC's interaction with informal actors, including fans and content pirates.

Chapter 2, 'Entrepreneurs', introduces people who have built businesses at the border of formal and informal economies. We discuss four influential and archetypal categories: the geek entrepreneur, the hip hop mogul, the pirate kingpin and the enterprising enthusiast. Telling the stories of how particular individuals have worked across the formal–informal boundary, sometimes in illegal ways, this chapter aims to revise and extend the ubiquitous heroic histories of media innovation. It shows how particular economic identities are fostered in entrepreneurial media culture. Along the way we meet a range of colourful characters, from Kim Dotcom to Jay-Z.

Chapter 3, 'Work', is about labour. In contrast to the glamorous entrepreneurs who straddle the lines between formal and informal media economies, there is the banal, often exploitative reality of everyday labour in media industries. In this chapter we consider some of the controversial labour arrangements observed at the fringes of the media economy, and the issues they raise for workers and policymakers. We also discuss how freelancing, outsourcing and other modes of informalization fit into the wider patterns of media globalization. These issues are considered in the context of the wider creative labour debate, whose key tenets we examine critically. The final section of the chapter considers policy solutions and the sometimes unpredictable effects of labour regulation in media work.

Chapter 4, 'Geographies', looks at the spatial dynamics of international media trade. Here our focus is on the issue of parallel importation, and how it fits within the market segmentation strategies that formal media companies have developed over the years to organize their global operations. Practices of unauthorized or unlicensed trade bring into focus the tensions that arise at the interface of formal and informal markets, and of discrete national borders. We discuss examples that demonstrate the multifaceted nature of this relationship – from the Thai textbook trader Supap Kirtsaeng, and his role in one of the most important US copyright cases in recent memory, through to electronics retailers in Hong Kong, India and China.

Chapter 5, 'Regulation', explores the governance strategies that seek to control media activity. Media and technology cultures are governed in complex ways, from direct state oversight through to private enforcement and technological codification. There are also informal modes of regulation, in which ground-level participants are enlisted as agents of governance. In this chapter we offer three case studies, each illustrating a different aspect of these processes. First, we look at the rise of app-enabled transport network companies like Uber and Lyft, exploring the policy questions they present for regulators. We then consider the case of wireless spectrum allocation, and how current regulatory approaches to open spectrum wireless have created a delimited space for informal innovation. We also look at the sphere of copyright enforcement, an increasingly privatized realm, and the regulatory failures that have led to the rise of new enforcement industries.

Chapter 6, 'Brands', returns to intellectual property, one of the most fundamental aspects of the formal economy. Brands have a remarkable formalizing power: they lend a degree of stability and organization to inherently chaotic consumer markets. Trademarks offer a legal structure to brands, but they remain vital elements in the informal economy. Successful brands are leaky; they rely on a type of circulation that is necessarily impossible to totally control. This chapter explores how brands 'work' in the hazy space between formal and informal economies, with examples including the complex IP management of James Bond and Sherlock Holmes through to controversies around trademark violation in adult cinema, brand clans in Brazil and pirate videogame brands in Colombia.

Chapter 7, 'Metrics', is about the politics of measurement. A characteristic feature of the informal media economy is that people are always trying to measure it: media companies, government institutions and market researchers have all created techniques for quantifying illegal downloading, social media chatter, unregistered media imports and consumer appropriations of brands. Whole segments of the media industries – from media ratings to brand protection – have emerged to satisfy this desire for data on informal activity. In this chapter we consider connections between these media-specific phenomena and long-running debates among social scientists and economists about how to measure informal phenomena.

Finally, in the Conclusion, we survey some recent developments in informal economies debates and likely future tendencies.

In contemplating alternative paths for media industries research, this book looks forward, sideways and also backwards. Media studies has a tendency to want to reinvent the theoretical wheel with every new technology, as though social networks or mobile phones required a whole new conceptual apparatus. In this book we hope to show

how media studies can profit instead from the accumulated wisdom of four decades of theorizing in an adjacent social science field. As media scholars, we have inherited a largely unused set of tools for thinking through the relationship between formal and informal economies. Many of these insights are directly relevant to current debates and problems in our fields. We feel it is time for media researchers to start engaging with the extraordinary conceptual and empirical resources generated around the problem of informality, so this book offers some concepts and ideas to get the discussion started. We hope you enjoy the experiment.

1

Formal and Informal Media

Television is a strongly regulated and centralized medium that has long been crucial to modernizing projects. From the early state control of television broadcasting before the Second World War, to technological developments drawing on wartime research and development, and the medium's mass appeal in postwar consumer economies, television was born in a period of remarkable formality. Today, many of these formal features are still in play. Broadcasting is a clearly defined global business with high barriers to entry and a limited pool of competitors. It attracts considerable scrutiny from state regulators, civil society groups, unions, business competitors and consumers. In most nations, broadcasters adhere to strict conditions regarding content and advertising and pay licence fees to the government. States control their radio spectrum and, in many cases, fund, or otherwise expect public broadcasters to fulfil, cultural policy objectives. Commercial television is the province of large, consolidated and diversified companies like Comcast and BSkyB (controlled by News Corp). These are among the most profitable, stable and regulated media companies in the world.

But this is not the end of the story. Throughout the television sector there is a wide variety of informal actors, from unlicensed broadcasters to pay-per-view pirates and grey hardware vendors. Anyone who has ever downloaded *Breaking Bad*, purchased a smart card from a stranger or leeched off a neighbour's cable connection has, wittingly or not, encountered the informal TV economy. Sometimes this informal economy dwarfs its legal counterpart, effectively becoming the norm. India is famous for its intricate system of off-the-books cable connections, run by local entrepreneurs – cable *wallahs* – who provide cheap, customized programming to their neighbourhoods. Pirate DVDs provide a bounty of content, and homes are connected using intricate networks of DIY wiring. Revenues – if declared at all – are underreported, and retransmitted content is probably unlicensed. Nonetheless, this system is massive and ubiquitous. More Indians get their TV from a local cable *wallah* than directly from any corporation. Nobody really knows how many viewers the informal cable economy serves in India; nor do we know how many programmers, card vendors, installers and repairers it employs. But the numbers are likely to be higher than the equivalent numbers for the legal cable business. Ravi Sundaram describes this economy as a form of 'pirate modernity': 'private enterprise without classic capitalists, or classic workers, or legal industrial estates, without brands or legal monetary rents to the state' (2009: 104).

It is perhaps tempting to think of these two worlds – the formal economy of corporate broadcasting and the informal, off-the-books TV economy – as existing in parallel, like train tracks that never cross, but this is not the case. Formal and informal economies are connected by exchanges of personnel, ideas, content and capital (we call these *interactions*). If we look back at the history of television we see that many formal companies started out as signal pirates before transforming themselves into legitimate operators, some even changing the rules of the game to suit themselves. Other formal companies rely on informal agents for market intelligence, technological innovation or free labour. Conversely, pirates depend on formal businesses for most of their content. Many also aspire to a career in the legitimate media sector, and frequently collaborate with established players when it is mutually beneficial to do so.

Understanding informality and formality in this way – as connected and co-dependent – invites us to view media in a new light. Too often, media industry change is presented as a singular trajectory: according to one reading, a one-way process of consolidation, corporatization and rationalization; according to another, ongoing fragmentation and disintermediation. In what follows, we offer a different kind of story about media industry history, which emphasizes the way formal and informal actors, from the largest corporations to the fly-by-night sole traders, are intertwined and interacting. This chapter introduces some analytic tools that can usefully interpret these interactions. Beginning with a simple binary (formal/informal) we build up to a dynamic model. Most examples are from one particular area of the media landscape, television – a relatively formal industry with enduring informal dimensions. Through these examples we tell a more general story about how formal and informal activities interact as a medium emerges, establishes and adapts.

From Binary to Spectrum

Analysing interactions between formal and informal media worlds requires us to think holistically about the media environment. A useful starting point is to ensure that our horizon is as inclusive as is possible, that it includes both the multinational broadcasters and the pirates. Most models for media industry analysis restrict their focus to the formal players, and if the informals are represented at all, they are merely noise around the regular system. We prefer to think about the informal economy as already integrated into the wider landscape, and to view media industries as encompassing both formal and informal sectors from the outset.

To represent this diversity, imagine a simple one-dimensional spectrum with formal systems located at one end and informal systems at the other (see Figure 1.1). Rather than a binary division, this schematic views informality/formality as a continuous line. Differences between the systems are variances of degree rather than fundamental oppositions. The line that connects the cable pirates and the CEOs is continuous, and – as we will see later – circuitous. From this starting point, we can begin to see systems, entities, actors and economics that combine formal and informal elements. Our 'mid-spectrum' example, YouTube, has both elements. The platform functions as a promotional vehicle for professional producers and a distribution system for unauthorized uploads and amateur content. The middle ground has not been easy territory: in fact, YouTube's position in this media landscape has been hotly contested. Broadcasters, producers and distributors have all sued YouTube at various points, challenging the legal status of this open, video sharing platform. YouTube survives because it has won most of these battles, but many other internet-based media services have failed. The attributes that distinguish the formal and the informal are often the result of such

Figure 1.1: a spectrum of formality

conflicts. When we look closely at the establishment of boundaries, through legal change, regulatory realignment, corporate fiat or other forms of official power, we find that the boundary between formal and informal actors – between pirates and legitimate broadcasters, for example – often turns out to be movable and permeable.

The history of cable television in the United States provides a clear example of the contingency of these boundaries. Early cable companies like Bob Magness's Tele-Communications Incorporated (TCI) were essentially free-riders: they rebroadcast the free-to-air signals of the national TV networks (Robichaux 2003). Entrepreneurs prospered by picking out neighbourhoods where over-the-air signals were poor, then installed basic cabling and energetically signed up TV-deprived residents for low monthly payments. They did not have permission from broadcasters to use their signals in this way. From the point of view of the major networks, this was piracy or 'signal theft'. Carriage disputes of this kind remain endemic in multi-platform television systems. Since 1992, US law has required 'transmission consent', formalizing a system of payments back to the networks. A similar conflict – with a different outcome – has marked the emergence of internet streaming services. Former Paramount and Fox executive Barry Diller backed a company called Aereo, a 'loophole

Bob Magness. Image: Denver Post via Getty Images (© 1985)

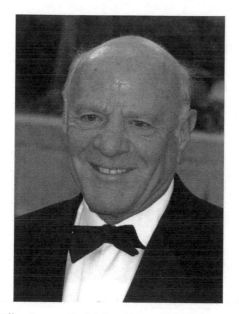

Barry Diller. Image: David Shankbone (CC BY licence, 2009)

start-up' that began by allowing its subscribers to watch live broadcast TV over the internet. Aereo's service was useful for cable 'cord-cutters' and for people who live in areas with poor reception or have no free-to-air antenna, but the legality of Aereo's business model was always uncertain. Aereo did not pay networks for their signals; it presented itself as a personal video recording service, using 'farms' of thousands of tiny antennas (one per subscriber), capturing broadcast signals that were then streamed to the devices of individual customers. Predictably, the networks sued Aereo for copyright violation. Aereo won the first round, but a Supreme Court ruling in 2014 disagreed and spelt the end of Aereo's operations.

This story of regulatory uncertainty and mobile legal boundaries is common to many parts of the world. Throughout Mediterranean Europe, broadcasting was an extra-legal activity for decades. Greece had a tightly state-controlled TV environment until 1987 when it underwent a rapid and messy process of deregulation. The result was a proliferation of local operations run by aspiring moguls. Unlicensed stations sprang up overnight. These operated as legitimate businesses, screening advertisements for clients and creating their own programming, but were technically illegal because they had no official authorization to broadcast. Around 50 per cent of the movies they screened may also have been pirated (USTR 2001). Italy is another interesting

Silvio Berlusconi. Image: Roberto Gimmi (CC BY-SA licence, 2006)

case. Since the 1970s, Italy's loose system of television licensing meant the distinction between legal and illegal media business was uncertain. Alongside the state-owned national broadcaster RAI, private broadcasters were permitted to broadcast their signals locally. This right to broadcast was allocated on a first-come, first-served basis, resulting in a flood of entrants into the market; by 1985 Italy had more than 1300 TV stations – the highest number per capita in the world (Noam 1987; Balbi and Prario 2010). Silvio Berlusconi built a huge media empire in the cracks between Italy's chaotic broadcast laws. Shuttling videotapes around the country, he stitched together a national advertising system and openly flouted the ban on country-wide broadcasting. His company Mediaset would become one of Europe's most powerful conglomerates, with operations in every corner of Italy and throughout Eastern and Western Europe. RAI's monopoly was effectively broken. In 1990 Italy's media laws were completely rewritten to favour Mediaset, meaning that a RAI/Mediaset duopoly was effectively authorized by the state. Built outside the law, Berlusconi's media business was given the imprimatur of the Italian parliament, and an informal empire was formalized. As Noam notes, Italy's 'transformation from state-run to privately owned TV is not the result of government policy, but was caused by the entrepreneurial initiatives of broadcast "pirates" whose efforts were later sanctioned by the nation's courts' (1987: 19).

The history of broadcasting is full of such examples, where the lines between legal operators and pirates are hard to make out. The purpose here is not to question the reputations of those businesses, but to emphasize the contingent boundary between the formal and the informal. Many private TV stations were informal because the wider broadcasting industry and culture were as well. What is currently formal may not always have been that way. Informality can be typical rather than exceptional, reflecting a nation's broader political economy, technological development and regulatory environment. In these circumstances, media business occurs in a regulatory flux where rules have yet to solidify. When they do, those in a position of power become the winners in a metaphorical game of musical chairs: they emerge victorious, able to reinvent themselves as legitimate captains of industry.

Disaggregating the Spectrum

So far we have introduced a spectrum of formality, demonstrating that there are many shades of grey between the poles rather than two neat categories. We also showed how the boundaries that differentiate formal from informal are historically contingent; they can be redrawn with changes in law and policy, as was the case in Italy. The informal economy in this sense can be pre-legal or extra-legal as well as non-legal or illegal. In the words of criminologist Stuart Henry, informality is 'integrally bound up with the process whereby law is constructed and maintained' (1983: 32). In analysing relations between formal and informal media economies, the next step we need to make is to disaggregate formality and informality into their constituent variables.

A starting point is to note the many informal practices that exist within formal organizations. These can take many different shapes. Sometimes strategic informalities are required to keep things running smoothly: workarounds are used when formal processes prove to be cumbersome or ineffective. Television networks often broadcast amateur footage of an unfolding emergency, for instance, whether or not a licence to do so has been granted. Rough-and-ready 'rule of thumb' agreements – as well as copyright law provisions in certain nations – enable TV networks to use material from other broadcasters. These arrangements are often vital to the effective operation of an industry. Other informalities are about harnessing the spontaneous and flexible aspects of enterprise, to enhance the more codified aspects of a business. Management textbooks dispense advice on how to harness the productive qualities of informality in the workplace, suggesting everything from paintball tournaments to casual Fridays. Whole areas of contemporary management are about creating strategies for eliciting *the right kinds of informality* from people. Finally, there are instances of informal practices within major companies that verge on the corrupt or the criminal. Mediaset is a fascinating example: it was Italy's largest and most powerful media company, with thousands of employees and enormous revenues (this was no off-the-books business), but it was also rife with questionable practices, including pay-offs to politicians, bank accounts in the Caribbean, and close links with the mafia (Stille 2006).

Rupert Murdoch's pay TV businesses provide another intriguing example. According to the financial journalist Neil Chenoweth (2012), who spent years researching the story, News Corporation's pay TV wing pushed the boundaries of the law. Chenoweth's revelations refer to NDS, a subsidiary of News Corporation that makes conditional access systems (the complex anti-piracy technologies that prevent consumers from accessing TV signals without payment). In this industry, the integrity of the system is everything: the pay TV business model depends entirely on restricting access to the signal to paying customers. If a conditional access system is hacked, unlocking keys can be posted online and counterfeit cards can easily be manufactured and sold, with potentially drastic losses to the broadcasters involved. Chenoweth's account suggests NDS used hackers to facilitate the widespread distribution of keys and counterfeit cards for use on competitors' systems. The alleged aim was to cripple News Corp's rivals in the pay TV and conditional access industries, thus boosting the market value of NDS and other News Corp businesses. The suggestion is that senior staff at NDS set up 'honeypot' websites to trick signal pirates into revealing their secrets, put friendly hackers on the payroll and threw others to the wolves, and used a shadowy division called Operational Security, run by former British cops and Israeli spies, to conduct surveillance, as part of 'a global policy of industrial espionage by a major wing of Rupert Murdoch's empire' (Chenoweth 2012: xiv).

Just as informality exists within corporate media, formal activities also occur within the informal economy. It is rare to find systems that are informal in every aspect. Only the most small-scale media worlds fully resist the trappings of formality; most others have at least some organized, regulated aspects. Online systems for translating TV programs offer a useful example here. The practice of fansubbing (the production and distribution of homemade subtitles, which are screened alongside shared video files) has grown exponentially in recent years, as open-source subtitle formats like SubRip (SRT) proliferate. Networks of multilingual volunteers, motivated by the

Subscene, a fansub sharing site

cultural capital that comes with being a successful fansubber, spend hours translating popular TV shows from one language into another. One can now easily download Turkish, Farsi, Mandarin or Bahasa subtitles to popular US shows within days or even hours of the programme's initial broadcast. Fansub networks are especially dynamic and efficient in East Asia, where fan-made subtitles for popular Korean, Chinese and Japanese dramas appear almost instantaneously. Websites such as Subscene, OpenSubtitles and Shooter (a popular site for Chinese subs) allow these subtitles to be easily shared between producers and fans.

As experts note (Ito 2012; Hu 2013; Mendes Moreira de Sa 2013), fansub crews are mostly informal: they exist outside the media industries in a world of ephemeral internet forums and pseudonymous identities; they infringe on the intellectual property rights of producers; they are unpaid amateurs (mostly students) without translation training. But the crews also have important formal aspects. Fansubbers are typically subject to sophisticated forms of self-regulation, driven by competition between subbing groups. Work schedules are tightly organized and rationalized, with chunks of a TV programme divvied up among the volunteers by a senior group member. Those who fail to deliver their allocated dialogue on time find themselves ejected from the group. Group membership is strictly monitored via a gatekeeping system designed to weed out inferior or inefficient creators of subtitles.

Recent developments in fansub media show an ever more complex integration between the formal and the informal. The multilingual streaming site Viki, founded by Korean students at Harvard and Stanford in 2007, is a case in point (Dwyer 2013). Viki began as an

unlicensed fansub repository that used an innovative system to divide
and allocate chunks of programming among volunteers. The site now
has more than 100,000 volunteer subbers on its books, working in
a vast array of languages. It has shed its amateur skin and become a
fully fledged media enterprise, with offices in Singapore and San
Francisco and venture capital from Indian and US investors. It was
sold in 2013 to Japanese e-commerce giant Rakuten for an estimated
$200 million (Swisher 2013). Viki's current business model involves
legal licensing of content from broadcasters – mostly anime and Asian
TV dramas from East Asian TV networks – and using its army of
volunteers to translate the content into various languages, then
streaming the subbed content to international audiences. Revenue
sources include in-programme advertising, premium subscriptions
and IP licensing (several Korean TV networks, impressed with the
quality of translation, have purchased the fan-produced Viki subs for
their own DVD releases). The end result is a slick, Hulu-like service,
built on an informal labour force, which – controversially – does not
receive a share of the revenues.

There are a few implications here for our model. The examples
above show a mix of the formal and the informal: fansubbers have
tightly organized labour practices, but weak adherence to copyright
law; major media companies are subject to formal financial regulation, but regularly employ informal practices on a day-to-day basis
(use of tax havens, for example, or secret executive payouts). Hence,
we have an array of possible criteria against which formality or
informality can be judged: we can look at a company's financial
affairs, their workplace practices, their size and scale, or the degree
of regulation. Using some of the components relevant to the fansubbing example, the schematic shown in Figure 1.2 visualizes these
possible criteria as well as the divergent results along each axis.

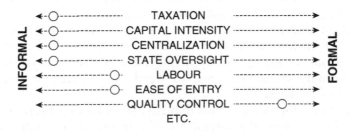

Figure 1.2: Disaggregating the spectrum

Breaking down the spectrum like this shows how constituent variables of media systems take up different positions along the spectrum simultaneously, even though they may cluster towards one end. So, while fansub groups will be positioned towards the informal end according to most criteria, many of the top groups find themselves closer to the centre when their labour practices, or the degree of organization and rationalization in the way they work, are considered. If we were to compare the fansubbers with another entity or a formal company, we might start to see unlikely connections in terms of where the dots sit along the spectrum. In other words, disaggregating the formal and informal in this way reveals structural similarities between what otherwise appear to be unconnected and incomparable media systems. Borrowing an idea from Bruno Latour's (1991) revisionist account of the modernist project, we might say that even the most established media companies *have never been entirely formal*; instead, they are a collection of activities, strategies and techniques that range across the spectrum, perhaps clustering at one end, but not very ontologically different from their informal counterparts.

Time and Transformation

Media economies are dynamic rather than static. They change over time, and so does the relation between their formal and informal elements. To account for these changes, we need to add a temporal dimension to our spectrum.

One direction of change is *formalization*, in which media systems become progressively more rationalized, consolidated and financially transparent. This can happen as a result of increased state intervention in a particular industry, which finds itself dragged into the light of regulation and accountability. Alternatively, it can occur when formerly small-scale media concerns become integrated into larger-scale structures. Specific financial arrangements, such as disclosure and reporting requirements for publicly listed companies, have a putatively formalizing effect. Particular technologies may also have formalizing properties when they become central to media businesses – for example, advanced data systems (people-meters, point-of-sale tracking). The aspiration here is towards transparency and data analysis, in contrast to informality's characteristic opacity.

Deformalization – when media activities become increasingly less transparent, centralized or governed – is also common. Regulation may be withdrawn or suspended, opening up a space for informal activity. It may overreach, with the same result; this can happen when

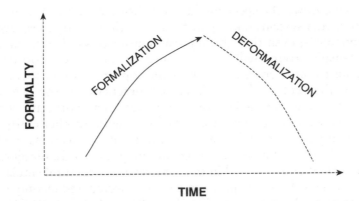

Figure 1.3: the spectrum over time

states lack the power to enforce the existing laws, or when technological change means that official systems of regulation play a catch-up
game with new fast-moving technologies and the practices of early
adopters. Media producers or distributors may even find it expedient
to relocate their activities from the formal to the informal zone, par-
ticipating in a voluntary flight from formality. These and other kinds
of deformalization occur in different kinds of media systems, across
digital and analogue platforms, and in diverse spaces and historical
periods.

Neither formalization nor deformalization are teleological processes, and neither one nor the other is dominant. A sense of history
is important here. Any claim about degrees of change will depend on
the timeframe selected for comparison. Depending on when we start
counting, the television industry may appear to be either formalizing
or deformalizing. For example, a deformalization narrative seems
appropriate when looking at television in the period from around
2002 to the present: there have been massive changes to distribution
structures, disruptive technological innovations, the emergence of a
new breed of nimble 'post-TV' companies, failing attempts at global
market segmentation, and other changes that have had the effect of
making the system less organized and settled (though the power of
many big players has not been substantially weakened). In contrast,
if we look at the industry from 2000 to 2002, when the Time Warner-
AOL merger was under way, a more centralized and top-heavy future
for television, characterized by 'a wave of massive mergers'
(McChesney 2013: 110), seemed plausible. As we have seen in this
chapter, different variables within an industry may be subject to
dynamic formalization or deformalization, so the story can be told

at a more fine-grained level as well. Consumption of TV content has been marked in recent years by deformalization, due to digital piracy. Infrastructure is a different story: the ownership of cable infrastructure in many nations, and its convergence with internet industries, is dominated by large-scale corporate structures and alliances. TV production has its own peculiar economy, marked by a dispersed array of small production companies coexisting with larger, more regularized outfits (Scott 2004b; Curtin 2003).

Given these caveats – neither direction of change dominates, neither is inevitable, and neither is infinite – how do time and transformation fit into our analytical model? Thinking about change over time requires clarity about degrees of formality, about the natural or necessary presence of formal or informal traits and about now versus then (Helmke and Levitsky 2012: 95). This emphasis on the contingencies of informality avoids the tendency to see informal systems as remnants of more organic societies, or as more truthful expressions of human creativity or freedom that exist outside history. Many informal systems are thoroughly modern in the sense that they take full advantage of and are enabled by – changes in digital technology, patterns of economic integration and leading-edge consumer behaviours. Formal and informal media economies dance together under the sign of technological modernity.

Understanding the Interactions

So far, we have set out several ways to think of formality and informality not as two discrete and mutually exclusive categories, but as a series of spectrums and dynamic trends. The emphasis on continuities and blurry boundaries arises from a belief that media systems involve both formal and informal elements; that informality is present at many levels, both outside and within even the most regulated and rationalized environments. One must also take into account the temporal dimensions of media industry change. At any given point in time, and across longer periods, particular elements of media industries may become more or less formal. Informal and formal elements may work in harmony, or they may pull in opposite directions. The next logical step is to consider the *interactions* that govern these relations – how entities, actors and activities in the informal and formal economies connect.

In Keith Hart's work (2009), we find a model for the boundaries and behaviours that divide the formal from the informal. There is the division, bridged in Hart's account by money, between paid work and domestic life. There are relations of content (the informal, unspecified 'workarounds' within formal organizations that we have already discussed); there is the negation of formality (breaking laws); and there is also the parallel coexistence of putatively residual, 'legacy' practices that may persist alongside formal models of regulation, as noted earlier. It is not hard to find instances of all these in the media, from the separations between media consumption in the workplace and the household, to certain kinds of piracy as a mode of negation, to the ethical norms and forms of shaming and exclusion that govern conduct in online communities such as the fansubbers.

Drawing on these typologies, we can identify three kinds of interaction that are particularly useful for the analysis of media industries. These three categories – *functions*, *effects* and *controls* – provide a way of thinking about the boundaries and linkages between formality and informality, across multiple dimensions. *Functions* are ways that informal elements get used within a formal media market. Functions do not of themselves change the boundaries of the formal and the informal. *Effects* describe what may happen to a particular media economy or to the broader ecosystem when informal elements are incorporated into formal systems over time. *Controls* are ways of managing, organizing or understanding informality. A few relevant examples of each interaction are set out in tables 1.1, 1.2 and 1.3. These reflect an illustrative sample of each phenomena, rather than a full taxonomy.

Functions are critically important because they show us that apparently different ways of doing things may in fact connect with each other. In other words, they reveal the enduring role of informal practices within formal systems. *Gap-filling* is perhaps the most obvious way in which informal activities are used in formal contexts: this is a kind of 'workaround' scenario, similar to Hart's (2009) notion of 'content'. This involves people using common sense and informal tactics to fix systemic problems. Some examples might be consumers sharing infrastructure, such as satellite dishes, or network employees adjusting their work schedules to suit project deadlines (staying late on a tight deadline then leaving early the next day).

Incubating is when skills and ideas developed in informal contexts are taken up in formal industries. Non-professional radio, film, theatre and musical performers are cherry-picked by established companies; start-up companies selling rights for new digital innovations are bought up by major broadcasters or media conglomerates, as a cheap means of R&D; professional content producers borrow ideas and styles from the street. In these ways, skills and concepts from the informal sector can enrich the formal.

Table 1.1   Functions: What Informal Activities Do in Formal Markets

Function	Definition	Example
Gap-filling	Informal 'workarounds' to solve practical or informational problems	Personal referral networks; rule-bending and 'practical sense'
Incubating	Growth in informal sector of skills, ideas, styles, processes that may move to formal sector	Community media organizations, amateur performance, backyard tech development
Outsourcing	Creating lower paid, more flexible labour markets outside institutional structures	Casual and freelance work, offshoring of low-value work
Taste-testing	Gauging consumer demand for a product or work outside established markets	Using informal media for market intelligence
Priming	Using informal practices to promote demand in formal markets	Viral promotions using social media
Educating	Educating consumers or businesses in the possibilities of new technologies and business methods	Crowdsourcing, social network-based messaging services, online shopping

Outsourcing (which overlaps with *incubation*) occurs when the formal sector acquires services or skills from the informal zone, or under informal conditions, because it is more efficient to do so than to rely on the usual models. Many freelance creatives in the media world work on an informal basis – compared to permanent staff, they are more flexible, paid on an output basis (resulting in fewer overheads) and can be dropped easily. Increasingly, crowdsourcing is used as a basis for efficiency-motivated outsourcing, as when users of social media platforms are called upon to contribute to branding and market research efforts for major corporations ('help design our new logo and win a $20 iTunes voucher'). The thorny ethical issues around these practices are discussed in detail in Chapter 3.

A related function is *taste-testing*. This is when formal media companies use the informal economy to measure the appetite for their products, or to assess the viability of new initiatives. The open architecture of the internet makes this kind of research easy: content producers can study download patterns or fan activity as a way of gauging market demand. A number of companies, including Netflix and the Australian publisher/digital media company Fairfax, have publicly acknowledged monitoring the most downloaded shows on BitTorrent networks as a way of estimating the market for future productions. Netflix reportedly bought the rights to *Prison Break* on this basis (Kelion 2013).

Priming is another way for formal actors to exploit informal activity: this is when the generativity of the informal economy is harnessed for promotional purposes. Jenkins, Ford and Green (2012) document many instances of corporate/crowd cooperation, as when 77 million people viewed Susan Boyle's *Britain's Got Talent* audition on YouTube. Rather than staying in the informal realm, much of this energy tends to seep back into the formal system through increased broadcast audiences, ratings and advertising spends.

Finally, *educating*. Informal services are sometimes the first places where businesses and consumers acquaint themselves with emerging technologies, services or products. Commercial social media, for example, build on the legacy of online forums and bulletin boards. The open Internet Relay Chat protocol and its predecessors demonstrated the demand for both public and private instant messaging in advance of its contemporary commercial implementations in Twitter and the direct messaging services now deployed by Apple and many others. Informal media plays a role in building popular literacy within changing technological environments.

The interactions we labelled *functions* imply some degree of intent. Even if there is no simple deployment of informal activities in the service of the formal sector, these activities are being used in some way. We call the second group of interactions *effects*, and they are generally more diffuse. Effects are changes to the original, formal market as a result of interaction with informal elements. They may concern the formal market's scope, main players or scale. Effects might involve redistribution of activities, roles, power and value between the formal and informal sectors, between different locations, and between different groups of people. It is likely that for any given example, more than one of the effects described here may be relevant.

What kind of effects can be seen in current media economies? Table 1.2 contains a few examples. *Substitution* is a term used in economics to refer to two inputs, goods or services that can be used interchangeably. In the context of interactions between informal and formal media systems, the substitution process could describe the changes when one technology or medium emerges to provide a

Table 1.2   Effects: How Informal Activities Change Formal Markets, and Vice Versa

Effect	Definition	Example
Substitution	Relocation of activity into the informal zone (or vice versa)	Lost sales as a result of piracy; direct messaging substituting for SMS
Dispersal	Market activity moves around in ways that are difficult to track	Informal streaming of TV content creating value for advertisers, internet service providers and platforms (but not networks)
Extension	Creation of additional market demand in the formal sector	Shazam sales monetizing public music listening
Revaluation	Value changes due to circulation in informal economy	Counterfeit hardware diluting brand trust; subcultural circulation increasing brand cachet
Redeployment	Take-up, in the formal sector, of technologies and methods developed in the informal sector (or vice versa)	Formal peer-to-peer networking applications, such as Skype
Reconfiguration	Change in the organizational logics of a formal market	Movie distributors reducing prices of DVDs to compete with competition from pirates

comparable service, overtaking the previous standard (examples might include the eclipse of LPs, VHS, CDs and others, or the replacement of SMS texting with internet-based direct messaging). It could also describe broader market shifts, such as loss of revenue through file sharing, in which case paid transactions appear to move into the informal zone as unpaid reciprocal exchange. Additionally, it could describe the substitution of one group of workers for another (see the description of *outsourcing* above). Analytical precision is important here. Sometimes, substitution involves a shrinking or disappearing market, as when the *Encyclopedia Britannica* was killed by Wikipedia – a classic example of a dying formal industry replaced by a free, informal structure. This was bad news for *Britannica* but good news for pretty much everyone else: Wikipedia's 'consumer surplus' is enormous. At other times, what looks like substitution may be the overall growth of a media industry. An example here is the emergence of home video rental in the 1970s and 1980s. Hollywood worried that video would cannibalize the revenue stream from theatrical exhibition, and went to great lengths to contain the video medium; but it is now generally understood that video led to overall growth for the industry, by opening up a profitable new revenue stream for Hollywood content. In retrospect, video appears to have had a substitution effect on certain parts of the theatrical sector, such as second- and third-run local cinemas, but elsewhere led to market *extension* – the creation of new markets on top of existing ones. Successful media technologies such as YouTube (which has created new advertising markets around uploaded content) or the track-recognition app Shazam (which allows smartphone users to identify then purchase the tracks they hear in stores, clubs and bars) are indicative of this kind of market extension. In the case of YouTube, as with video, this has also involved some substitution; the two effects can coexist.

In other scenarios the trend may be towards *dispersal*, when market activities are replaced by activities in a different category, or transactions move into many diffuse areas of the economy simultaneously. Sometimes transactions go overseas, or into a parallel market, or move across to a neighbouring technology, in ways that are difficult to track. The rise of home internet and mobile data subscriptions has dispersed other kinds of consumer spending, such as movie admissions and (increasingly) cable subscriptions, and has also moved much of this expenditure out of the category of 'entertainment' and into 'communications' or 'infrastructure' spending, making things harder to track. Similarly, some (but not all) of the money we used to spend on CDs has relocated to other parts of the music economy – merchandise, marketing tie-ins, and especially touring (Page 2011); and many ex-record label staff have resurfaced in fields like branding, touring, niche marketing and data analytics. Here we have a kind of substitution, but also a dispersal: revenue seems to disappear into the four winds but is actually relocating elsewhere.

At the level of individual media properties, *revaluation* can occur. Quantitatively, economic value can increase, or decrease, due to informal activity. Qualitatively, intangible value may change depending on what happens to them in the informal economy (increased street cred on the one hand; brand dilution on the other). Other common effects worth mentioning are *redeployment*, where particular elements originating in the informal economy are taken up in formal commerce (as in the use of free and open-source software within large organizations), and *reconfiguration*, when formal players restructure their business models in response to informal competition. In all cases, we must be careful not to think in a zero sum way: just because changes take place in one industry, it does not mean that an equal and opposite activity will crop up elsewhere. Formal–informal interactions are more complex than this.

A final category of interactions is controls (see Table 1.3) – strategies by formal actors that seek to manage, contain, organize, systematize or curtail informal activities. There are various possibilities. Disciplinary and enforcement mechanisms seek to reduce or contain informal activity. We have called this category of action *restriction*.

Table 1.3   Controls: Mechanisms for Managing Informal Activities

Control	Definition	Example
Restriction	Reducing informal activity through the enforcement of rules	Litigation on the part of rights owners against ISPs and individuals
Codification	Rule-making that formalizes patterns of informal activity	Digital rights management technologies, that enable limited but not extensive sharing within a household
Authorization	Extending legal and bureaucratic frameworks to encompass new phenomena	The classification of digital games; licensing community television stations
Measurement	Generating information about the size and nature of the informal sector, enabling regulation and other formalizing strategies	Government and corporate monitoring of social media and peer-to-peer platforms
Promotion	Targeted interventions to encourage particular informal practices	Government endorsement and promotion of informal activities, such as geoblock workarounds

Anti-piracy enforcement is a classic example; so too are government
censorship and rules about media conduct, such as anti-sexting laws.
A related mechanism is *codification* that involves creating new categories, rights and limitations around informal activities, thus allowing them to be controlled while also permitting a certain scope of
informality. Governance is not just top-down; other approaches seek
to bring informal activities into the fold, moving them from the
informal to the formal zone via some strategy of *authorization* (such
as licensing schemes, classification and other official recognition).
Some strategies of authorization, like broadcast licensing, not only
recognize pre-existing entities but also create a space for new media
institutions to emerge.

Measurement does not involve direct action of a positive or negative nature, but simply information-collection (though this is often
the first stage for other governmental actions). The informal media
economy is subject to a very high level of scrutiny by governments
and corporations, with techniques from torrent tracking to household
surveys. We will return to this issue in more detail in Chapter 7.
Finally, governments can also publicize the energy of the informal
economy as a solution to a pre-existing problem (*promotion*). Public
institutions in some countries are now actively encouraging their citizens to make the best use of informal technological workarounds so
as to counteract unpopular forms of market segmentation (HRSCIC
2013). Here, the innovative energies of the informal economy become
a solution to other governmental problems produced by the formal
sector.

We can make some general observations about these controls.
They can produce formalizing and informalizing consequences simultaneously: by imposing taxation, for example, governments create
not only more transparent and administered systems, but also the
incentives to work around them. The market effects, and some of the
functions, are clearly shaped by a search for lower costs or access to
markets, whether for producers in the form of cheaper labour, for
distributors as new market channels, or for consumers as lower
prices. Highly regulated media sectors such as broadcast television
necessarily erect barriers to would-be competitors; the informal sector
can sometimes provide ways of circumventing constraints. As that
example suggests, the role of government is plainly also essential: far
from diminishing the importance of states, any fluid study of informal
media must make regulation, taxation and administration central
concerns. But here we are also dealing with the broader category of
code as well as law. The rules embodied in technological designs, such
as those intended to protect the interests of rights holders, may be

just as important as statutes or official policies. Lawrence Lessig (1999) famously captured this in his epithet, 'code is law'. (Given our observation of the informal economy, we would add the word 'sometimes'.)

The approach we have proposed here in summary requires (a) imagining a spectrum, (b) disaggregating the spectrum, (c) factoring in time and (d) analysing the interactions. By doing this, it gives us a set of categories and ideas to work with. What does it look like in terms of actual media? We offer the following illustration.

Formal–Informal Interactions in Television: The BBC Case

The BBC is the quintessential formal media organization. The world's largest and most influential public broadcaster, it has long been a model public enterprise, born during a time – the interwar years – of institutional experimentation and increasing state involvement in the economy. It remains a creature of liberal government and a legacy of empire, with a Royal Charter providing its constitutional basis. It has a great national civic and cultural remit to 'inform, educate and entertain', its own governance institutions (the BBC Trust, BBC governors), extensive internal regulation, a funding stream based on its own special form of taxation (the TV licence fee) and a large (although recently reduced) workforce. The BBC is at the centre of UK media policy debate, and much of the argument is necessarily about the BBC's consequences for other formal media. To its detractors, including commercial competitors and economic reformers, the BBC's dominant position in Britain crowds out private investment and innovation – an argument that goes back to its establishment as a monopoly broadcaster. For its defenders, the BBC is a bulwark of stability and integrity against the excesses of the market.

Like most other media organizations, the BBC is engaged in a series of complex interactions with the informal realm. These occur right across the organization's extraordinary array of production, distribution and market activities. Far from compromising its purpose, these interactions are in many cases strong expressions of the Corporation's public service remit. For instance, the BBC works extensively with user-generated content, from news and current affairs to entertainment and documentary. It uses amateur footage to cover natural disasters, wars and terrorist attacks. It works with fans who promote BBC programmes in their own unexpected ways. It piloted an open-access archive, the BBC Creative Archive, encouraging users to 'rip it, mix it, share it'. It attracts talented performers and producers whose skills have been honed in comparatively informal settings: stand-up comedy, university drama, community broadcasting, YouTube or Vimeo. Strategies such as these produce several of the effects we have discussed earlier: the redeployment of informal methods and material in the formal sector; and the extension of the BBC's markets and the expansion of its audiences. In the case of some informally produced content, such as amateur news footage, it may even be that we are seeing an organizational reconfiguration, deeply affecting the conduct of journalism.

These informal and formal interactions have intensified in recent years as the BBC attempts to build on its online presence, globalize its operations and derive revenue from international audiences. One site where we see them in action is iPlayer, the BBC's internet-based service for on-demand 'catch-up' viewing. Catch-up services, enabling viewers to stream or download recently broadcast programmes, are notable features of the new digital media landscape. In our terms, they can be seen as a mechanism for formalizing the hitherto informal practices of personal recording and playback which depended on consumer equipment such as video cassette recorders or, later, hard disk recorders – in other words, they are an attempt to incorporate previously informal practices within a formal, regulated architecture. Personal recorders have given viewers a measure of control over scheduling, but they introduced a level of complexity into household audiovisual technology that could also be frustrating. From the perspective of copyright owners, recording devices opened the door for pirates; for broadcasters, viewers of recorded programmes were lost audiences, uncounted for the purposes of ratings. From the mid-2000s on, the broadband internet and the improving economics of cloud computing gave broadcasters the opportunity to regain some control. They could give viewers the chance to see programmes they missed. They could solve the piracy problem by using digital rights management to retain control over sharing and redistribution, and they could solve the metrics problem by using server data to track viewers across devices and platforms, and thereby augment traditional audience measures.

The iPlayer has not been an unqualified success. In fact, it has generated a series of controversies relating to its effects on competitors, its reliance at certain stages of development on proprietary and restrictive software platforms, and its lack of international availability. These controversies have fuelled informal responses: hacked or open source solutions for unsupported platforms, for example, when the service was restricted to Windows XP, and a proliferation of technical workarounds enabling international access (British expats and global BBC fans often use VPNs – virtual private networks – to stream iPlayer content). At the same time, in terms of the framework introduced in this chapter, we can see the iPlayer enacting some of our key governing mechanisms in a previously unregulated space: the authorization by the BBC Trust of a new framework for public service internet television, the restriction on access outside the United Kingdom, the development of new measures of audience activity and the codified rules relating to household sharing.

While the BBC itself is subject to governance from above – in the form of the BBC Trust, the BBC Board of Governors, and various legislative instruments – a more interesting issue for us is how it seeks to manage the conduct of other producers in the media economy. Intellectual property regulation is a particularly important area for today's BBC. A prolific and prodigious producer of programmes, genres, web content, stars, books, TV formats, channels, merchandise, live events and media franchises, the BBC has a lot to protect, and many rights holders to manage. Its super-brands (such as *Top Gear* and *Dr Who*) are particularly valuable. In the past, the BBC has been content to tolerate infringing consumer activity around its content, sometimes even partnering with fan organizations to promote its shows. Bacon-Smith (1992) notes that the *Dr Who* Fan Club of America had an arrangement with the BBC to become, in effect, an 'authorized' distributor of branded merchandise. As the BBC has come under increased pressure to pay its own way, it has moved to a more restrictive strategy, with active enforcement and exploitation of its copyrights and trademarks, especially within its commercial spin-off, BBC Worldwide. Non-commercial infringers, including fans who post *Dr Who* knitting patterns online (Doctorow 2008), now receive cease-and-desist letters. The BBC has hired the freelance anti-piracy company Entura International to send out internet takedown requests (TorrentFreak 2013b). Yet, as a rule, it remains tolerant of small-scale infringements, and has a general reputation for being less demonstrably muscular in enforcing intellectual property rights than most media organizations of its scale.

This attitude opens up a limited, safe space for creative interaction with BBC content, and also catalyses the production of new kinds of content around the BBC ecosystem. One small example of an informal spin-off from regular BBC broadcasting is the UK-based audio streaming website Test Match Sofa, which represents a fascinating mix of formal and informal broadcasting models. Test Match Sofa was the idea of an IT manager who had lost his job in the global financial crisis. Streamed live from his actual living room in Tooting Bec, the show began as a vehicle for alternative cricket commentary, a spin on the BBC's venerable *Test Match Special* programme, famous for its idiosyncratic and sometimes meandering style. Test Match Sofa was produced entirely outside the heavily controlled sports media industry. It is and was made by enthusiasts simply watching televised games and generating their own incisive and partisan descriptions and analysis in the form of an audio stream. In cricket journalist Gideon Haigh's words (2010), the Sofa reinvented sports broadcasting by bringing an unashamed amateurism to bear on a hyper-professionalized business, 'turning work into play, play into work'. But somehow along the way, Test Match Sofa has become a genuinely alternative source of cricket media. In 2013, when the Australian team toured India, the Indian cricket board refused to license a radio broadcaster for Australian audiences, leaving only Test Match Sofa as a provider of audio comment on the games – an ironic result, given the Sofa's comically unrestrained anti-Australian bias.

From our perspective, Test Match Sofa's relationship to the mainstream sports media involves several interesting elements. Clearly the site is a kind of tribute to a BBC programme and a certain style of mainstream media broadcasting, with parallels to fan sites developed in other genres. The effect of sites such as these is generally not to undermine or devalue the source of the inspiration, but to sustain and stimulate demand, cultivating the formation of groups of highly motivated listeners and performers. In this sense, the site is an example of what we are calling *priming activity*. If its function shifts – for example, it becomes more important as a source of information as a result of the Indian cricket board's commercial overreach – something else is going on. A different audience uses the site as a kind of workaround, to make sure that a flow of news is maintained despite the breakdown in the formal system. In this situation, and without any particular intent or design on its part, the Sofa fills a gap. None of this threatens the audiences or the viability of licensed broadcasters; any large-scale substitution of the Sofa for formal media channels seems unlikely. But there are positive possibilities: for redeploying the talents displayed on the Sofa in mainstream coverage, for extending the audience for cricket through more humorous, less reverential and formulaic treatment, and for demonstrating the feasibility of streamed audio services over the web. So while our typology attempts to describe and categorize a series of likely relations between the formal and the informal, the Sofa shows how these are combined and mixed in an actual informal media practice.

Uses and Implications

This chapter has outlined a lexicon for media industry studies – a way to talk about how industries change and how the various parts within them interact. One of our aims has been to provide an alternative to some of the more totalizing accounts of industry evolution: the drama of fragmentation, revenue loss and piracy that comes through in industry public relations; the seemingly inexorable process of consolidation and corporatization that marks political economy accounts; but also the hollow utopianism of 'digital democracy' and Web 2.0 discourse. Understanding media industry change requires an approach that can make sense of a range of effects and functions: some major, some minor, some good, some bad. We may have emphasized the positives more than the negatives, partly in response to the excesses of the industry-driven 'piracy debate' that forms the backdrop to this book. But if there is one thing that we would underscore in our account, it is that informality produces *differentiated* outcomes.

The informal economy is often good news for consumers: it means lower prices, more competition, free stuff, and better access. The informal economy also plays a significant role in the distribution of taste: it provides alternative channels of communication, together with access to content, that cross the boundaries of conventionally defined market segments. Where no formal supply exists, informal markets can satisfy demand – and by virtue of their dynamism, create further demand – for content that would otherwise not be available. In this sense, the informal media economy is an enormous reservoir of textual experience. For cultural producers in the formal economy, however, the prognosis may be more mixed. The informal economy, despite its generative capacities, can mean undercutting revenues and regulated working conditions. Substitution of formal transactions for informal ones is still common, and producers have a right to be concerned about revenue losses. (Although we must bear in mind the fact that the squeakiest wheels do not represent whole sectors.) The other thing to consider is what informality means for institutions. As we have seen in the case of the BBC, institutions can interact profitably and productively with informals, but it is very hard to create institutions from scratch using *only* the resources of the informal economy, at least not in the short term. Only a handful of significant media institutions, such as Wikipedia, have emerged this way. So, while the informal media economy means diversity and dynamism, it usually also means ephemerality, fragility, undercapitalization and – sometimes – inefficiency.

Innovation is another key theme: a vital role for the informal sector lies in providing environments where new ideas can emerge and are tested without the constraints and costs of regulatory and institutional structures. A corollary of innovation is uncertainty and unpredictability. As we've seen, cable services begin as simple infrastructures for retransmission, but without the bandwidth limits imposed by over-the-air broadcasting, they evolve into an entirely different kind of media. We have chosen not to describe technological disruption as an effect, even though new technologies play an unquestionably large part in making both informal and formal innovations feasible. This is because we see technological shifts as conditions of possibility, not as formative in themselves. Many of the transformations we are describing could not occur without the common ingredient of modern digital networking technologies, but these technologies do not explain the nature or direction of the industry changes that may follow their implementation in one or more forms. This is a key point: any given technology may be embodied in both formalizing and deformalizing innovations. Media streaming, for example, is an integral component in the architecture of YouTube, as well as the innumerable illegal streaming sites. It is also fundamental to mainstream 'on demand' or 'catch-up' video services such as Hulu and the BBC's iPlayer, both designed to bolster traditional broadcasting industry models.

Finally, a point about regulation. The connections we are describing here align with those found in the broader scholarship of informal economies, where they also help explain the persistence and dynamism of the informal sector. In that literature, considerable emphasis has been given to the ways in which the informal sector sits outside regulatory systems, and the opportunities for governments to formalize industries through taxation, licensing, measurement and the expansion of property or other rights. Because of this alignment, we would argue that there is also something to be learnt in the media context from the broader policy debates surrounding informal economies. Understanding the diversity of the interactions connecting the formal and informal economies should caution us against overly simple diagnoses and prescriptions. In the field of development studies, policymakers and researchers have often assumed that the informal sector is disorganized and unstructured, and that better statistics and more targeted regulatory interventions would underpin fairer and more prosperous industries. In practice, informal activities often turned out to be much better organized and managed than policymakers understood (Guha-Khasnobis, Kanbur and Ostrom 2006). The work of Elinor Ostrom and others on community-based rules for managing common resources provides a well-known example. In the digital environment, we see some of the same sophistication, creativity and productivity in informal networks. This complexity helps explain the failures of broadly framed, industry and government-driven campaigns against informal activity, such as 'the war on piracy'. It underlines the need for careful, longitudinal research: sometimes the copying and sharing activities that industry groups assume are substituting for formal consumption turn out to be playing more of a market-priming role.

In the chapters that follow, we apply and extend the ideas presented here to contentious and challenging problems, events and people. We consider the issue of measurement, and the task of quantifying the apparently unquantifiable; we explore the double-edged quality of contemporary media brands; we return to the problems of regulation, of cultural trade and labour on our new Grub Streets. Before these, we turn to the ways in which we understand agency and action in media change. With the informal economy plug-in, our next chapter looks at the entrepreneurs who seem to have shaped our contemporary media histories.

2

Entrepreneurs

From Alexander Bell to Carlos Slim, Ted Turner to Marissa Mayer, Berry Gordy to Lady Gaga, the story of media is often taken to be the story of the people at the top. Countless words have been devoted to the biographies of individual entrepreneurs: their humble and not-so-humble origins, their rise to power and enduring legacies, their daring deals and great escapes, their philosophies, personalities and peccadilloes. When we consider media businesses, we often think about these heroic individuals. Reflecting our inclination for human stories over structural interpretations, this way of conceptualizing the media economy – as a series of individual achievements by Great Men (and the occasional woman) – personalizes impersonal processes and transactions, condensing the contingency of commerce into bite-size stories of action and agency. The other side of the coin is the critique of great men, which is an integral element of much media studies. The celebratory lives of media entrepreneurs have their counterpart in critical business biographies and journalistic exposés that are just as focused on the singular individual as agent of change and control.

Understanding the rhetorical power of these histories is especially important in an internet economy, when the digital entrepreneur has become a paradigmatic figure for the 'new' business way. In *Fortune*'s 2012 list of the greatest entrepreneurs of our time, four out of the top five positions were claimed by internet industry figures: Steve Jobs, Bill Gates, Jeff Bezos and Google's founders Larry Page and Sergey Brin. These individuals index a conceptual shift, in which media entrepreneurs come to putatively embody, and sometimes foreshadow, wider economic and social change.

With this aim in mind, the present chapter turns a critical eye to the image of the entrepreneur and what it means for media industry analysis. Considering the commercial trajectories of some familiar and some less familiar figures, we explore how these stories crystallize particular ideas about informal media. Our argument here is that the category of the media entrepreneur necessarily includes a wide range of informal actors (YouTube celebrities, backyard technicians, informal booksellers, street vendors, virus writers, cyber-fraudsters, and so on), as well as people who work *across* the formal–informal boundary, moving activities and transactions from one zone to the other – a business model they share with peers located in the formal media economy.

It should be clear that our approach is not a celebration of media entrepreneurialism. Twenty years ago the sociologist Paul du Gay felt the need to warn cultural critics that the 'discourse of entrepreneurialism' was inextricable from 'the New Right project of an enterprise culture' (1995: 67). He was referring to the UK's post-Thatcher era of privatization and diminishing social provision. In the intervening decades, in line with du Gay's prescient study, a new raft of enterprise cultures have appeared, together with new entrepreneurial identities: the West Coast internet starter-upper, the creative industries impresario, the social sector entrepreneur, the streetwise promoter. Each embodies particular ideas about how power works in the media industries, and invites analysis on this basis.

The Entrepreneur in Context

In his unfinished *History of Economic Analysis*, first published in English in 1954, the Austrian economist Joseph Schumpeter offers an influential definition of the entrepreneur. Tracing the term's origins to the eighteenth century, Schumpeter considers the entrepreneur as the central figure of capitalism – 'the pivot on which everything turns' (1996/1954: 555). In contrast to the merchant or the landowner, the entrepreneur was a risk-taker, the harbinger of creative destruction, a visionary who creates value where it did not previously exist, and a revolutionary force in what Schumpeter felt was a potentially static system.

The Schumpeterian view of enterprise is today central to everyday economic discourse. It finds its apotheosis in flamboyant billionaire Richard Branson, whose early ventures – the recording of Mike Oldfield's *Tubular Bells* and the establishment of Virgin Records in the early 1970s – became the basis for an eclectic business empire that

Richard Branson. Image: David Shankbone (CC BY licence, 2010)

now includes 400 companies, from fitness centres to financial services. Branson is arguably the quintessential media entrepreneur of the baby-boomer age, and ticks all the boxes of the contemporary stereotype of this figure: his highly polished good looks, his private jets and his reputation for extravagant projects like space tourism. One of his accomplishments has been to relocate the libidinal energy of rock 'n' roll into the corporate sphere, making media commerce 'sexy'. Of course, relatively few people who make their money in the media business can be described as entrepreneurs in this way. Some of the most successful media businesses of the twentieth century are decidedly *un*-entrepreneurial, such as the giant East Asian *zaibatsus* and *chaebols* like Sony and Samsung, where innovation has a more collective character. As demonstrated in Chapter 1, economic concepts have a tendency to be redefined according to the values of the day.

One way to track these shifts of meaning is to compare today's discourse about the media entrepreneur with earlier images of disruptive media industry figures, such as the media mogul, kingpin or baron. In a classic 1982 study of the newspaper business, historian Piers Brendon defined the press baron in terms that seem both familiar and remote to today's understanding of the entrepreneur. For Brendon, the press baron – typified by characters like William Randolph Hearst and Lord Northcliffe – was 'a tyrant with an all-consuming appetite for success', a 'vicious, unstable, despotic' disposition, and a loathing of government interference (1982: 3–4). These individuals are still with us, of course: think of Rupert Murdoch with his Rolodex full of politicians' phone numbers. As an image of media power that evokes a feudal kind of monopolistic power, this figure is akin to the robber barons of gilded age America. Compare this archetype to the more diffuse idea of creative entrepreneurialism that was at its zenith in the late 1990s and early 2000s. Creative industries policies, widely adopted by governments in the United Kingdom, Australia and various other nations, were organized around what Kate Oakley (2011: 287) describes as a 'belief in the inherently democratic nature of small-business ownership and the liberating power of entrepreneurship'. This was a quite different idea of what being an entrepreneur entailed – a world of work that was all about small-scale start-ups, subcultures, collaboration and urban redevelopment. Self-employed DJs, designers, dance instructors and other DIY creatives were the paradigmatic entrepreneurs of this period. This media entrepreneur certainly was here to get rich, but was equally interested in being cool. Readers in the United Kingdom may recall the Channel 4 program *Nathan Barley*, which parodies this subjectivity: its main character is a DJ, webmaster, filmmaker, Apple fanboy and – in his own words – a 'self-facilitating media node'.

Today's West Coast internet entrepreneur is a different beast again. These are geeks who make millions early then downshift to enjoy philanthropic, new age pursuits. Schooled in new management thinking, they speak the language of 'empowerment, smart sanctions, thought leaders, change agents, cultural autonomy, [and] ecopreneurialism' (Chopra 2012). In an absorbing article, Heller (2013) profiles some of the new powerbrokers of San Francisco's new media economy. 'The word "entrepreneur" has undergone a redefinition', says one 25-year-old whiz kid, who goes on to describe 'a whole flourishing of people who are starting different kinds of businesses – who are having pride in a *small* business that gives them autonomy'. One venture capitalist remarks, 'I can't tell you how many times I've called a C.E.O., and it's like, "I'm at a meditation retreat!" or "I'm tied up for the next three months!"'

The sociology of enterprise provides some useful concepts through which we can approach entrepreneurship analytically. Experts regularly make an analytic distinction between *productive* and *nonproductive* entrepreneurs: those who create new markets for their goods and services versus those who muscle in on existing turf. An inventor who patents a new gadget would be considered in the former category. In the non-productive category we find patent trolls (traders who buy up IP rights to particular technologies at a steep discount and then use them to sue other companies) and internet free-riders (like 'mugshot entrepreneur' Rob Wiggen, who scrapes police websites for images then charges people for their removal [Kravets 2011]). The discourse of innovation holds that creating new markets is good, while cannibalizing existing ones is bad, but the boundary between the two is contested, as we saw in Chapter 1's discussion of

substitution versus market extension. Daniel Ek, the Swedish founder
of the music streaming service Spotify, claims his business is all about
'growing the pie so the artists can go back to making a meaningful
amount of money' (Sloan 2013), while Radiohead and other artists
regard Spotify as having a cannibalizing effect on record sales, arguing
that the pie is now much smaller than it ought to be. Another ambigu-
ous category of entrepreneurs comprises the inventors of 'scalping
economy' (Leonard 2014) apps that exploit public systems for private
profit, by auctioning off parking spaces or restaurant tables. Productivity, like beauty, is in the eye of the beholder.

Another question in the entrepreneurship debate is whether entrepreneurs are born or made. Many Marxist scholars view entrepreneurialism as being differentially distributed along lines of economic
advantage, foregrounding structural issues like class and education
rather than personal or biographical qualities (Peterson and Berger
1971). There is plenty of evidence to support this view. A Reuters
survey of 88 Silicon Valley venture capitalists revealed that most come
from affluent families and benefit from social networks forged during
years of expensive college education; McBride (2013) concludes that
'unknowns from modest backgrounds, like [Netscape founder Marc]
Andreessen and [Steve] Jobs, are relatively rare among today's Valley
start-ups. Much more typical are entrepreneurs like Instagram
co-founder Kevin Systrom, who followed a well-trod path from Stanford to Google to start-up glory.' A structural interpretation of entrepreneurialism sits uncomfortably with the myth of the change-making
individual who rises above their circumstances.

Entrepreneurship and the Informal Economy

Scholars of the informal economy have had a lot to say on this issue.
Economic anthropologists and development economists who studied
the informal economy in the 1970s and 1980s, a period when the
research had a structuralist flavour, rejected the individualist explanation of economic achievement. Manuel Castells and Alejandro
Portes famously argued that the informal sector often functioned as
a holding tank for people squeezed out of the regular workforce,
and that the kinds of enterprise to be found there consequently had
a compensatory character: 'The informal economy evolves along the
borders of social struggles, incorporating those too weak to defend
themselves, rejecting those who become too conflictive, and propel-
ling those with stamina and resources *into surrogate entrepreneurship*' (Castells and Portes 1989: 27; our emphasis). Castells, Portes,

and their collaborators provide examples of surrogate entrepreneurs, from self-employed carpenters to market traders. They argue that informal enterprise is best understood as a by-product of the informalization of advanced economies, linked to the erosion of organized labour (weakened unions, watered-down workplace regulation, and so on). This has influenced the subsequent social science. Experts now regularly distinguish between *opportunity* and *necessity* entrepreneurs. Opportunity entrepreneurs are those who can see and act on market opportunities, and are the classic self-starting go-getters. In contrast, necessity entrepreneurs often find themselves barred from this kind of action because they are locked out of certain markets or lack the required capital to get a conventional business set up, or as a result of some kind of discrimination. They improvise and get by however they can. Everyday work takes on a quality of individual, ad hoc enterprise, whether they like it or not.

All this provides a useful qualification and augmentation of Schumpeterian discourse. Outside the corporate and institutional sectors of advanced economies, much labour has the character of informal, 'own-account' micro-enterprise (International Labour Office 1972). These are minor strategies of survival rather than heroic innovation. An ideological gulf organizes the entrepreneur debate: one side gives a romantic, individualist explanation for economic advantage, while the other sees entrepreneurialism as a class privilege. Middle-range accounts strike for a compromise, noting the co-presence of necessity and opportunity and the indistinct line between these two things (Cross and Morales 2007; Gurtoo and Williams 2009; Williams and Nadin 2010). Rather than a binary division between heroic (formal) entrepreneurs and necessity-driven (informal) entrepreneurs, a fluid definition that captures the traffic between the extremes is useful for our purposes.

Media Entrepreneurs Across the Formal/Informal Divide

A common theme when researching these figures is that many of the most important media entrepreneurs have worked *across* the border of the formal and informal economies. Rather than operating solely within the regulated spheres of formal industry or the netherworlds of informality, many work in the space in between – at the frontiers of the formal and informal economies. Often their success is linked to this very mobility, allowing them to move activities and transactions from one zone to the other.

For example, the Hollywood moguls of the studio era were *formalizers*: they built a vertical empire out of a chaotic industry, creating a structure for standardized media production. More than half a century later, Blockbuster – under the control of Wayne Huizenga, a waste management specialist turned media entrepreneur – would do the same to the home video market, applying supermarket-styled rationalization techniques to what was previously a chaotic, mom-and-pop kind of business (Greenberg 2008). Other movie business entrepreneurs specialize in behind-the-scenes transactions. National Research Group founder Joseph Farrell introduced a raft of standardized metrical techniques to the industry during the 1970s, such as test screenings and sociodemographic analyses of audience segments, making millions in the process.

Some entrepreneurs formalize systems while deformalizing markets. Take Jeff Bezos, known for a kind of meticulous logistics that would make Henry Ford's production lines look positively disorganized. In his years with Amazon, Bezos has built the most sophisticated supply chain of any media business in history. In Amazon warehouses, robots pluck packages from conveyor belts; staff prowl the aisles with barcode scanners; and everything is timed and measured to within an inch of its life. Yet Bezos is also, in some senses, a deformalizer: he has re-engineered the book trade by opening it up to a range of small resellers and second-hand traders and by undermining the market segmentation on which global publishing has been founded. (We return to this topic, and to Amazon's contradictory tendencies, in Chapter 4.)

What other varieties of entrepreneurial identity are at work in today's media economy? Let's start in the obvious place.

Geeks

In Silicon Valley, a specific idea about entrepreneurial innovation is hardwired into the way business is done. Steve Jobs founded Apple in his parents' garage in 1976. The image of Jobs clad in jeans and turtleneck, now burnt into the popular imagination, is representative of a wider folklore: his mythical status as the visionary of the digital age relies to an extent on his outsider status, a thriving biographical industry (Jobs's early death instigated a form of secular canonization), and ongoing debate about the precise nature of his Schumpeterian contribution. Much of this turns upon what we think we mean when we celebrate Jobs as an innovator or a disrupter. Walter Isaacson's 2011 biography provides many of the ingredients: the West Coast

The young Steve Jobs. Image: © Tony Korody/Sygma/Corbis, 1981

counter-culture; the Hewlett-Packard legacy of the 'start-up'; the radical vision of combining creative and technical innovation. Centrally, there is a question of authorship and originality: how much credit should Jobs take for Apple's breakthrough devices? Were they breakthrough devices, or triumphs of marketing? If Jobs is now secular 'Saint Steve', is he a saint of innovation or of public relations?

Malcolm Gladwell (2011) offers the standard contrarian view of Jobs's career and significance. The dazzling successes of Jobs, together with his signal failures as a technology entrepreneur, were not the result of great vision or technical genius. Instead, Jobs's significance lies elsewhere. He was an adept appropriator of other people's ideas. He unfailingly recognized failure in other people and things. He had a perfectionist's love of 'closed systems' – that is, he could not relinquish control over the uses and applications to which Apple's devices might be put. The machines that Jobs introduced and helped invent (the computers, phones, tablets and music players) embodied both his strengths and his weaknesses; they were and are distinguished by being both brilliantly designed and obstinately difficult to adapt, extend or modify. From Gladwell's perspective, Jobs's real significance is as a flawed example of a specific kind of technology developer and marketer. He is the archetypal tweaker, rather than an original inventor: an improver of other people's ideas. His skills are editorial, not inventive; his products are derivative, their development driven not by an original vision on Jobs's part, but by a caustic, unerring grasp of the weaknesses of his competitors. Nothing Jobs did, in this account of things, was entirely new. The Mac's great original selling points – its graphical user interface and bitmapped screen – were borrowed from technology developed by Xerox. The first versions of tablet computers were produced elsewhere, as were smartphones and music players.

Jobs's tale, then, is about adaptation and appropriation, and for Gladwell these attributes turn out to be the essence of economic progress. Far more than the breakthroughs of visionary inventors, it was the work of engineers and technology entrepreneurs in taking ideas from elsewhere and improving them that powered the industrial revolution in Britain through the nineteenth century. As an entrepreneur in this vein, Jobs achieved great things. So far, so good for the informal economy. But his approach has an unusual characteristic: his perfectionism, which was necessary to his success, also led him to jealously refuse others the freedom to adapt and modify that he enjoyed. He was a tinkerer who perversely created obstacles to the tinkering of others, whether amateur users or firms wanting to make products that would work with his. Jobs steadfastly resisted suggestions that the early Apple computers should include more (or any) expansion ports for third party add-ons; he struggled with the idea and consequences of licensing operating systems at Apple and NeXT; he tied the iPod to the iTunes store, and would not allow other music stores access to the device. More recently, in the case of the iPhone and iPad, the development and distribution of third party applications has been strictly controlled through the App Store. At the same time, Jobs was enraged when others copied his ideas: he sued when Microsoft copied the Mac's 'look and feel'; he was furious when Google launched the mobile operating system Android, because he felt it stole ideas from the iPhone.

In Gladwell's account, Jobs was an innovator who lacked the self-awareness to understand his own role and achievement. He was a tweaker (no dishonour in that) who imagined himself a visionary. Famous from early on for his 'reality distortion field', he deceived himself and became an innovator who stood in the way of innovation. Other contemporary commentators on technology have taken this theme further: in Jonathan Zittrain's *The Future of the Internet (and How to Stop It)* (2008), the iPhone is a salutary contrast to the 'open' architecture of the classic PC, which, for all its faults, could be far more readily adapted and modified by users and third party businesses. Here we find an old line of argument, that 'openness' (and the associated goodness of 'open source') is the real recipe for innovation and inexpensive distribution. In the case of computing, it is hard to argue with this: even deep within the iPhone, there is POSIX, and elements of BSD Unix.

The striking thing is that the closed iPhone has itself sparked an amazing wave of formal and informal innovation. The App Store's standardization of small-scale software distribution (it appeared after Zittrain's book) encouraged new kinds of software, including locational media and games, educational, creative and social software. All this new software is now also spreading to a host of other phones and tablets, including freely licensed (if not precisely open source) Android machines. And this points to another aspect of Jobs's legendary passion for combining technology with design. For someone with a focus on control, the ownership and development of original design is a notoriously weak area of intellectual property protection. Apple's minimalism has spread far and wide.

Today's internet industries are still swayed by the figure of the renegade innovator: the CEO in Converse trainers (or, in the case of Jobs, Issey Miyake turtlenecks), the anarchic impresario, the hungry entrepreneur prowling the edges of industry, looking for the 'new new thing' (Lewis 1999). These icons of informal innovation provide libidinal energy that keeps the industry running. Robert McChesney (2013: 27) argues that tech industries have re-engineered the iconography of capitalist enterprise, replacing the 'bad old days of Ebenezer Scrooge, John D. Rockefeller, Mr. Potter, Exxon, Goldman Sachs, and Walmart' with the infinitely more palatable 'hacky-sack-playing CEOs at Google and Facebook'. One cannot help but think of Mark Zuckerberg, who has been less successful than others in his public relations, and who embodies a very different position from Jobs in the entrepreneur hall of fame.

Like many dotcom moguls, Zuckerberg embodies a certain relationship to informality, a strategic leveraging which bundles informal work practices and origin myths into disruptive business models that can be scaled up to reorganize the status quo. Yet, despite his seemingly accessible image (omnipresent sneakers and fleece sweaters), Zuckerberg is an ambivalent figure. Facebook began as a start-up incubated in the Harvard geek culture of the early 2000s. Questions arise as to who came up with the idea and when. Zuckerberg's

Facebook founder Mark Zuckerberg. Image: JD Lasica (CC BY-NC licence, 2012)

informal beginnings are also less wholesomely linked to the objectionable excesses of his early Facemash program, where Harvard listings became a grotesque game of 'pick-the-hottie'. Aspects such as this established Zuckerberg's reputation as a rising star within a nascent economy where the lines between adolescent pranksterism and media commerce were barely distinct. Even after Facebook's corporatization, a reliance on informal ways of working remained. A moment from David Fincher's film *The Social Network* captures this in-betweenness: a Californian bungalow that doubles as a sweatshop for the production of Facebook code is full of geeks, bongs and blondes. As one of the geeks is about to jump off the roof and into the pool, Zuckerberg is about to catapult into the *Forbes* rich list.

Where do women fit within this male-dominated world? Sheryl Sandberg's bestselling book *Lean In* (2013) is a reminder of the gendered nature of informal innovation in Silicon Valley. Sandberg is herself a successful business executive: she held senior positions at Google and is now Chief Operating Officer at Facebook, with an estimated personal fortune of US$400 million (Rankin 2013). While *Lean In* is about the place of women across the Fortune 500, many of Sandberg's most challenging examples concern the IT sector, where there is ample evidence of a particular problem. Only 11 per cent of companies that received venture backing in 2009 had a female CEO or founder, according to Dow Jones VentureSource. A tiny 9.1 per cent of the board members of Silicon Valley companies are women, compared to 16 per cent across the top 500 companies (Streitfeld 2012: BU1). Sandberg's approach is to interrogate prejudicial stereotypes (the 'bossy' female) and then to identify concrete changes that will enable and support women – a liberal feminist response to the Valley's boys' club environment.

Bestselling author and Facebook executive Sheryl Sandberg addresses the World Economic Forum in Davos. Image: WEF (CC BY-NC-SA licence, 2013)

One example of personal history appears early in Sandberg's book, and becomes a motif for the power and potential of small, positive steps. Sandberg joined Google in its early days as a start-up; she stayed with it, managing online sales and operations, while the company workforce grew into the thousands. In an instructive episode, a pregnant, nauseous Sandberg finds herself struggling to negotiate Google's ever-expanding carpark in time to attend an important meeting with a client, an experience which makes her feel even sicker. A later conversation with her husband Dave elicits the information that Yahoo provides convenient parking for expecting mothers. Why can't Google do the same? The next day Sandberg visits Larry Page and Sergey Brin's office, 'really just a large room with toys and gadgets strewn all over the floor' (2013: 4). Sergey is there, in a yoga position in the corner. He agrees immediately that Google should provide pregnancy parking.

Sandberg's story adds a gender dimension to the male ethos of the technology enterprise in two ways. It reminds us that professional exclusion usually operates through informal means. The Silicon Valley boys' club reproduces itself through personal networks, word-of-mouth recruiting and late-night coding parties. It also highlights the potential of formalization for counteracting the worst excesses. Sandberg's suggestions are often about adding some structure to arrangements that are otherwise rather loose (for example, sponsoring up-and-coming female colleagues). In our terms, these are controls: forms of codification and authorization. There is also, interestingly, a certain promotion of the informal: Sandberg wants women to engage positively with the chaotic, unpredictable, risky aspects of work. She describes herself as someone who, in her personal life, 'like[s] things to be in order' (2013: 60); she files documents in coloured folders and does not 'embrace uncertainty'. But work is different. Sandberg believes that many women are too conservative in their career choices.

Sandberg relished her entry into the messy boys' room of Google because of its potential, which was necessarily uncertain. Her story of the carpark is also about knowledge: she asks herself why she had not realized earlier that Google needed the pregnancy parking. Sergey Brin observes that he had never thought about this before, and Sandberg wonders why other women had not raised the issue earlier. These questions imply an ethos of investigation and questioning, where what matters is not so much the content of the problem or its solution (in this case, a simple model readily borrowed from a competitor), but a higher-level systemic analysis – why didn't we recognize this was a problem in the first place? The Yahoo solution was there for the taking; the Google solution involved wrapping the problem in a puzzle. Curiously, in Google's case, the extension of the start-up culture of questioning to the organization of the workplace appears to be a necessary precondition for formalizing improvements to equity and diversity.

Moguls

In May 2014, the announcement of a multi-billion dollar corporate deal between a Silicon Valley tech giant and a headphone manufacturer highlighted some of the unlikely connections between formal and informal media enterprise. The tech giant in question was Apple. The headphone manufacturer was the Culver City-based company Beats, founded in 2006 by rapper Dr Dre and former Interscope Records boss Jimmy Iovine, and known for its colourful (and expensive) headphone line Beats By Dre, as well as a fledgling streaming service. When Apple announced it would purchase Beats for a jaw-dropping US$3 billion in cash and stock, industry observers were

Dr Dre, with Beats headphones, in 2010. Image: © CJ GUNTHER/epa/Corbis

quick to hail the emergence of hip hop's first tech billionaires. A video recorded by R&B singer Tyrese Gibson at a post-deal Beats party captured the vibe. Dr Dre looks into the cameraphone and proudly anoints himself 'the first billionaire in hip hop – right here from the mothafuckin' West Coast'. 'They need to update the Forbes list', says Gibson. 'Shit just changed.'

Dre, born Andre Romelle Young, is one of hip hop's veritable entrepreneurs. Raised rough in Compton, he followed many of his 1990s hip hop peers by forging a savvy career as label boss and scene Svengali, launching the careers of Snoop Dogg, Tupac and Eminem, and trying his hand at a range of other commercial pursuits. Dre is now enjoying the fruits of his dalliance with Silicon Valley. The Beats deal marks Dre's inauguration into what Gibson dubbed the 'billionaire boys club'. It also has wider implications for the media industries generally, as it reflects a deepening integration between the media hardware, content and tech industries, and points the way towards more durable revenue streams (hardware, streaming subscriptions) for popular culture industries in a context when the always precarious pay-per-track digital music model seems to be on the wane.

The hip hop mogul epitomized by Dre is a flamboyant artist and businessman with a cross-media empire, encompassing music, fashion, advertising and sometimes videogames. Always male, he is 'tethered, either literally or symbolically, to America's disenfranchized inner cities' (Smith 2003: 69). Artists like Dre, Sean 'Puffy' Combs and Def Jam founder Russell Simmons are exemplary in this respect, as they have all made the transition from the street to the boardroom, mapping a path of economic ambition. Hip hop's iconography is all about this movement, evoked by the juxtaposition of icons from America's bifurcated urban economies: Fubu and Louis Vuitton, handguns and gold watches, Coors and Courvoisier. For our purposes the hip hop mogul is interesting because it is a classic example of

Jay-Z in concert. Image: Penn State News (CC BY-NC licence, 2009)

media entrepreneurs working across the formal–informal divide. The *mise en scène* is different from the Silicon Valley scenario – from suburban garages to inner-city projects – but a particular way of engaging the informal economy comes to the fore.

Shawn Carter (Jay-Z) is another hip hop entrepreneur of the first order. A talented artist and businessman, his rise across multiple areas of the entertainment industries is predicated on an informal origin story that has become central to his personal mythology. Carter grew up in the notorious Marcy projects in Brooklyn's Bedford-Stuyvesant neighbourhood. He was involved in gun crimes as early as the age of 12. As he describes it in his autobiography: 'My life after childhood has two main stories: the story of the hustler and the story of the rapper, and the two overlap as much as they diverge . . . I was on the streets for more than half of my life from the time I was 13' (cited in Gardner 2011). He started selling Jay-Z CDs from his car boot before founding Rock-A-Fella Records, arguably the most influential and successful rap label of the past two decades or so. The label name of course evokes America's most famous industrial dynasty, providing some indication of the scale of Carter's ambitions (here, as elsewhere in hip hop, the 'robber baron' figure endures). Carter's empire expanded rapidly in the late 1990s and today includes not only the record label, but also the fashion label Rocawear, film production ventures, the Brooklyn Nets basketball team, cologne brands and a chain of sports bars. Revenues from his ventures are estimated at around half a billion dollars a year (Gardner 2011).

Streetwise business methods remain a part of the Jay-Z story. In 1997, Carter stabbed rap rival Lance Rivera reportedly because he believed Rivera was selling bootlegs of his tracks. For rap's predominantly white audience, these periodic irruptions are the necessary co-presence of violence, crime and regular business. Likewise, for Curtis Jackson (50 Cent) – an ex-drug dealer with a bullet-scarred face – the relation between opulence and crime is explicitly indexed in the title of his first album, *Get Rich or Die Tryin'*. Jackson went on to prove this point by expanding his business empire from rap into a host of new areas, becoming a 'rapper turned entrepreneur, pitchman, author, philanthropist, actor, and movie producer' (Robinson 2011: 75). In this sense, the 50 Cent story is a classic narrative of informal-to-formal entrepreneurship as it moves between the two privileged spaces of the record industry: the streets and the executive suite (Negus 1999).

Informality has had specific consequences within black popular music in the United States. At an industrial level, informal business practices are hardwired into the industry. Norman Kelley (2002) shows how the music business has been built on expropriation of black labour – a 'structure of stealing'. White-owned blues and R&B labels signed artists up to dodgy contracts, made token one-off payments or offered 'gifts' (a Cadillac or flashy suit) in lieu of intellectual property rights (Dannen 1991). Here, the notoriously informal nature of the record industries, characterized by impulse decisions, handshake deals and contracts written on the back of a coaster, dovetails with a longer history of racist exploitation. The result has been a deep and far-reaching dispossession of black artists. The legacy of this informality is still felt in the US music industries today, where black-owned labels are few and far between. In this context, the passionate entrepreneurialism of the hip hop mogul needs to be understood as, at least in part, a parodic response to a situation where capacity for entrepreneurship and economic mobility are distributed along race and class lines.

Pirates

In the lexicon of enterprise studies, the difference between productive and non-productive entrepreneurs stands in for a wider values distinction: between healthy greed (involving the creation of new markets and an expansion of productive activity) and bad greed (associated with theft, redistribution and substitution). Commercial pirates are located in the latter category, and are therefore textbook cases of negative enterprise. These are the scheming shysters who 'reap financial gain at the expense of . . . hard work, investment and ingenuity' (MPAA 2011). Quintessentially non-productive, piracy is seen as 'the domain of slavish reproduction, without any transformative act of creativity' (Liang 2009: 19). Liang's own work extensively deconstructs this binary between the productive and the non-productive.

Kim Dotcom and dancers at the Mega launch in Auckland. Credit: Anthony de Rosa (CC BY-NC-SA license, 2013)

Taking a closer look at some famous pirates reveals interesting complications to this narrative. The flamboyant German hacker Kim Schmitz (aka Kim Dotcom), and his 'metamorphosis from cyberspace outlaw to new-economy hero' (Williams 2001) is an irresistible subject of study. Founder of the notorious cyberlocker Megaupload and an array of associated ventures – including the encrypted file hosting service Mega, the defunct streaming sites Megavideo and Megarotic, and mooted 'legal' subscription service Baboom – Schmitz seems to embody the most flagrant excesses of the entrepreneur. Since his arrest in Germany for phone card fraud in 1994, he has financed a lavish lifestyle through a string of questionable online businesses and venture capital deals. He shuns the pseudonymity of hacker culture for tabloid celebrity stunts. Images of him cavorting with swimsuit models, throwing extravagant parties, and boastfully showing off a private helicopter are all over the internet. In his adopted homeland of New Zealand, Schmitz decked out his rented mansion in the style of a James Bond villain, with LCD screens for walls and a fleet of expensive cars in the garage with personalized number plates such as GOD, MAFIA, GUILTY and HACKER.

Schmitz projects an image of entrepreneurial excess that is so exaggerated as to be self-parodic. His rhetoric is a mix of naked ambition and digital communitarianism, honed around a vehement opposition to the 'copyright Taliban' (Twitter, 15 February 2013). 'After we win our [Megaupload defense] case', he tweeted (11 February 2013), 'I am going to buy an Olympic size swimming pool . . . filled with the tears of copyright extremists.' As one journalist memorably put it, Schmitz's greatest achievement has been 'to take the absurdity inherent in the dotcom craze and elevate it to high comedy' (Ewing 2002). Like the hip hop moguls, he embraces the contradiction of his condition by projecting himself as a parody of capitalist excess.

In recent years, Schmitz has been the bête noire of US entertainment industries. The general narrative is of a non-productive entrepreneur piggybacking on formal business. This is not inaccurate, but there is more to the story. Schmitz's biography and the history of his ventures display a strategic oscillation between the formal and informal economies, combined with an attempt to reposition the supposed non-productivity of pirate entrepreneurialism as vanguard digital innovation. While he loves to play the pirate provocateur, Dotcom's CV contains some interesting dalliances with more conventional IT business. In the mid-1990s he ran the Munich-based business Data-Protect, which hawked digital security products to corporate clients. Subsequent projects included the venture capital outfit Kiminvest, and a stake in the UK shopping website LetsBuyIt. Dotcom is no anti-capitalist, and his rabid entrepreneurialism reflects a strategic relationship with both formal and informal economies.

Within the history of piracy, oscillation between formal and informal enterprise is not unusual. Even a world leader – former Ukrainian Prime Minister Yulia Tymoshenko, who was an informal media entrepreneur in her younger years – has followed this path. The businesswoman, economist and academic, who rose to global prominence as a figurehead of Ukraine's 2004 Orange revolution, served as Prime Minister between 2004 and 2005 and again from 2007 to 2010, and was later imprisoned for many years in a state hospital in northeastern Ukraine, having fallen foul of the regime. As a young woman, Tymoshenko ran one of the most successful video piracy operations in Eastern Europe, using smuggled VCRs to dub bootleg copies of popular movies. Her father-in-law Genady Tymoshenko was a party official in charge of a string of state movie houses, with rare access to Western videos and hardware. In the early 1990s the Tymoshenkos established an informal media business in Yulia's living room consisting of 'a dozen VCRs cranking out hundreds of pirated cassettes daily' (Brzezinski 2001: 137). In time, this informal start-up evolved into a thriving enterprise, and their best-selling product was a *Rambo* bootleg. Using capital from her video business, Yulia later moved into the energy industry, amassing a multi-billion dollar fortune as the Soviet Union crumbled, and then into politics. The rest is history.

While Yulia Tymoshenko's early video business was certainly informal, piracy may not be right word to describe it. In the Soviet Union there was no intellectual property system as it is now widely understood, and Hollywood movies were considered a perfectly acceptable target for reproduction and sale. Crucially, Tymoshenko was not breaking the law. In the absence of strong regulation, all media trade necessarily has an informal dimension. Tymoshenko's

Yulia Tymoshenko in 2008. Image: European Parliament (CC BY-NC-ND licence)

brand of entrepreneurialism was in line with the wider economic context in the post-communist societies of the former Soviet states, in which many forms of trade took the shape of barter between individuals or exchange in black and grey markets. The anthropologist Caroline Humphrey (2002) has written eloquently on this topic, noting the blurry lines between formal and informal, and the diverse range of institutions – including private companies, neosocialist corporations, postsocialist corporations and state institutions that act like corporations – spanning this boundary. In the post-Soviet context, distinctions between legal and illegal conduct, between productive trade and non-productive piracy, and between formal and informal economies are inevitably leaky.

Entrepreneurs working in the grey and pirate economies often shed their informal skins once they reach a certain level of power. From this point onwards, the 'pirate' tag may be something of an embarrassment. It is therefore interesting to consider media entrepreneurs who, although having the opportunity to set themselves up as legitimate operators, prefer to move *away* from formality, respectability and the media establishment. One example is Alki (Alkiviades) David, the unbelievably colourful businessman who built a career in the grey areas of the internet. David is a provocateur-entrepreneur in the Larry Flynt mould. A British citizen born in Nigeria to Greek-Cypriot parents, he is the heir to a multi-million dollar soft drink bottling empire that stretched across 28 countries, and is estimated to be worth US$1.7 billion (Gardner 2012). Rather than indulging in the benefits of his privileged upbringing, David instead has poured his formidable energy into an online video site called FilmOn, a retransmission service that the major US broadcast giants (including Fox, NBC Universal, ABC and Disney) have accused of 'flagrant infringement' of their copyrights.

Alki David at the FilmOn antenna farm. Image: © FilmOn

Like Barry Diller's Aereo before it, FilmOn has an uncertain legal status. Part of its business model has been to record and rebroadcast network television to paying subscribers. The company's headquarters in Beverley Hills has millions of tiny TV antennas on its roof, which it used to provide an online TV streaming service to individual subscribers. It also streams a wide variety of other content across multiple platforms, including broadcast material from non-US jurisdictions (streaming 'stations' include Sports, Latino TV, Greek Live TV, Horror TV and Bikini Babe). At the time of writing, FilmOn's live TV operations are in doubt following US Supreme Court rulings. While the 'cable cowboy' approach worked for the early pay TV entrepreneurs like Bob Magness of TCI, David may not be so lucky, at least not in the United States.

David has all the trappings of an eccentric media entrepreneur: a swimsuit model wife, a fleet of sports cars and an entourage of high-profile mates such as Ice-T and Charlie Sheen. He is also an actor, specializing in bad-guy roles in movies and TV series such as *Spooks/MI5* or *The Bank Job*, and even produced and directed his own movie, *Fartacus*. He is also fond of creating media spectacles. In a show of anti-copyright solidarity, he pledged to pay the legal costs for another alleged copyright infringer, TVShack founder Richard O'Dwyer. He also delights in provoking Diller, his former competitor in the live streaming industry, by using the URL barrydriller.com to promote FilmOn. There is nothing rational about how he conducts his media business; his ventures play out like the script of a B-movie. Whether or not all this counts as a productive or cannibalistic activity is a matter of some debate. What is clear is that in the informal media economies, innovation often comes from unexpected places and people.

Enthusiasts

So far this chapter has discussed opportunity entrepreneurs, driven people who create new or parallel markets in media worlds. Another category of informal media entrepreneurs consists of people who turn their love of a particular media practice into a business. This more quotidian entrepreneurial subjectivity is grounded primarily in pleasure rather than need or greed: pleasurable pursuits morph into a source of revenue.

Consider Yoshi, a marginally employed Japanese youth who wrote Japan's first cellphone novel, *Deep Love*, triggering a massive popular culture phenomenon:

With an investment of $1,200 (¥100,000), Yoshi launched a website where he posted his novel. To promote his novel, he distributed leaflets to female high school students in Shibuya. News of Yoshi's novel spread by word of mouth, and within three years, the site had received 20 million hits. In 2002, Starts, the largest publisher of cell phone novels, sold 2.5 million copies of *Deep Love*. Yoshi's story of a teenage girl who contracts AIDS in the course of her involvement in sex work (*enjō kōsai*) was adapted as a movie and a television drama. Matsushima Shigeru, Yoshi's editor at Starts, told me that Yoshi was successful because he was a clever entrepreneur. Yoshi invested heavily in promoting himself; he also maintained control over his media image by giving interviews only when he was allowed to weigh in on which portrayals of him appeared in the media. (Lukacs 2013: 47–8)

Yoshi is one of the relatively small but significant number of content producers who have hit it big in the amateur jackpot economy. His peers include first-time, informally published writers (recently, *Fifty Shades of Grey* by E. L. James), celebrity bloggers (such as Illinois high school student Tavi Gevinson, who runs the massively popular fashion blog RookieMag), and many other non-professional producers.

Traditions of amateur content production are long and durable, and we have explored this history elsewhere (Hunter et al. 2012). But much of the explosion in user-generated and amateur content is recent, in the sense that it has its roots in particular technologies that allow monetization of non-professional content. Google has played a vital role here. First, its AdSense advertising platform has opened up paid advertising opportunities to virtually any website, creating a revenue stream for non-professionals with audiences. AdSense's two-line text advertisements began appearing across parenting blogs, cycling forums and cooking sites in the early 2000s. Then came YouTube, which Google purchased in 2006, and its partner programs designed to incentivize and monetize non-professional production. This kind of structured revenue sharing between users and platforms is now hardwired into the digital media economy, appearing on a vast number of websites. Google has effectively entrenched this model of media enterprise as a commercial norm, creating new entrepreneurial subjects along the way.

Many people have come to the world's attention through these platforms. Video bloggers like western Sydney's Natalie Tran use YouTube as a platform for personal broadcasting, spawning successful cross-media careers along the way. A notorious case is Lonely-Girl15, the popular video blogger who was later revealed to be a professional actress – her case brings into focus the strategic uses of amateur aesthetics for building careers in the formal media economy. A different variety of entrepreneurialism can be found in the figure of celebrity linguist Marina Orlova and her massively popular YouTube enterprise, *HotforWords* (Burgess and Green 2009b). Orlova's specialty is providing etymologies for everyday English speech, explaining the linguistic roots of common phrases and words. The unique selling point is that Orlova happens to be an attractive Russian blonde and delivers her mini-lectures while wearing low-cut blouses and posing in a range of provocative positions. Her blend of education and titillation has been a big hit, and her YouTube channel is among the most popular in the site's history (Burgess and Green 2009b). Readers of *Wired* magazine voted her the sexiest geek of 2007, and she is now a 'branded personality to be extended into a potentially endless stream' of commercial spinoffs (Vonderau 2010).

In their pioneering study of YouTube, Burgess and Green (2009b) describe the commingling of the formal and the informal in YouTube channels. They note that 'amateur and entrepreneurial uses of YouTube are not separate, but coexistent and coevolving' (2009b: 103). This is a helpful way to think about the kind of entrepreneurial subjectivity that emerges in and around new media sites. Vonderau (2009: 120) has also explored the interzone between the enthusiast, the professional and the entrepreneur, arguing that while 'YouTube served as a rationale providing new role models, with a clear strengthening of the entrepreneurial side of creative work', it also shapes our activities in ways that complicate both individual-centred theories of enterprise and the determinist accounts of technological disruption. In recent years, YouTube has ramped up its activities on this front, extending its commercialization logic to new hinterlands of non-professional activity. The site recently announced a range of new features, including the crowd-funding platform YouTube Fan Funding and the data and analytics platform YouTube Creator Studio (Glotzbach and Heckmann 2014).

While we often think about self-made digital stars as the paragons of entrepreneurial enthusiasm, there is another way to approach this category. The etymological root of 'enthusiasm' is the classical Greek *enthousiasmos*, meaning possession by a divine being. Like other superficially secularized ethical categories, in current English-language usage the term obscures this religious layer of meaning, but the trace of divinity is important because media commerce often overlaps with spiritual motivations. Early European print culture was organized around the church. The boundary between commerce, spirituality and public and private life was faint (naturally, the church was enmeshed in all layers of life). Print technologies and industries were structured around enthusiasm for God. It was not an opposition between market and non-market, as these lines did not exist, but rather a network of monetary and non-monetary interactions radiating out from the church as society's central institution.

In industrial modernity, most media industries are ostensibly secular in nature, as are the many modes of enthusiasm that regulate our engagement with these industries but which retain a trace of religious affect (passion, fandom, technophilia, cinephilia, internet 'addiction'). But there is a parallel history of faith-based media evolution that has as much to do with the accumulation of divine capital as economic capital. US televangelist entrepreneurs like Billy Graham and Jerry Falwell were media institutions in their own right, commanding huge audiences across the media of television, publishing, radio and the internet. Today's evangelical pastors, like Joel Osteen, reach millions weekly with televised sermons. In the Islamic worlds, the Egyptian *da'iya* (caller to Islam) Amr Khaled is a veritable superstar, transmitting his lectures around the globe via satellite TV, audiotapes and the internet. In the process, he has built up a multifaceted media career as 'television host, author, motivational speaker, interfaith mediator, entrepreneur, doctoral candidate and an international media celebrity' (Moll 2010: 2). In Nigeria, evangelist Helen Akpabio (head of Liberty Foundation Global Ministries) is a prolific film director and producer, releasing a constant stream of religious-themed movies and playing a central role in Nigeria's booming movie industry (Okome 2007). Australia's fast-growing Hillsong Pentecostal church is famous for its media spectacles, and runs its own music and film production side businesses: its in-house band, Hillsong United, has sold 1.9 million CDs and DVDs without a major label contract (Cuneo 2010), and has its presence felt in the formal media economy via the domination of a season of *Australian Idol*. (Four out of eight *Idol* finalists in 2007 were Hillsong members.) These huge faith markets and the enterprising enthusiasts who supply them are a curious combination of the formal and the informal: ordered, organized and professional, yet relatively autonomous in relation to the established systems of media production.

Conclusion

From pastors to pirates, the informal media economy is full of unusual people. Perhaps the best way to think about the very different entrepreneurs described in this chapter is that they all have a special expertise in manipulating boundaries: between legal and illegal, commercial and non-commercial, formal and informal. Their distinction lies in their mobility across border zones and their talent for relocating transactions from one side to the other. While most of our entrepreneurs have this in common, there are also differences between them. Most migrate, or at least shift residency, from the informal to the formal, but some move the other way.

In contrast to many accounts, we see no clear correlation between formal practices and opportunity-driven enterprise, on the one hand, and necessity-driven entrepreneurs and informality, on the other. Divisions between particular motivations and particular modes of economic organization – like the boundaries between profit, passion and pleasure – are not easily drawn. This underscores the limitations of our standard media industry histories for describing motivation and action. Many aspects of everyday media practice appear at first glance to be highly irrational: the amateur subtitler who spends every evening producing text for free, the hacker risking jail time to impress a tiny circle of peers, the unemployed scriptwriters who wait tables while waiting for their big break. With its mute categories of producer, consumer, distributor, firm and market, the toolkit of orthodox media industry analysis cannot fully capture what happens in daily practice. In adapting a category from this toolkit and fleshing it out with some counterintuitive examples, we hope to have demonstrated one way in which we can productively modify established categories. Here, perhaps, media industries scholarship can contribute to wider debates about economy, enterprise and society.

3

Work

In the previous chapter, we met some of the entrepreneurs who operate in the space between formal and informal media. Many of these individuals have colourful biographies, big personalities and outlandish schemes. There is a lot of money to be made in this line of media work. But the formal–informal borderland is not always a glamorous or easy place to be. For many people involved in the actual labour of media production and distribution, much of which is repetitive and lowly paid, informal media work has a real downside: it can mean insecurity, overwork and low pay. This is especially the case for freelancers and other workers at the bottom of the food chain, where the boundaries between flexibility and exploitation can be very leaky.

As an example, let us introduce the freelance web content creator Ken Muise. Muise, a non-commissioned US army officer and part-time journalism student, spends much of his free time writing short articles for online 'content farms' such as Associated Content/Yahoo Voices, HubPages, Textbroker and other websites that commission articles based on common web queries (how to bake brownies, groom a dog, or change a tyre). Some of these sites pay writers on a per-word rate of 1 or 2 cents, or sometimes higher; others offer a fixed fee per article (often around $15), or a share of advertising revenue (Bakker 2012: 630). Muise also finds work on online recruitment platforms such as Elance, one of the new institutions of the digital freelance economy, where thousands of writing jobs are advertised on any given day ('Need a 50 healthy muffin recipes writer', 'Ghost-writer for a semi fiction screenplay'). Rates and conditions vary considerably. Some advertised jobs are legitimate, offering decent rates for one-off writing, editing or translation work. Other jobs are clearly exploitative, cashing in on writers' desire to build a resumé, and offering little to no pay. Per-word rates can sometimes go as low as a quarter of a cent.

In his Yahoo Voices article 'Freelance Writing: How to Write a 300 Word Article in Under an Hour and Avoid the Traps of Distraction!', Muise (2011) explains his system for making a living in this unconventional industry:

> If you're a freelance writer like myself – just starting out and working on your game – then you NEED content engines to supplement income while you are acquiring a private client base. If you are writing for content engines then your top pay is around 1 or 2 cents per word (I currently make a penny per word at TextBroker and 2 cents a word at Independent Publishing) then you really should try to become more efficient and do those jobs in under an hour – *way* under hour. I would say you need to be doing 300–400 [word] articles in under 20 minutes, with 15 minutes being my personal goal.

Muise's article goes on to provide more advice to writers hoping to get a start in the content production industry. Writers need to write what they know. In Muise's case, this means sports, animals, travel and military life (his articles for Yahoo Voices include 'Best exercises to strengthen your core' and 'Baltimore's best karaoke bars'). Writers also need to understand search engine optimization. And they need to work *very* fast. Muise does not complain about these conditions. He urges his readers to make the best of the situation. 'Just do your best work,' he advises, 'give nothing for free, and discipline yourself to making some system – any system – work for you.' His long-term goal is to move into a higher pay grade, so he can earn $12–$18 per hour. This plan has worked well for Muise. By 2014 he was no longer writing for the penny-a-word platforms and had moved up to sites offering better pay and higher standards.

Non-professional, ultra-freelance media work like this raises a number of issues pertinent to our book. For example, we can see here a distinctive combination of *formal* media enterprise and *informal* employment. Sometimes owned by major media companies (the *New York Times* owned About.com, a major content farm, until 2012), content farms tend to employ a core of full-time, well-paid programmers and executives based in US cities, while outsourcing the writing to thousands of non-professionals with local topic knowledge, some of whom are located in low-wage countries. These writers are encouraged to think of themselves not as employees but as 'associates' or 'contributors'. There are no minimum pay standards, unions or other formal protections. Remuneration schemes are designed as incentives for people to do what they love doing, rather than taking the form of a salary paid to workers in return for a certain amount of time and effort.

This new freelance writing industry has attracted criticism for its low-pay model. *Harpers* journalist Thomas Frank (2010) calls it a 'literary maquiladora' that 'deprofessionalizes journalism'. Bakker (2012) describes content farms as 'digital sweatshops'. For professional journalists, this whole industry is an affront that devalues research and writing and floods the internet with rubbish. Google seems to agree: since 2011 the search engine giant has been tweaking its algorithm to push low-quality sites further down its search results. Content farms also call to mind the wider neo-Marxist critique of digital free labour (Terranova 2000), which holds that the 'dominant capital accumulation model of contemporary corporate internet platforms is based on the exploitation of users' unpaid labour' (Fuchs and Sevignani 2013: 237).

Clearly, there are some important issues to be explored here. Do content farms and freelancer sites exploit writers and erode the working standards of the writing profession? Or do they provide a previously non-existent opportunity for amateurs to get paid – albeit modestly – doing what they love? What are the ethics of using non-professional labour in this way? How can we distinguish work from pleasure, and pleasure from self-exploitation?

These are some of the questions we address in this chapter, which focuses on informal modes of media work. As noted in the Introduction, the informal economy means different things to different people. Viewed from the perspective of consumers, it seems benign and often very useful; but from the producers' perspective, it often represents a threat to hard-won standards and entitlements, or a race to the bottom. To get to the heart of these issues we need to connect media labour debates with informal economy debates, something rarely attempted within current media research. We begin with a critical review of recent academic writing on creative labour. We then consider what an understanding of informal economy dynamics can add to this debate. We conclude by discussing prospects for the regulation and formalization of informal labour.

The Creative Labour Debate

Labour is an increasingly prominent concern for media research. As Toby Miller noted: 'There would be no culture, no media, without labor. Labor is central to humanity, but largely absent from our field' (2010: 99). It is absent no longer. In the past few years, a growing academic literature has explored current working practices in cultural and media industries, building on longer traditions of labour analysis from the political economy of communications tradition (Garnham 1990), economic geography (Christopherson and Storper 1989; Scott 2004a), and other areas of social science. For the purposes of this chapter, we refer to this conversation as the creative labour debate. The terms of this debate extend beyond media industries, but here we focus specifically on media-related labour issues.

This critical field is complex and fast-moving. Scholars of culture and communication have produced important books on labour issues (Banks 2007; Deuze 2007; Hesmondhalgh and Baker 2011; Mayer 2011; Stahl 2013). Within media studies, a 'production studies' movement is foregrounding labour issues (Caldwell 2008; Mayer, Banks and Caldwell 2009; Mayer 2011; Szczepanik and Vonderau 2013). There is also a more general post-Marxist critique of knowledge and creative industries labour across the theoretical humanities (McRobbie 2002; Rossiter 2006; Fuchs 2013). At the risk of generalization, a few observations about this body of research and critique can be made. One of the main concerns has been about the unpredictable and insecure aspects of work in the cultural, creative and media industries, and how this affects ground-level employees in these industries. There is a strong awareness of the gulf that separates the fantasy of a creative lifestyle from the reality of everyday work experiences in these industries. As Mark Banks notes, 'in most firms cultural workers are not "stars", nor are they rich or even particularly successful – in fact, the majority of cultural workers toil in relatively anonymous enterprises, either living off the erratic incomes from "projects" or more conventionally on low or subsistence-level wages' (2007: 10). Scholars involved in this debate also explore the connection between flexible (informal) creative labour and knowledge-economy capitalism, often arriving at the conclusion that 'employment in the new creative economy is being intentionally imagined and structured in neoliberal ways that are antipathetic to traditional [labour] organization' (Ross 2007: 39).

Where did this wave of interest in media labour come from? Precedents exist throughout communications research and sociology, but much of the recent scholarship emerged as a response to boosterist arguments regarding creative work and creative industries. The paradigmatic text here is Richard Florida's book *The Rise of the Creative Class* (2003), which extended and popularized a longer tradition of thinking about the 'new' knowledge economy (Bell 1973). *The Rise of the Creative Class* was not about the creative industries per se, but about elite creative workers across a range of professional sectors, such as IT and management; the book nonetheless became totemic as a general argument for flexibility as the defining characteristic of knowledge economy work. Florida emphasizes the mobility and lifestyle orientation of today's professionals. His book begins with a tableau of images from a new industrial paradigm, where remote working and the Blackberry replace the punch-card and tea-room: '[O]ffice workers dressed like folks relaxing on the weekend . . . individuality and self-expression . . . valued over conformity to organizational norms . . . a time when the old order has broken down, when flux and uncertainty themselves seem to be part of the everyday norm' (2003: 4–5).

This claim suggests that today's most in-demand knowledge workers *choose* to work in a less routinized way than previously, enjoying a permeable boundary between work, private life and leisure. Informality takes on a positive character, associated with freedom, autonomy and liberation from Fordist routinization. Creative and media industries – especially recorded music, writing, design and advertising – figure in this account as crucibles for such new labour models. Indeed, *The Rise of the Creative Class* itself echoes arguments from UK creative industries research, such as the 1999 Leadbeater and Oakley report, *The Independents*, which defined the new creative enterprise through its *distance* from formal employment:

> The Independents thrive on informal networks through which they organise work, often employing friends and former classmates. . . . They have few tangible assets other than a couple of computers. They usually work from home or from nondescript and often run-down workshops. Their main assets are their creativity, skill, ingenuity and imagination. Across Britain there are thousands of young Independents working from bedrooms and garages, workshops and run-down offices, hoping that they will come up with the next Hotmail or Netscape, the next Lara Croft or Diddy Kong, the next Wallace and Gromit or Notting Hill. (1999: 11)

These and other accounts from the late 1990s and early 2000s, the peak of creative industries thinking in the United Kingdom, emphasize the entrepreneurial character of creative work and signal the emergence of a new kind of subject – equal parts worker, artist and entrepreneur. Leadbeater and Oakley were upbeat but also nuanced in their assessment of the new industrial zeitgeist: they acknowledged that flexibility produces 'fragile, low-growth companies' with 'high turnover of talent and ideas' (1999: 19). However, the general theme of many of the major creative industries documents (e.g., Howkins 2001) was excitement about the flexibility of new working cultures.

Florida's 'pleasurable flexibility' thesis provoked many rebuttals. Critics pointed to the more problematic aspects of informal work in the creative industries, including underemployment, unhealthy working conditions, unpaid overtime, self-exploitation, discrimination and the lack of unionization and minority representation. They stressed the unglamorous nature of much creative work, and the fact that employers often force flexible work upon employees, not the other way around (McRobbie 2002; Ross 2003, 2009; Banks 2007; Deuze 2007; Caldwell 2008; Gregg 2011; Hesmondhalgh and Baker 2011; Mayer 2011; Lee 2012). Gill and Pratt list some of the issues that concerned these researchers:

> a preponderance of temporary, intermittent and precarious jobs; long hours and bulimic patterns of working; the collapse or erasure of the boundaries between work and play; poor pay; high levels of mobility; passionate attachment to the work and to the identity of creative labourer (e.g. web designer, artist, fashion designer); an attitudinal mindset that is a blend of bohemianism and entrepreneurialism; informal work environments and distinctive forms of sociality; and profound experiences of insecurity and anxiety about finding work, earning enough money and 'keeping up' in rapidly changing fields. (2008: 14–15)

Arguably the most prominent voice within creative labour critique is New York University professor Andrew Ross. In *No-Collar: The Humane Workplace and Its Hidden Costs* (2003), Ross documented the working lives of media professionals in Manhattan's cluster of internet start-ups, Silicon Alley. Enjoying many of the benefits of 'new economy' work, such as flexible hours and creative freedom, his respondents also experienced an array of old and familiar problems, including overwork and exploitation. One informant was a writer employed by a trendy digital media company, who said this about her experience:

> Definitely, there was a certain coolness to being in a kind of sweatshop, a coolness to staying late into the night. It was intoxicating at first. Look at me! I'm in New York and I'm working really late! Then, of course, you realize that it sucks. But, even then – and this was the strange part – it was still a rapturous feeling. (Kathy Vanderstar, cited in Ross 2003: 76)

Recent scholarship has continued to document this unusual mix of pleasure, dissatisfaction and self-exploitation. Game development, a creative field built on labour-intensive programming work, is emerging as a particular site of tension. The ugly side of this industry was revealed when Erin Hoffman, the unhappy partner of an Electronic Arts employee, took to the blogging site Livejournal in 2004 to voice her dissatisfaction at her partner's Dickensian working conditions, particularly the unpaid overtime that programmers are expected to contribute (see Miller 2010 for an analysis). Her blog on this topic attracted several thousand comments – the discussion is still continuing, more than a decade later – along with follow-up articles in the *New York Times* and *Salon*. Here are a few excerpts from Hoffman's post:

> Electronic Arts offered a job, the salary was right and the benefits were good, so my SO [Significant Other] took it. I remember that they asked him in one of the interviews: 'how do you feel about working long hours?' It's just a part of the game industry – few studios can avoid a crunch as deadlines loom, so we thought nothing of it. When asked for specifics about what 'working long hours' meant, the interviewers coughed and glossed on to the next question; now we know why.
>
> Within weeks production had accelerated into a 'mild' crunch: eight hours six days a week. Not bad . . . When the next news came it was not about a reprieve; it was another acceleration: twelve hours six days a week, 9am to 10pm. . . . Now, it seems, is the 'real' crunch, the one that the producers of this title so wisely prepared their team for by running them into the ground ahead of time. The current mandatory hours are 9am to 10pm – seven days a week – with the occasional Saturday evening off for good behavior (at 6:30pm). This averages out to an eighty-five hour work week. (ea_spouse 2004)

Here, the glamour and pleasure of creative work provide a foil for extraction, creating consensual forms of domination in which workers are eager participants. Critics have therefore been at pains to emphasize the *subjective* as well as structural preconditions for creative self-exploitation, or what Caldwell describes as 'the local conditions and cultural scenarios that enable, facilitate, and legitimise our increasing shift to blackmailed or unpaid creative work' (2013: 92).

In contrast to Hoffman's complaints about too much work, some scholars also emphasize the experience of *precarity* – economic and subjective insecurity caused by lack of work – which is widespread in creative sectors, especially the performing and literary arts. The precarity critique emphasizes the difficulty of piecing together a living from project to project, and the general condition of underemployment experienced by many aspiring entrants to the creative workforce, and even by many skilled veterans. Anyone who has tried to break into fields like television or advertising can vouch for the willingness of employers to exploit the oversupply of aspiring entrants to these industries. Young hopefuls in many fields (particularly fashion, television and publishing) are often obliged to do unpaid work experience for months at a time, with no guarantee – and in some cases, no prospects – of a job at the end. David Hesmondhalgh and Sarah Baker (2011: 115) have documented people working for free for up to 12 months. Dissatisfaction with this state of affairs has been acute in the United Kingdom, where a campaign against exploitative internships by groups such as Intern Aware has resulted in a boycott of unpaid internship advertisements by major recruitment and media companies, and proposed – but ultimately not passed – legislative reform. Labour MP Hazel Blears introduced an anti-unpaid internship bill in 2012.

This problem has generated its own popular culture, such as Lena Dunham's HBO TV series *Girls*. Dunham plays Hannah Horvath, an unpaid intern at a trendy Manhattan publishing house, who embodies the cultural archetype of the precarious twenty-something. The unemployable Hannah has few useful skills but is willingly humiliated in the hope of landing a real media job, while her parents pay the bills. She seems oblivious to the fact that she has no prospect of a creative career, despite her many months of free labour. Poking fun at Manhattan's trust-fund creative wannabes, the character of Hannah captures the experience of many aspiring media workers with working lives full of uncertainty and (self-)exploitation.

A radical strand of the precarity literature stresses the links between irregular labour in cultural and creative work and a more generalized

Girls: Lena Dunham as unpaid intern. Image: © HBO

condition of instability that is bound up in the logics of late capitalism. This critique is strongly influenced by Italian autonomist Marxism (Virno 2004) and the work of Hardt and Negri (2000, 2004), and began to infuse critical social science debates about creative labour in the late 2000s. In a special issue of *Theory, Culture and Society*, Rosalind Gill and Andy Pratt (2008: 3) defined precarity as a double-pronged condition, comprising not only 'all forms of insecure, contingent, flexible work – from illegalized, casualized and temporary employment, to homeworking, piecework and freelancing', but also 'the multiplication of precarious, unstable, insecure forms of living and, simultaneously, new forms of political struggle and solidarity that reach beyond the traditional models of the political party trade union'. Neilson and Rossiter (2005) add to this definition the existential dimension of precarity, how it 'extends beyond the world of work to encompass other aspects of intersubjective life, including housing, debt and the ability to build affective social relations'.

For these critics, precarity is not specific to the creative industries, although it is especially visible in that domain. Rather, it is a side effect of late capitalist restructuring, deregulation and dematerialization of labour. Precarious creative labour therefore came to be seen by some critics as a symptom of wider political-economic problems. In his book *Nice Work If You Can Get It: Life and Labor in Precarious Times*, Ross makes the case for a structural link between flexible creative industries employment and minimum-wage work in service industries:

> Though they occupy opposite ends of the labor market hierarchy, workers in low-end services, both formal and informal, and members of the 'creative class,' who are temping in high-end knowledge sectors, appear to share certain experiential conditions. These include the radical uncertainty of their futures, the temporary or intermittent nature of their work contracts, and their isolation from any protective framework of social insurance. (2009: 6)

These are powerful claims, which suggest political possibilities. If precarity is a common condition, can it also be a starting point for a cross-class movement? For Ross, as for Neilson and Rossiter, the experience of precarity provides the potential ground for collective mobilization across national borders. In its more radical version, this discourse seeks to build a new kind of class formation and class politics, interfacing with existing activist movements and imagery such as the San Precario mobilizations in Europe, Euro May Day marches and the Occupy movement.

Across this literature, we see a range of critical positions from boosterism to reformism to radicalism. While the disagreements are passionate there is also much common ground. Most accounts accept the connection between postindustrial flexibility and informal employment practices, and note that flexibility can be liberating (for those who choose to work this way) and exploitative (for those on the receiving end). Differences of opinion are about the extent and scale of precarity and involuntary flexibility, the class politics that might emerge from it and the degree of inevitability or contingency of such employment practices within a context of late capitalist knowledge economies.

Limits of Creative Labour Critique

Reflecting on the creative labour debate so far, it is clear that the discussion has already achieved a number of important things. We have seen the beginnings of meaningful reform in some countries, including boycotts of exploitative employment practices. There has been important consciousness-raising work, with labour being put on the media studies research agenda in a new way, enabling connections (conceptually, though less often in practice) between creative workers and other social movements. And there has been a range of provocative intellectual interventions leading to reappraisal and renewal of labour theory. All this has been productive for media industry studies. Critics have done vital work in foregrounding unsexy industrial issues like the role of unpaid training and self-education, the unevenness of industrial protections and the limited reach of organized labour in creative fields. They have also shown the deep embeddedness of informal practices – cronyism, word-of-mouth recruiting, lack of transparency – within formal media industries. Among the most important consequences of the debate is a general diversification of what we understand as work in the creative industries and an acknowledgement of the highly variable conditions under which such work is performed. Whereas once labour economics restricted its focus to the kinds of salaried jobs that could be counted in the national statistics, we now have a much more textured understanding of the range of work that goes on in the creative and cultural sectors, and thus a conceptual apparatus that is closer to the realities of how people work in these parts of the economy.

At the same time, there has been overreach in some areas of the debate, particularly in the precarity literature. While the precarity critics draw attention to the structural links between creative industries and service sector workers, in positioning creative workers as vanguards of an emergent condition, they also unwittingly con- struct an exceptionalist discourse around them which sometimes stretches the boundaries of credibility. (Should the situation of under- employed graphic designers really be compared to McDonald's employees or abattoir workers?)

Cunningham (2013) considers this problem in a detailed response to the precarity argument. He suggests that the precarity critics over- look important aspects of current creative employment – for example, that a very significant proportion of creative workers, including designers and multimedia artists, are located *outside* the creative industries, in sectors ranging from automotive to financial services, and thus escape some of the deprivations common within the creative sector proper. Citing Australian census data, he also suggests that creative jobs are still growing overall as a proportion of national employment, and that creative workers are better educated than most workers elsewhere, and thus have more options. 'While the creative workforce may be clearly distinctive in the degree of "flexibility" seen in its labour market,' Cunningham argues, 'creatives are also gener- ally remunerated well for their services . . . and have "options" and mobility due to their qualification levels and experience in project- based work' (2013: 147). He goes on to explain that other areas of the national workforce – including agricultural and automotive workers, whose jobs are disappearing as those industries transform – 'face a much more precarious future than do creatives'. Cunning- ham's data is Australia-specific, but the general point helps to keep things in perspective. Beyond the creative industries, in other sectors of the economy, many people have it worse.

There is a gender dimension to precarity that has yet to be fully explored. McRobbie (2011) and Gill (2013) note that the entrepre- neurial jackpot economy of creative work is especially hard on women, who are often excluded from the homosocial rituals of cre- ative industry workplaces and on whose shoulders the work of child- rearing and other care duties unequally fall. Feminist analyses of creative labour have been important in foregrounding not only the structural biases of creative industry employment practices (single mothers cannot go to networking parties every night), but also the ontological assumptions of the precarity critique, which prioritize certain experiences over others. For example, Fantone (2007) notes that what is now being called precarity is in fact an age-old condition of economic insecurity with which women are well acquainted. The discourse of precarity may mark the expansion of this condition across the gender boundary: it seems to have emerged at the historical moment when flexibility is starting to hurt white-collar men. This is another reason to be careful when using the kind of critique that 'threatens to generalize precarity as a ubiquitous and therefore undifferentiated condition' (Nyong'o 2013: 158).

Additionally, there is a geographic aspect to the precarity debate. While some contributions apply the ideas to contexts outside the global North – Franco Barchiesi's book *Precarious Liberation* (2011) about labour relations in South Africa is one example – most research has been concerned with the working conditions of tertiary-educated workers in the industrialized world, where instability hurts precisely because of the relatively more expansive experience of economic security afforded by minimum wages, the welfare state and other prizes of modernization and the formal economy. This social safety net is the result of a long labour struggle and should be defended at all costs. But we should not forget that for many workers in the global economy, the experience of economic security cannot be taken for granted. What is understood as precarity in the North may elsewhere be understood as the predictable turbulence of the informal economy – as business as usual, the way things work, a routine economic experience.

Jaron Lanier's book *Who Owns the Future?* (2013) is symptomatic of some of these problems. Lanier, a computer programmer and cultural critic, is widely read in internet circles and his work offers a critique of aspects of the information society. A topic of concern for Lanier is labour; he argues that the social web is a driver of deformalization: it 'hollows out every industry' (2013: 2). The book begins with a provocative question:

> At the height of its power, the photography company Kodak employed more than 140,000 people and was worth $28 billion. They even invented the first digital camera. But today Kodak is bankrupt, and the new face of digital photography has become Instagram. When Instagram was sold to Facebook for a billion dollars in 2012, it employed only thirteen people.
>
> Where did all those jobs disappear to? And what happened to the wealth that those middle-class jobs created? (2013: 2)

This is a powerful image, but the reasoning behind it reflects the narrow national frames in which a lot of this discussion takes place. In Chapter 1, we noted how certain economic processes could be mistaken for others: what looks like substitution can sometimes actually be dispersal. The phenomenon of disappearing jobs is also often a function of where we look for them, what counts as employment and who counts as a worker. Lanier's rhetorical question brings this problem into focus, because the industrial transformation of imaging industries arguably has more to do with displacement and offshoring than with hollowing-out. Imaging jobs have not gone away; the productivity gains enabled by low-cost digital photography have contributed to their continued expansion. But these jobs are no longer concentrated in the large industrial conglomerates. They are dispersed through the economy, across the very many sectors where images and visual communication are important. Many of them are also new *kinds* of jobs, involving new technical skills and career trajectories. Some of the former Kodak jobs have also moved offshore, especially those related to the manufacturing of imaging equipment. So a facetious (but serious) response to Lanier's questions would be this: some of the Kodak jobs have moved to China. A question to ask in return would arguably be whether that is necessarily a bad thing, and if so for whom – American or Chinese workers?

The Ethical Drama of the Informal Economy

Another example of this displacement problem can be found in our earlier discussion of freelance web content creation. A lot of the criticisms of the 'race to the bottom' concern the new breed of freelancer recruitment websites like Elance and oDesk. On these websites, employers announce contracts, describe the work involved and specify payment terms. Many jobs involve writing web content of various kinds, sometimes general-purpose clickbait, or the repurposing of existing material for commercial (sometimes borderline illegal) ventures, such as online manuals or summaries. Most work advertised is low-paid, repetitive and decidedly uncreative. Here is a typical contract:

> Location: Anywhere
> Start: Immediately
> Budget: $50–$75 . . .

> I want to summarize and review a 466 pages book called 'Sycamore Row' by John Grisham.
> I need at least 40–50 pages of content.
> Time delay 1 week

a) Intro to book
b) History/Biography of author of original book
c) If this book is part of a series give a recap of the previous stories up to this instalment.
d) Outline and summarize the events/lessons/ideas of each chapter, one by one.
e) Discuss the Critical reviews of the book. Quote several critics making points that could be seen as both positive and negative about the book.
f) Recap the book and give your impression of it in a final summary.
g) Refer them to your other books and to join your fan club/notification list etc.
h) The book has to be in a kindle format 5x8 inches.
(posted on Elance com, 2 November 2013)

The employer offering this job has commissioned similar summaries on Danielle Steele and Dan Brown novels that can be seen in their Elance user history. The aim of these projects is to produce Kindle-format summaries of popular books that can be sold cheaply on Amazon to lazy students and book club members – a venture of dubious creativity and questionable legality, but which has many precedents in publishing history. We estimate the work involved in reading a book and doing the requested summaries at a professional level would likely take 20–30 hours. At maximum speed and minimum quality, it would take perhaps half that time. For a US$50–$100 payment this would amount to somewhere between $1.60 and $10 per hour. So it may not come as a surprise that the winning bidder was from Bangladesh. The content was delivered within a week for a flat payment of US$65.

If we view this kind of work as a deviation from a professional norm – a deformalization of professional writing – then yes, it seems like a race to the bottom. The Elance netherworld of clickbait commissions, fake product reviews and crackpot entrepreneurs becomes a site for minimum-wage labour extraction in which workers from low-wage Anglophone countries (India, Pakistan, Kenya and Bangladesh) are brought in to do the heavy lifting under insecure and exploitative conditions. But the other side of this story is that sites like Elance may possibly be opening up opportunities for a certain kind of middle-class media work in low-income countries – work that is commissioned with the worst of intentions, but also safe, accessible and, in the context of many countries' average GDP, relatively well paying (average weekly earnings in Bangladesh are US$16 per week). Someone like Lanier sees in Web 2.0 the disappearance of middle-class jobs, but from the perspective of highly skilled, lowly paid knowledge workers in the global South the story may actually be about the *expansion* of a certain kind of media work. This is more than another iteration of the trickle-down debate; it is also about an epistemological question of who counts as a media worker, where and under what terms, and who the creative labour debate is really for. Is it reasonable for us to expect writers in Bangladesh to fight battles on behalf of creatives in industrialized countries?

There are a number of risks here. On the one hand, there is the risk of embracing flexibility and therefore justifying the dubious business models of free-riders and freelance recruiting websites, which willingly facilitate extractive outsourcing. Let us be clear: the intentionality behind the low-pay/no-pay work model is extremely dangerous. But in taking the opposite stance and rejecting the global ecology of piecemeal media work, there is also the risk of unwittingly rolling out in all directions a set of conditions and expectations about labour that are specific to industrialized, high-wage countries in the global North, and to a certain kind of formalized, professional media environment that has never been universal even within those countries. Both these risks are real, and both make us uncomfortable. It will be a challenge for creative labour critics to develop a truly global critique of knowledge and media work that takes seriously the extractive potential of offshoring and outsourcing without simply reproducing a Eurocentric discourse about good work that is of limited relevance to workers outside those professions and regions.

Factoring in the international divisions of labour within new media work is a way to add some geographical complexity to the discussion. Another way that the issue of creative labour could be more deeply contextualized would be to draw the same kind of connections across *time* – to consider the precarity issue over the long term. Is today's precarity totally new, or is it a remix of older forms of insecurity? Has there ever been a time of non-precarity (Neilson and Rossiter 2008)? What connections can be made with workers in other historical moments? What were the issues then, and what were the outcomes? These are difficult questions that require historical excavation. One response would be to note the enduring precarity of most creative professions. The Grub Street bookseller, a paradigmatic figure of the eighteenth-century English press, is a historical archetype of a precarious overexploited cultural producer. And, as Robert Picard (2010) reminds us, there are precedents in early journalism for the kind of penny-a-word content creation we see in content farms (though it is alarming that pay rates are now no higher). There are also historical precedents for the kinds of critical arguments that are now appearing. Susan Luckman (2013) notes that John Ruskin and the Arts and Crafts movement in England at the end of the nineteenth century prefigured today's debates with their critique of alienated cultural labour. Neilson and Rossiter (2008) make a similar point when they stress that, within the long history of capitalism, insecurity and informality are constant features.

This is a version of an older argument about the contingency of the formal economy that is regularly made by social scientists. Harding and Jenkins put it this way:

> History may be viewed as the progressive encroachment of formality upon widening areas of social life, as a consequence of literacy and the introduction of ever more sophisticated information technology, on the one hand, and the increasing power and bureaucratization of the state, on the other. [Hence] an absence of formal regulation is the historical norm. (1989: 15)

In other words, formalization has been uneven, across time and space, and so therefore is the experience of precarity, if we understand this in terms of the decay of the economic bargain struck between citizen, state and industry. Precarity, in this context, might be a concept which can only make sense in a postindustrial context, where social and economic security was once, but is no longer, regarded as attainable for all.

Informal economy research is well placed to help us navigate through these conundrums. A useful move at this point in the debate would be to open up a dialogue between the creative labour debate and the informal economy debate. For example, if we extend our analytic schema from Chapter 1, we would see that formal–informal interaction can take a number of different shapes and is not just about cannibalization of existing structures and conditions The argument that content farms compete with journalism presumes a *substitution* model, whereas content farms may also be a *market extension* that does not compete with news sites but, instead, monetizes users' time and clicks in a different way. In other words, content farms could possibly be growing the pie of writing work rather than cannibalizing it. Such unpleasant propositions need to be taken seriously.

The example of content farms and freelancing sites also brings into focus the tension between workers *inside* the formal news media, copywriting and professional communications sectors, who feel threatened by these developments, and informal workers *outside* those traditionally well-paid professions, who have nothing to lose and possibly something to gain from the easy-to-enter content farm industry. Without defending the extractive intentions of many websites, it is worth noting the historical parallels between the content farm situation and older labour struggles, in which formal workforces – maritime and manufacturing workers, for example – defend themselves against informal workers who wish to enter those industries by the back door, and from overseas competition. The history of labour is full of such conflicts, which frequently have racialized overtones. These are some of the political complexities of formal–informal interaction that the creative labour debate would do well to confront.

Formalization: Prospects and Pitfalls

This chapter has focused on problems, but what about solutions? How can media labour markets be organized to minimize exploitation and maximize decent work? What strategies have worked successfully in the past and might do so again in the future? While we do not offer a policy blueprint for this area, from our observations of informal economies and media industries we can make a few general comments about different ways of intervening in media labour markets and what outcomes these might produce.

It is important to base any policy interventions on the understanding that creative and media production systems are unevenly industrialized. The discourse of creative industries and creative labour has been useful in that it reminds us that this is work, not (only) pleasure, but in using this language it implies an imaginary coherence and suggests that these industries can be regulated like any other. In reality, creative industries are a mix of formal and informal working practices, organizational cultures and firm structures. Some areas such as television production are indeed industrial in nature, and should be treated as industries (with all the attendant normative claims made in this regard – for employer obligations, protections, wage standards and other entitlements). Other parts of the creative industries are not industrial in that sense and look more like entrepreneurialism, self-employment, patronage or personal creative endeavour for pleasure and prestige.

A lot of the mixed messages in the creative labour debate arise as a consequence of extending the normative standards around formal economy sectors to what are essentially informal activities outside the regular economy. As David Hesmondhalgh (2011) has argued, we need a *differentiated* model of labour that is flexible enough to account for these complexities. In this sense we would be able to distinguish unpaid work that generates a surplus for somebody else, from unpaid training undertaken for strategic career reasons, from community-minded volunteering, from personal hobbies, and so on.

Having established such a baseline and identified those areas that should and should not be treated as labour markets, the next task would be to assess prospects for formal regulation. Creative labour critique has tended to evaluate informal employment negatively and formal employment positively, precisely because the latter is usually better regulated with better conditions. Gill (2013), for example, makes a strong argument against the informality of creative industries employment and the regulatory failure, lack of transparency and nepotism that haunts this sector. She argues that

> informality is the structuring principle in which many small and medium-sized new media companies seem to operate: finding work, recruiting staff, getting clients are all seemingly removed from the formal sphere governed by established procedures, equal opportunities legislation, or union agreements, and located in an arena based on informality, sociality, and 'who you know'. (2011: 256)

Likewise, proposed solutions to the creative labour problem generally call for formalization of workplace and recruitment practices, along with better and more extensive government regulation. Hesmondhalgh and Baker (2011) place a strong emphasis on formal measures like unionization and a basic guaranteed income as a means to reform, as well as individual commitment not to self-exploit.

What other kinds of formalization are possible? In Chapter 1, we set out a series of common control mechanisms for informal media activity, including authorization, restriction, measurement, codification and promotion. Regulatory approaches to informal media labour, where they exist, have typically involved a mix of these strategies. Minimum wage levels and industry-wide bargaining apply formalization approaches honed throughout longer histories of labour struggle, and aim to restrict and police noncompliant work practices. Codification of transactions is quite visible in the case of freelancer websites: it involves the division and organization of labour into units and activities that can be traded. The same principle can be easily used for regulatory purposes (feedback mechanisms, systematized complaint systems, Google's algorithmic campaign against low-quality content). Measurement is a vital policy instrument. Plausible estimates of the extent of informal labour and employer abuse are essential as prompts to policy and legislative reform. Classification is another option. Rennie, Berkeley and Murphet (2010), for example,

have proposed a standardized labelling system that would help consumers and participants distinguish commercial operations from
genuinely community-based media operations in the messy online
space – and therefore distinguish ethical institutions deserving of free
labour from unethical ones.

These are all different types of formalization, and they all have
their place within creative labour markets. But formalization is never
value-neutral. Research on informal economies has documented some
of the things that happen when economic arrangements are formalized. From this research we know that if you formalize an informal
system, you end up changing the system in certain ways – how it
operates, what it can do and not do, and so on. In the case of greater
regulation of creative employment, there are very important benefits,
but there will also be trade-offs that we need to take seriously.
These can include subtle changes to the experience of creative industry workplaces (formalization may result in a more regularized
experience, removing some of the energy and dynamism that people
find attractive about these industries), or changes to the amount of
work available (formalization may in certain cases mean a *smaller*
number of better paid and more secure jobs). Any intervention
needs to be assessed on a case-by-case basis, with an understanding
that formalization is never value-neutral. Nor, for that matter, is
deformalization.

A best-case scenario would involve the creation of regulatory
systems that enable the most productive and rewarding kinds of
formalities and informalities to coexist. In terms of the precarity
issue, the best-of-both-worlds approach could involve micro-policy
and regulatory strategies akin to the much-debated notion of 'flexicurity'. This term entered the social and economic policy lexicon in
the 1990s as a way of thinking about how the social democratic states
of Northern Europe might adapt to increasingly competitive, and
rapidly changing economic conditions. It was easy to assume that the
flexibility apparently demanded by modern labour markets posed a
profound, dialectical challenge to the social security at the heart of
the European postwar settlement. But a series of academic and public
sector analysts noted the many ways in which these macroeconomic
and social objectives could be conceptually related and connected, if
the abstractions of 'flexibility' and 'security' were sufficiently disag-
gregated (Viebrock and Clasen 2009). For instance, in terms of flexibility, firms need to be able to adjust workforce numbers ('external
numerical flexibility') and to change the mix of, for example, full-time
and part-time workers ('internal numerical flexibility'). They need
also to be able to modify the range of skills in the workforce, and

levels of remuneration on the basis of productivity and performance. Employees need flexibility as well, including access to training opportunities and the capacity to adjust workloads in the light of health issues or family commitments. Security for employees also takes many forms: security in a particular job, in employment more generally and in a predictable level of income. Combinations, contradictions and trade-offs between these elements of the flexibility–security matrix can then be better understood. So if external numerical flexibility increases when controls on hiring and firing are reduced, job security is diminished, but employment and income security may be sustained, if, as in Denmark, unemployment benefits are sufficiently generous, and if there is meaningful support for continuing training. The European Commission (2007) promulgated a series of broad policy principles enshrining strategies for flexicurity in 2007, and proceeded to track progress towards them thereafter.

Understanding the nature of the mix is, of course, entirely different from getting the mix right. In Europe, the policymakers of the early 2000s had no way of knowing that a protracted economic downturn would heighten social tension, increase economic conflict and jeopardize high-level aspirations for economic and social policy coordination everywhere. Crisis has also obscured the question of whether such coordination is ever possible. The problem is that in the European discourse, 'flexicurity' is used to describe desirable aspects of the diverse patchworks of national social and industrial settlements that have evolved, and a set of programmatic policy principles. The power of the flexicurity idea depends on an agreement that diverse aspects of economic and social life are best considered as connected: interventions or reforms in one domain, such as attacks on 'middle-class welfare', can be understood in a broader framework; the futility of policy measures that work at cross purposes may be more obvious, and the benefits of continuing investment in training programs, or in programmes that encourage labour mobility, may be more widely accepted. But if circumstances change and the positive models are no longer seen as successful, or if consensus evaporates in the face of a serious downturn, these arguments lose traction.

At the micro level of firms and industry sectors, the same problems arise. In high-risk media industries or anywhere, very few working environments have *both* the positive, secure aspects of formality *and* the flexibility of informality. Those that come close are often large corporations rather than small, adventurous companies or public institutions. Google's famous '20 per cent time' is one well-known instance. There is great scope for more initiatives of these kinds, and for industry and government measures that improve prospects for temporary and part-time workers, especially in the knowledge-intensive environment of the contemporary media and information sectors. But consensus is fragile and trade-offs are inevitable – and if these contingencies are rendered more clearly by ideas such as 'flexicuirity', so much the better for both workers and employers.

There is an unresolved contradiction in the scholarship here, and it haunts the creative labour debate like an evil spirit. Progressive cultural critics of creative industries want it both ways: we want the stability of the industrial model as well as the seductive informality of the art, fashion and dotcom worlds; we want state support for workers without paternalistic bureaucracy; 9-to-5 wages without 9-to-5 drudgery. It may be possible to build systems that let these things coexist, although few would assume the probability or even possibility of that outcome. We first need to see this apparent conundrum at the heart of the debate – the utopian claims for coexisting formality and informality – brought into the open and discussed, rather than repressed.

4

Geographies

So far in the book, we have met a range of participants in the informal media economy, from black-hat hackers to altruistic fans. This chapter adds a new layer to the analysis by focusing on the geographic aspect of informal media trade: how such trade is spatially organized and regulated, and how (and where) it interfaces with formal media systems.

As we will see, the informal media economy has a distinct and fascinating geography premised on the strategic leveraging of formal market differences for profit. Wherever there is a border of some kind and a corresponding difference in prices, quality, regulation or enforcement activity, there will also be informal media trade. Understanding these linkages between informal activity and pre-existing formal market structures can help add complexity to our analysis of global media flows.

The Kirtsaeng Affair

We begin our inquiry into informal media geography with the story of Supap Kirtsaeng, a part-time cultural entrepreneur who became reluctantly famous in 2012. Kirtsaeng specialized in one of the oldest and most enduring informal trades: parallel book importing. His career as a book trader began when he moved from Thailand to the United States in the late 1990s to pursue his education: in his case, a maths degree at Cornell. Kirtsaeng held a Thai government scholarship, which required him to return to Thailand after his study and

teach there for 10 years. He duly completed his degree, and then a
PhD in maths at the University of Southern California, before going
back to Thailand to teach. Clearly, Kirtsaeng was a good student; of
more interest to us, he was also an informal media entrepreneur who
supplemented his scholarship through a simple and successful business reselling textbooks purchased cheaply in Thailand. It was this
uncomplicated trade that became the focus of one of the most important US copyright cases in recent years, and in the process made
Supap Kirtsaeng famous.

There is nothing unusual in selling second-hand textbooks: textbooks are expensive, and cash-strapped students sometimes need
them for just a single subject of study. Most large university campuses
support a healthy trade in used books. Resales help defray the cost
of new purchases and ensure that the benefit of a good textbook will
be shared as long as the book is current. Much of this trade sits
towards what we call the informal end of the book business: sales of
physical books are organized through personal networks, local stores,
university noticeboards or online forums, and are generally unregulated by the kinds of rules that seek to control the circulation of more
recent cultural goods. Such sales are rarely measured, infrequently
taxed, and no royalties are paid to authors or publishers. This means
that although prices can be low, profits for dealers may be high. One
of the legal ideas at work here is known as 'first sale', or 'exhaustion',
the theory being that the intellectual property rights of authors or
publishers expire after a copy of a work is sold for the first time,
leaving the owner to dispose of the physical object as he or she
wishes.

Supap Kirtsaeng took full advantage of the first-sale principle,
using eBay as a platform for a transnational import and resale business. Friends and family in Thailand would buy cheap English-language textbooks in Thai bookshops and ship them to Kirtsaeng in
the United States, who would then resell them for a tidy profit online.
Kirtsaeng was exploiting a basic feature of international markets: the
fact that goods are usually priced differently in different places
because people's capacity and willingness to pay varies greatly
between different countries. Despite the putative flattening effects of
globalization, the price of books and other cultural goods still varies
dramatically around the world. Kirtsaeng benefited from this price
discrepancy, as it enabled him to buy low and sell high. As court
documents later revealed, he sold $900,000 worth of books this way,
making a profit of around $100,000.

Textbook publishers were not impressed. New Jersey-based publishing house Wiley and Sons, whose Asian subsidiary produced the

textbooks in question, called in their lawyers. A lengthy court case followed, with well-known companies filing briefs on either side. Costco and eBay – whose business models rely on the same parallel import principles – lined up in support of Kirtsaeng. Copyright holders and industry groups, including the Business Software Association and Motion Picture Association of America, pitched in for Wiley. The end result was an historic Supreme Court judgment in March 2013 that found in favour of Kirtsaeng, concluding that his first-sale rights took precedence over the parallel import restrictions built into US copyright law – a decision that pleased second-hand book traders, libraries and civil society groups, while enraging copyright holders.

The Supreme Court case brings into focus some spatial aspects of media trade. The legal dispute, which came down to a technical distinction between geographic and non-geographic readings of US copyright law, is one of many conflicts that arise at the borders between media markets, and at the interface between formal and informal systems. Scholars of the informal, including Tom O'Regan (1991, 2012) and Adrian Johns (2009), regularly foreground these geographic tensions in their analyses. O'Regan's (1991) analysis of global VHS markets in the early 1990s is a notable case. He distinguished between three kinds of market formations: a largely legal market for movie playback (in the United States, Japan, Canada and Australia), an informal market that functioned as an 'extra, partially underground TV service' (typical of the Eastern Bloc), and a 'substantially illegal' hybrid model (in the Gulf states and Latin America). Video circuits, while taking different forms in different nations, had a common effect in terms of the way they built up a global market structure: the medium's 'porousness', according to O'Regan, was also 'a powerful factor integrating markets on a global scale'. Here we see the paradoxical logics of fragmentation and recentralization across space that characterize many new media forms. eBay, as used by Kirtsaeng, may be performing a similar function for book markets.

There are geopolitical implications to these market border disputes. Most debates about cultural trade are about access to national markets and local regulation. Countries identified with powerful media and cultural industries – those that are the great exporters of intellectual property – generally want more access to foreign markets, and stronger protections for rights holders in all jurisdictions. Producers in small or developing countries, where they exist, face the problem of competing with much larger global businesses. In response, they argue for protection on cultural, social or national development grounds. Contemporary trade agreements, and the industry and regulatory structures that are constructed around them, are often described as 'liberalizing' or 'neoliberal' reforms. In the context of media industries, however, we see them also as formalizing interventions, because they revolve around creating cross-border regulatory structures and corresponding national property rights regimes.

Informal trade adds another layer of spatial market complexity, shaped by evolving technologies, market structures and patterns of use. Kirtsaeng's case is interesting in the light of this cultural geography because it reminds us of the ubiquity of informal economies. Momentarily at least, it brought global information policy debate back from its contested edge in Southeast Asia to its US centre.

Disaggregating the Market

To understand the issues in play within the Kirtsaeng story, it helps to distinguish between *primary* and *secondary* media markets. The fact that books can be and are being parallel imported and resold through large, well-organized secondary markets is one of those obvious but often overlooked dimensions of the industry. Overlooked, but important, for at least two good reasons: second-hand books provide affordable access to knowledge for students and others without the resources to buy new books. And the second-hand trade also ensures that obscure and out-of-print books continue to be accessible. It is not surprising, then, that the second-hand trade survives even as the prices of new books fall and as digital books appear to be turning the industry upside down. The internet has contributed to the second-hand business, with aggregating websites such as AbeBooks (now owned by Amazon) providing even small, out of the way stores with a global market.

This has implications for how we think about media markets. While it is common to speak of the market for a media technology or product as a unitary field ('the book market', 'the tablet market'), what we are talking about is an array of many different markets that interact and cross-pollinate. Each has its own spatial dynamics. Consider the textbook market so expertly managed by Mr Kirtsaeng: as the Wiley case demonstrated, it has many moving parts. We could represent a few of them in a simplified fashion (see Figure 4.1)

Book markets are both typical and exceptional. As the oldest media commodity, the book is at the centre of an extraordinary system of markets, non-market and institutional structures, from public libraries to mail-order book clubs. Historical studies by Elizabeth Eisenstein (1979) and Adrian Johns (1998) have successively

A customer at Gould's bookshop in Sydney. Image: Ella Horsfall (CC BY-NC-SA licence, 2011)

Second-hand books on sale in Old Havana, Cuba. Image: Gerry Balding (CC BY-NC-ND licence, 2013)

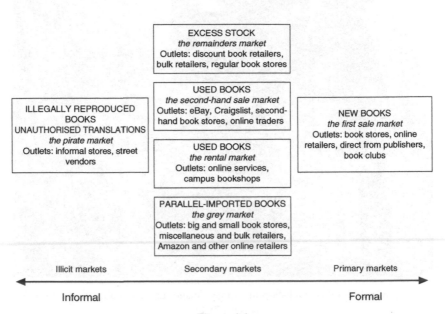

Figure 4.1

revised the multifarious history of the print trade, while the sociologist John B. Thompson (2010) has begun to trace the contemporary impact on it of digital media. One of the many insights to emerge from this body of work is an understanding not only of the multiplicity of book markets, but of how formal and informal, primary and secondary markets have historically interacted, and the tensions that spring up at market boundaries. Although the cultural form may be old, some book markets are new and volatile. Agents within them may occupy highly contested spaces in the broader industry. Like other markets, book markets depend on liquidity, so they must get their stock – and their sales – from somewhere. In the second-hand textbook trade, students provide a predictable flow of both. But some markets are more favoured than others: textbook rental businesses, for instance, may find publishers unwilling to offer them the same terms for new stock as others.

The emergence of online portals for second-hand book dealers demonstrates the importance of geography in this evolution. Abe-Books.com is a well-known example that enables book buyers to find and compare prices of used books across a global network of sellers. This site and others like it have upset the established order of the book trade in several interesting ways. It has weakened the position of publishers and the first-sale market by making a wide range of used books much easier to find. While second-hand bookshops have long existed, locating books in that market has often been a time-consuming and hit-and-miss affair. Buyers often relied on the acquired knowledge of particular outlets, and retailers frequently specialized (in textbooks, for example) in order to attract a larger clientele. The fragmentation and dispersion of second-hand stores created a form of natural protection for the first-sale trade. The portals, however, mean that special consumer knowledge of specific dealers was no longer required; a cheap second-hand book could be found and bought online in no more time than a pricier new one, and shipped for the same fee. Publishers and new bookshops have fought back with cheaper (and prominently branded) 'classic' editions.

AbeBooks also disturbed the equilibrium of the second-hand industry, hitherto a typically low-volume, high-margin trade built on personal networks. It increased the size of the market, and also introduced a new element of price competition. The effect of this was intensified by the introduction of new players, encouraged by the falling cost of entry (no need for a physical store) into what remained an attractive business. These new players behaved differently from established players in the trade: they did not see themselves as part of the same social and commercial networks. All that AbeBooks requires from a seller is a monthly subscription fee (from $25 in 2013) and an agreement to their terms. One 2007 post to an antiquarian booksellers' blog conveys some of the consequences:

> I vividly recall an incident a few years ago . . . A 'dealer' . . . got in touch, seeking a book we had. He insisted on a discount. We didn't know him so I wrote back saying that our criteria for providing a trade discount was simple: we don't extend discounts on first meeting and the discount has to be reciprocal. Since it appeared likely that he would never have anything we would ever be interested in, I respectfully declined his request.
>
> Oh, did he get bent out of shape by that polite refusal! He, apparently, believed that trade discounts were his God-given right. After all, he was 'a registered dealer on ABE!' (Gertz 2007)

The author of this comment went on to make the case for a special section of the AbeBooks website for 'the true rare and antiquarian book selling professionals'. They wanted the professionals to be distinguished from the 'cavalcade of amateurs and idiots . . . that currently overpopulate the site'. (AbeBooks does now have a separate search facility for Rare Books.) Amateurs perhaps, but AbeBooks clearly has a direct interest in the efficient management of its sellers' stock. The site offers its sellers free inventory control software, which includes price comparison tools and connections with the Amazon store. Software of this kind represents a further formalizing initiative. The effect and intent are to unify a fragmented, spatially dispersed industry sector into a single market through user-generated data and a series of linked websites. AbeBooks' unified market effectively requires every book buyer to be a parallel importer, creating – together with other such portals – a new economic geography for the second-hand trade.

First-Sale and Commodity Afterlives

Primary and secondary markets are interconnected rather than autonomous. A bookshop may buy some of its stock direct from the local, authorized representatives, while also parallel importing additional stock from overseas and acquiring bargain-bin items from a third-party distributor (the kind that specializes in bulk purchases of excess stock). This commingling of primary and secondary market activity is common in book and music retailing. As trade liberalization has enlarged the legal possibilities for parallel importation, vendors take an increasingly wide-angled view of their inventory and how it can be sourced. Some media retailers house new, grey and used goods under the one roof.

All this activity is premised on resale rights enshrined in the first-sale provisions of copyright law in the United States (or in similar provisions elsewhere). The ability to resell media commodities works to the advantage of both producers and secondary traders by adding value to the initial purchase. This principle underwrites whole sectors of the economy, such as the property market and the used car market. As such, it allows producers to charge a price that reflects this embedded value, with future resale value taken into account. This is as true of the media business as of the car business. Students buy expensive textbooks in the knowledge that at the end of semester they can take them down to the used bookshop or list them on eBay or Gumtree. In the earlier age of LPs and CDs, buyers knew they had a chance of getting at least a few dollars back from their purchase of the latest Aerosmith album when they traded it in at the local second-hand store.

Digital goods are a different story. Most digital books – including, of course, Amazon's own – are putatively licensed rather than sold: consumers 'buy' permission to read them for a certain time, on certain platforms and under certain conditions. Digital music and movie stores generally operate on the same principle. Technical obstacles prevent purchasers from sharing them or reselling the content they have acquired. Upon the death of the purchaser, the licence expires: goods are not transferred to the beneficiaries of an estate. To date, there are no large-scale secondary markets for digital goods. A few entrepreneurial companies have tried to create such systems, notably the MP3 reseller ReDigi, which briefly operated an online resale marketplace for unwanted iTunes downloads. However, a US Federal Court judge shut down ReDigi in 2013 on the grounds that first-sale provisions do not apply to digital media.

For consumers, the difference between purchased and licensed content is not obvious, and the lack of ownership rights is not necessarily a problem. Many people are happy with the way iTunes, Amazon and other e-retailers supply media. Licensing also has its advantages: the kind of low-cost, high-value service provided by Spotify and other streaming programs would be impossible under a digital sale scenario. But tensions flare up at the margins when system failures and vendor overreach remind us of the vulnerability of our digital libraries. In 2009, Amazon deleted e-books by George Orwell from customers' libraries because of legal problems with the original vendor (Stone 2009); *1984* was one of the books in question. The most serious objections to the new licensing regime are raised by librarians, who find e-books more restrictive than print. Some publishers now ask for per-loan payments rather than a one-off purchase price, meaning that the library must keep paying for popular titles well after the publication date.

The extent of secondary trade in physical media goods varies from commodity to commodity. Some have a very close relationship to secondary markets – limited edition merchandise, for example – whereas commodities like newspapers have little or no value beyond the first sale. The properties of particular technologies and the way they are used by people mean that the number, character and size of secondary markets vary from one media commodity to the next. Secondary markets for concert tickets are a controversial example. Ticket scalping (on-selling of tickets for profit) is sometimes held up by advocates of the free market as a natural experiment in supply and demand dynamics in which everybody benefits: consumers get a second window of opportunity, and entrepreneurs profit from their work. Certainly platforms like eBay and corporate ticket resale sites ViaGoGo have the potential to streamline and normalize such transactions (one no longer has to pay cash to touts outside venues). But others see scalping as a classic case of price gouging which results in much higher prices for some consumers. Attitudes towards scalping vary considerably from country to country; in the United Kingdom and the United States it is widely practised, whereas in Australia it is uncommon and bitterly resented by consumers. The distinction between opportunistic on-selling and predatory scalping is not always easy to draw. Witness the increasingly common phenomenon of retail websites (including Amazon and certain airlines) charging different prices for the same goods based on where you live, your buying history, and even what kind of computer you are using (Mac users pay more) (Mattioli 2012). The scalper's logic of strategic price elasticity clearly has a place within formal commerce as well.

Debates over secondary markets are happening in many different areas of the economy, from cosmetics to medicines to aeroplane parts. Understanding this point can help add some nuance to the way certain forms of secondary market activity are represented by media corporations. There is nothing inherently menacing or exotic about secondary markets per se; they are an integral part of modern (and, indeed, pre-modern) economies. However, they do make some aspects of formal business more difficult, such as measurement, regulation and supply chain integrity, and their presence may create potential for predatory activities. There is also a link between secondary markets and informality: multiple secondary transactions tend to move exchange further and further away from the institutions of the formal economy. The paper trail simply finishes. Again, this may be a blessing for consumers or a curse, depending on the context.

Diverging interests between producers and legal resellers are another source of friction. Goods in secondary markets have already returned revenues to their producers, but their subsequent distribution does not feed anything else back to these people; instead, it generates profits for entrepreneurial third parties. It is unsurprising that producers get annoyed seeing 'their' products making money for others. Conflicts inevitably arise, with each side claiming the moral high ground. Parallel importation is a particularly contentious area because it brings geography into play. Unlike a second-hand sale, a grey market transaction involves a leveraging of territorial differences: a layer of legal, economic and, in many cases, cultural and geopolitical complexity gets added to the transaction.

In drawing attention to the multiple and inter-related nature of media markets, we return to the opening premise of the book: that a thorough understanding of media commerce needs to factor in the informal. In this case, this means looking beyond the primary market. Media industries research has long focused on first-sale issues and, consequently, topics such as movie release timing and record sales patterns. In taking into account secondary markets – which are usually closer to the informal end of the spectrum – and treating them not just as an add-on but as an *integral component* of the media business, we can better understand the system as a whole.

Grey Technology Markets

Let us recap on a few key points. First: geographic differences and boundaries are great *drivers* of informality, for they provide an opportunity to leverage market and regulatory differences; producers and consumers alike exploit these differences in their own ways. Second: the globalization of formal media industries has produced global informal industries that respond to and sometimes even mirror the shape of their legitimate counterparts. While taking many different forms, grey markets obey a general logic: they tend to appear in sites where media commodities are expensive, scarce or unavailable. Wherever demand is high, cross-border arbitrage is legal (or the laws forbidding it are weakly enforced) and the commodity in question can be purchased cheaply abroad, a grey market is likely to emerge. Seen from this perspective, parallel importation is an in-built effect of the same global industry structures that seek to contain it, in the same way that 'illegal' migration is linked to border protection policy – border crackdowns inevitably produce evidence of more transgressions – and piracy rates increase as a result of stronger copyright enforcement. Parallel importation is similarly linked to wider phenomena: the globalization of national media and entertainment systems, and the trade structures that seek to regulate this unruly tangle of interconnecting markets.

Consider the retail ecology of the mobile phone. Trade in mobiles occurs across an intertwined set of markets. New handsets can be purchased direct from manufacturers, at electronics stores, malls and small retailers, or bundled with phone plans from telecommunications carriers. Phones are bought second hand from eBay, from traders specializing in second-hand handsets, or from friends who want to trade up to a new model. In many nations, grey market phones are widely available – these handsets are usually parallel imported (in which case the phone comes at a discount, reflecting the geographic price differential), they may have been sold to the retailer by legitimate distributors that specialize in disposing of excess stock or they may be factory overruns sold off in lots to distributors. It is also possible to buy counterfeit versions of phones that perform many of the expected functions but are manufactured without the manufacturer's consent. Additionally, there is the black market of stolen handsets which get routed back into the formal economy through pawn shops and chain stores specializing in reselling used goods.

A fascinating study by anthropologist Gordon Mathews (2011) has shed some light on the international grey trade in mobile phone handsets, a great deal of which has historically been routed through Hong Kong. Grey market phones are affordable options for consumers in developing nations priced out of most formal phone markets. In the 1990s a massive cross-border trading system emerged to supply, repair and resell these handsets. Hong Kong's Chungking Mansions building, a sprawling hotel and trade complex in Kowloon, became a central site for small to medium-sized trading companies catering to third world markets; here, African and South Asian traders would buy bulk shipments to be resold in their home countries. During the mid-2000s, around 20 per cent of sub-Saharan Africa's mobile phones – approximately 15,000–20,000 units a month – came from Chungking Mansions (Mathews 2011: 106). Many of these were shipped informally to Africa in the luggage of migrant workers. In his detailed study of the Chungking Mansions economy, Mathews introduces the people who run this trade and notes the assortment of different markets coming together in this unique building:

Electronics retailers at Chungking Mansions in Hong Kong. Image: Little_Ram (CC BY-NC-SA licence, 2012)

Shops often have their particular specialties: China-made branded phones such as G-Tide or Orion; China-made no-brand phones; China-made knock-off phones such as 'Sory-Ericssen'; China-made copies of European, Korean, or American brands exactly like the original; four-teen-day phones, which are European-brand phones that have been returned by their original owners and have been warehoused and eventually sent to Hong Kong and Chungking Mansions to be sold to developing-world buyers; or used phones. (2011: 111)

Mathews's account of this transnational mobile phone ecosystem underscores the remarkable geographic *centralization* of digital technology markets in particular trading hubs. Though the importance of Hong Kong and its trading places is diminishing with the rise of Southern Chinese cities like Guangzhou, the system Mathews describes here – which is informal but legal – has been the basis for an intricate set of grey-market interactions between phone wholesalers, traders, migrant workers and African consumers.

Another vivid description of grey technology markets can be found in journalist Scott Carney's (2006) account of shopping for iPods in Chennai in the mid-2000s. As in the rest of India, informal small traders dominate the electronics retail system in Chennai. The highest concentration of these traders can be found in Burma Bazaar, a well-established locale for electronics and disc trading. These marketplaces are noisy, hot and crowded, everything is paid for in cash and there are no warranties or receipts. To a touristic eye it appears haphazard, yet people who understand the system know that traders here run a finely tuned business that efficiently leverages cross-border differences and operates in ways suited to the local political economy. Perusing the Burma Bazaar in search of iPods, Carney discovered that those on sale were authentic and legal, but parallel imported from places like Dubai and Singapore. At the time, there was very little official supply of 'authorized' iPods in India: most units were bought abroad, shipped back home and sold informally. The grey market was the default trading system for this shiny new device.

The iPods sold at Burma Bazaar may have taken a circuitous route from wholesaler to consumer, but they arrived more quickly and could be purchased more cheaply than the official equivalents. This is because grey market iPads evaded the hefty sales taxes and tariffs that would apply were the same product to be imported and sold through formal channels. Customers also did not have to wait for the official Indian product launch, which may happen months after the product goes on sale in wealthier nations. Carney paid US$280 for his 30GB video iPod, which was 'only $20 cheaper than [one] you can get at Best Buy in the United States, but a whopping $160 cheaper than the $440 that authorized dealers sell iPods for in India' (Carney 2006). A more recent account suggests that USB sharing is drawing people away from the pirate disc economy of Burma Bazaar, and the rest of the traders at the centre, including the electronics traders, are suffering as a result (Kandavel 2013).

In their analysis of grey mobile markets in India, Rangaswamy and Smythe (2012) argue convincingly that, while informal, such markets are highly organized (see also Sundaram 2009; Srinivas 2003). Consumers have a choice between many varieties of the same phone: new, second-hand, reconditioned, or grey versions can all be found in the marketplaces. Of the grey phones, many are imported from Dubai and Malaysia. Pirated software programs are used to unlock the handsets and make them usable on local networks. Rangaswamy and Smythe's description of this extremely well-organized and internally governed system offers a kind of implicit management theory for the informal media economy:

> Markets, especially the more established districts in downtown Mumbai followed unwritten rules of organizational arrangements. This was firstly to brook peace among competing businesses by 1) channelizing allocation of various sales and servicing units, 2) harmonizing demand/ supply across the units, and 3) internally organizing dealers, wholesalers and clients to optimize business flow. Given the precarious legal status of the markets, these silent rules were critical to curtail disharmony and their public spill-over between business units. (2012: 302)

Such arrangements are not unique to India. Similar things happen in other nations where differential currency rates, pricing or enforcement structures make cross-border arbitrage attractive. Australia, a high-wage nation, has a very different media market from India but it too is a thriving centre for grey parallel imports, especially in software and information technology markets. The principal cause of this grey market activity is the relatively high local pricing. Australians pay A$1.19 per track on iTunes, compared to US$0.69 in the United States. (At the time of writing, the two currencies were close to parity.) Likewise, business software and IT hardware is around 50 per cent more expensive in Australia (Choice 2012; HRSCIC 2013). The trend has deepened even as the value of the Australian dollar has strengthened in recent years. The result is a broadly held anger over widespread price gouging: consumers resent paying what they call the 'Australia tax' for digital goods that are basically identical across the globe. The premium consumers pay for the local version is attributed to higher labour costs and value-added extras like strong warranty support; however, consumers are dissatisfied with this explanation when they see little evidence of local infrastructures. This buyer's experience is indicative of the wider sentiment:

> Last year I wanted to upgrade my Adobe Acrobat and Adobe Photoshop Elements and went to their web site for the price and to order the upgrades. When I put in my address it directed me to their Australian site and the price increased two and a half times. However this wasn't the end of my annoyance with Adobe, when the software arrived it had been posted from Singapore and I was billed from Dublin. (HRSCIC 2013: 81–2)

Complaints like this reflect the tensions that arise when two incompatible media geographies collide – the flat, friction-free geography of digital media where everything is just a click away, and the real-world geographies of corporate location, infrastructure, differential pricing and tax regimes. It is the 'flat' earth of economic globalization theory (Friedman 2005) versus the hilly terrain of corporate media *realpolitik*.

For a different example of how geography shapes media commerce, we can look to China, home to a billion aspiring media consumers. Here, state restrictions open a space for a flourishing grey market: gadgets have traditionally been bought in bulk in Hong Kong and carried over the border, or covertly shipped from the United States then resold for profit to local buyers. One 2011 estimate suggests around half the iPads sold are grey market imports (Kan 2011). In China, the iPhone has a mostly grey history because of the high levels of informal parallel importing that marked the early years of its presence there. Apple did not launch the iPhone in China until 2009, two years after its US debut. Even after its official launch, the iPhone was only available on a contract with the unpopular carrier China Unicom, and local versions did not have wi-fi connectivity because of government regulations. None of this provided a compelling value proposition and so, unsurprisingly, grey marketers raced to fill the gap. Media scholar Yu Shi has documented how this informal trade works:

> One path starts from the gray market in the United States from which Chinese retailers can directly mail order units already freed from AT&T's contract. Another way is to get the phones from a supplier in the United States who can buy a large number of units. The units are then delivered to Chinese retailers by tourists or flight attendants who earn US$10 to US$30 per phone. These mail-ordered or personally

delivered units are finally sold to Chinese consumers either in retail stores or through eBay-like websites in China such as taobao.com. (2011: 10)

Apple learned from its mistakes. In 2013, the iPhone 5 went on sale in China on the same day as the rest of the world, meaning that Apple fanatics in Shenzhen and Shanghai waited no longer than their counterparts in San Francisco. This substantially curtailed the parallel import business model, although opportunities for arbitrage remain in other consumer markets. Witness the unusual situation with games consoles: PC gaming is legal in China, but consoles like the Xbox or PlayStation 3 are banned. This law is the result of a government crackdown against games 'addiction' among China's youth, and has led to a pent-up demand which grey marketers satisfy through parallel imports of consoles (which are ironically manufactured in China in the first place, then shipped abroad before being shipped back by grey marketers). Another side effect of the law has been the emergence of 'non-console' gaming devices that work around the ban through crafty means. For instance, Nintendo's iQue Player, made specifically for the Chinese market, is a controller that plugs straight into the TV.

Other aspects of global gaming markets exhibit a similar propensity toward semi-formal secondary trade. The CD key business is well known to regular gamers, and is a legal but grey industry that involves reselling access codes to popular games. CD key codes are used to verify a legal purchase by linking the software to one individual. This is a variation of the system long used by software manufacturers, as readers who recall buying a copy of Microsoft Office from a computer store and then having to enter a long multi-digit code stamped on the box will attest. Game communities are increasingly shifting away from box retail sales to paid downloads and subscription models, so the CD key system is common; gamers are familiar with the ritual of entering these magical codes. The system also works well for bulk buyers such as internet cafés and LAN cafés that have to install multiple copies of a game and do not want to mess around with unwrapping boxes and loading discs.

While there is nothing illegal about this system, its reliance on alphanumeric codes transmitted over the internet makes it well suited to cross-border arbitrage – and therefore to grey markets. Online grey market resellers like CJS (founded by British teenager Corey Smith) buy their codes from game distributors in EU nations where games are priced low. Through their websites, they resell these codes to customers in higher-wage countries where games are more expensive. The end result is that savvy consumers in the United Kingdom and

Australia can save significant amounts of money on their game purchases. The CD key industry is a curious fusion of the second-hand and parallel import models. It makes life difficult for global companies that engage in price differentiation, leading to inevitable crackdowns and overreach. Game distribution giant Valve famously banned *Modern Warfare 2* codes bought from resellers, enraging thousands of users who believed they had bought legitimate codes (Good 2009). Another workaround involves transnational reselling of parallel imported boxed games. In online stores such as the UK-based ozgameshop.com, games can be half the price of the Australian boxed versions.

Proposed changes in international trade law may bring an end to much of this grey activity, or at least push it further underground. The Trans-Pacific Partnership (TTP), an international trade agreement currently being negotiated between the United States, Japan, Mexico, Canada, Australia and a number of other Southeast Asian and Latin American nations, is set to outlaw many parallel import activities currently permitted under international law. At the time of writing, leaked documents suggest that the TPP will feature provisions enabling copyright holders to block imports of cheaper foreign versions of their goods. The proposed restriction would apply to 'books, journals, sheet music, sound recordings, computer programs, and audio and visual works'. While many nations already have similar restrictions in place for particular media forms, this kind of blanket restriction is a definite upward ratchet for territorial copyright protection.

As technology retailing continues to move online, this raises the stakes of our original question: what role does geography play in media markets in an ostensibly borderless, digital age, and how does it mediate relations between the formal and informal media economies? To answer this question, we need to return to and consider the historical evolution of international media retailing, and the challenge digital technology presents to these models.

Boundary Trouble

As we have seen, the formal media economy has a layer of geographic organization, where markets are segmented through a territorial division of the globe into discrete spaces with their own pricing and retail structures. This enables media producers to price their goods according to local income levels, to control sequencing and to extract the greatest return from each market. The objective for media companies and trade institutions is to keep these zones separate and stop goods spilling over from one zone to another. The territorial segmentation of the market also has to be coordinated with other marketing strategies – for example, the segmentation of markets through multiple formats and platforms (the hardback book, the theatrical release of a movie).

This is a task of real complexity, and needs to be understood as an uneven and ongoing process rather than a *fait accompli*. It is not a necessary attribute of cultural markets. The early book trade crossed borders; copyright laws – even those based on natural rights arguments – enacted national, industry-based models for production and distribution that had to be established, consolidated, extended and defended. In the nineteenth century, European national print languages provided the basis for national media and cultural industries, and a degree of protection from production centres in larger, wealthier countries. Although we often assume that media industries are now global, copyright was (and remains) the creature of nation-states; from Berne to the World Intellectual Property Organization, international copyright is a matter of trade between nations, a question of competing national interests and competing interests within nations.

The problem of translation illustrates some of the issues involved in attempting to control international distribution through copyright. Eva Hemmungs Wirtén (2011) has recently described how the 'transformative practice' of translation reveals the divisions in copyright law and policy between nations that are primarily exporters or importers of intellectual property. Hemmungs Wirtén shows how small, 'importing' nations – often those with 'minor' languages – consistently argued for liberal translation rights to facilitate knowledge flows and build national cultural markets. Large 'exporting' nations such as France and Britain sought stronger translation rights, seeking their assimilation into a broader reproduction right (an objective achieved in the 1908 Berlin convention). But translation raised all kinds of problems for the conception of authorship that appeared to lie at the heart of copyright law. Was a translation a purely 'derivative work', or should it be treated as something closer to an adaptation, with elements of originality? Should developing countries have a right to translate foreign works freely? These questions resonate in the digital environment, where the scope for cosmopolitan adaptation, translation and redaction is greatly expanded.

Market segmentation can be realized through strategies of technological or economic control as well. Sweeteners designed to add value to goods purchased in the right places. At the technological level, there are strategies like regional coding, which makes it relatively difficult for DVDs, games, phones and even printer cartridges to be used outside the area of the world for which they were intended. The curious and complex geography of the DVD region scheme is illustrated in the maps below, combining, on the one hand, Papua New Guinea with Latin America, and, on the other, Japan with South Africa. Together with copy protection mechanisms, the aim of regional coding is to discourage parallel importation and resale. However, the widespread availability of region-free players and the reverse engineering of the DVD copy protection system has undermined regional coding for DVDs. A consolidation and simplification of region codes is evident in the later, higher-definition Blu-Ray system.

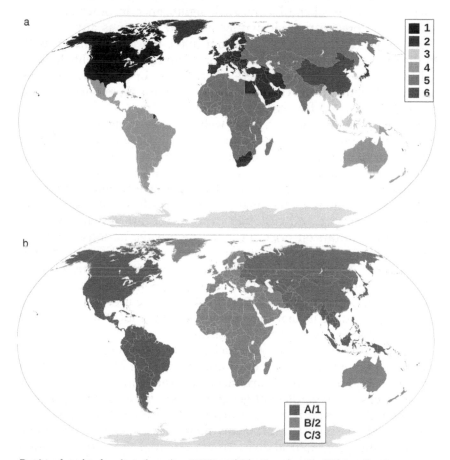

Regional codes for digital media: DVD and Blu-Ray. Image: Wikimedia Commons (GNU license)

These spatial divisions are technically and legally complex constructions. Underlying them are established market boundaries, distribution practices shaped by convention and a contentious international legal regime. Additionally, the *timing* of new releases is just as important as place. The problem for rights holders here is that while cultural trade is plainly global, the business retains some simple local and regional particularities. The entertainment industry competes for consumers' leisure time, but this time is not evenly distributed everywhere. In the United States, for example, the Memorial Day holiday at the beginning of summer is a traditional time to release blockbuster movies; the long weekend gives more people the chance to go to the cinema. This means the industry has an opportunity to attract large audiences at an early stage and to build market momentum. But this particular long weekend has no such significance in other countries at the same precise time. It may be as good a time as any for a de facto global release, but that does not make it a good time in itself. In theory, regional coding solves the problem by giving rights holders a lock on the 'when and where' of releases. In practice, the lock *invites* unlocking: it provides the opportunity for cross border retailers and consumers, file sharers and downloaders.

Media companies use carrots as well as sticks to encourage people to buy through authorized channels, thus maintaining the spatial separation of markets. Local warranties, customer support and troubleshooting, guaranteed delivery times and other customer-service goodies are some of the benefits of making a legitimate purchase. Electronics companies and many media retailers are increasingly focusing on service and customer experience, rather than trying to race to the bottom on price. In many high-wage nations, buying a parallel-imported camera on the grey market is significantly cheaper – sometimes by 40 or 50 per cent – than buying the same product through authorized local retailers, but many people still prefer to pay the extra money because they know they can take it back to the shop where they bought it, that they are covered by a local warranty and that they can ring a helpline for assistance.

In the domain of digital goods such as software programs or music, any consumer advantages in local distribution are likely to be much harder to communicate. Consumers buy the same goods on very similar websites, regardless of geography. Service is rarely a point of differentiation, especially in software; consumers are generally encouraged to solve any problems themselves, using international websites. But geographical divisions are essential to the organization of these businesses. While early theorists of the internet often pointed to its potential to work across borders, the emergence of global consumer markets for digital goods (and the computing infrastructures supporting them) have plainly made national market segmentation *more* feasible. At the time of writing, Apple's iTunes store sold digital music, movies, TV shows, books and apps in 155 countries, each with its own shopfront. Amazon, which began by selling physical goods and moved into digital more recently, has far fewer stores (12 country-specific sites in 2013), but the number of country-specific shopfronts is rising. These digital retail infrastructures allow for considerably more delicate and sophisticated market segmentation and price differentiation strategies than could be achieved in the world of physical media commodities.

For those consumers with enough skill and time, the informal economy provides workarounds to these barriers. Apple's approach – driven not only by its own pricing strategies, but also clearly by the international fragmentation of rights – has produced a thriving subculture of offshore gift cards, multiple Apple IDs, and fake addresses. While Apple tries to maintain trade in geographic market segmentation by using automated country-detection and requiring credit card registration, many consumers outside the United States who are disappointed with the high prices and limited range of their local iTunes shopfront go to great lengths to work around these blocks to access more bountiful and affordable content from the United States. They are not pirating this content, but, rather, they are taking a series of actions – ones that may violate Apple's terms – in order ultimately to pay for Apple content.

This is a very common practice in our home country, Australia (Barrington and Tilley 2011). The elaborate charade involves first

iTunes gift cards: an international media currency. Image: Anthony Agius
(CC BY-NC-ND licence, 2009)

setting up a US iTunes account, using a bogus address and phone number (often a hotel located via the web, or Apple's Cupertino headquarters). The next step is to acquire US dollar-denominated iTunes giftcards, which may be purchased from any number of vendors on eBay. If all goes well (and it often does not; these vendors can be unreliable) you will receive a code from the giftcard that you can then enter into your iTunes account for credit. After going through all these steps, non-US customers are generally able to purchase and view content through the US iTunes store. We are also aware of a vibrant system of friend-to-friend exchanges among Australians visiting the United States who buy numerous cards and bring them home to resell. A more expensive, but nevertheless popular, alternative ploy is the acquisition of multiple devices – such as Apple TV set-top boxes – each attached to a different jurisdiction and therefore offering different content at different prices.

Such activities provide informal workarounds to artificially imposed market blocks. If geographic market segmentation is a formal industry response to diverse national markets, then parallel importing and technological workarounds are a response to this response. All these responses are labour-intensive and time-consuming, and everyone involved wishes the charade was not necessary: enforcing market segmentation is a burden for media companies as well as for consumers. But for industry, the alternatives are even less palatable – so the charade must be maintained. Such is life in our un-flat global media market.

The Enemy Within

There are reasons why market segmentation would want to be protected as a principle. While it can be exploited for price gouging, the ability to price goods differently for different territorial markets may have some up-sides for consumers in nations with low wage levels or deflated currencies. In the case of intangible goods like a film or a book, pricing naturally has more to do with an assumption about what the market can bear and is not simply a calculation based on production costs. When market segmentation becomes impossible, there is a risk that media companies will simply opt for a strategy of price equalization, increasing the lower prices to match the highest ones and wiping out the incentives of arbitrage for grey marketers. For this reason, eliminating market segmentation could potentially introduce its own logistical and ethical problems. Price equalization may have the effect of putting formal media goods out of reach of many people in low-wage nations, contributing to a further deformalization of those markets.

At the same time, we need to carefully scrutinize both the pricing policies of media multinationals and their rhetoric about grey markets. Some of the arguments that come from the brand-protection industry – that alliance of marketers, lawyers and rights holders who make it their mission to stamp out parallel trading – arguably push the boundaries of credibility. If we follow the rhetoric on parallel trade by industry groups like the Anti-Grey Market Alliance, grey marketers are a spectral force that needs to be contained. Intellectual property lawyer David Sugden provides a representative sample of this discourse in his handbook on grey market containment strategies:

> Providing access to technology and company know-how has been devastating to various American businesses. Less than honorable partners will over-manufacture genuine goods, manufacture their own copycat goods, or share secret processes to other individuals or companies. The accounts of American business getting burned by foreign deceit are endless. (2009: 37)

Putting aside its xenophobic tone, let us consider the argument being made here about grey traders. The quote above frames this kind of business in much the same way as copyright discourse describes piracy. Of course, some grey trading *does* have a seedy element, as it involves the violation of implicit or explicit contracts with suppliers: there are plenty of cowboys out there. Sugden quotes one such operator, who describes the art of buying low and selling high in the sportswear market:

> What I . . . did was look for big brand names like Adidas or Lacoste or Nike and sell them into a country where they already have a distributor. It's called parallel trading. Many years ago when I started out, the big names turned a blind eye to the parallel market.
>
> It was convenient and good business to have one official and several unofficial distributors channeling your goods into a country where the demand was growing and the official distributor was going along just a little too slowly. When the official guy kicked up a fuss, the brand [owner] turned around and blamed the lying cheating little toe-rag who had misled them. 'We were told it was going to Nigeria,' they would protest, or 'these goods were sent to Poland, we have no idea how or what or . . .' After the dust settled and sales needed a boosting the whole process began again, followed by more threats and recriminations. (Cited in Sugden 2009: 70–1)

Accounts like this lend the grey trade a shifty allure. But they also suggest something larger and more interesting: a tacit cooperation between multinational corporations and informals. This is the other side of the story. As well as being a side effect of the market segmentation strategies of the formal economy, the 'problem' of parallel importation is just as often produced by media corporations through their own distribution and acquisition policies. The grey trader is a boundary figure who moves back and forth between legitimacy and illegitimacy, depending on circumstances at the time.

This ambiguity can be seen in a fascinating mid-1990s legal dispute between Apple and grey marketer David Braunstein, an American IT trader. Braunstein had offices in California and Tijuana and was in the business of buying Apple Powerbooks from Apple's Latin American division, then reselling them over the border in the United States. Because prices were significantly higher in the United States than in Mexico, Braunstein made a tidy profit. He was a big buyer, and spent around a million dollars a month with Apple. This scale of this grey trading could not remain a secret forever, and his activities eventually came to the attention of Apple executives in the United States. They were livid about Braunstein undercutting their US operations and causing brand-dilution in the domestic market, and called the Department of Justice. Braunstein was charged with fraud and money laundering. As the case made its way through the US courts, what came to light was the fact that Apple's Latin American arm was well aware of Braunstein's plans for the computers: it knew he was reselling them in the United States, and it knew this was against the rules. But because the Latin America division was under extreme pressure from its US bosses to meet sales targets, executives were happy to turn a blind eye. Their dealings with Braunstein were off the books – a classic informal strategy – to keep the transactions opaque. But they knew what was going on.

The Braunstein case paints a picture of Apple as a corporation at war with itself. The way the business as a whole operated clearly helped to *produce* informality. High sales targets and weak internal governance were a recipe for grey trade. Apple divisions appeared to be happy enough to overlook the activity when it was in line with certain strategic objectives, but also chose to cry foul when it undermined other objectives. By changing the way they run their businesses – reducing price differentials, stopping exports, rebadging product for overseas markets, and so on (Clarke and Owens 2000: 284) – corporations may be able to contain grey trade, but this will come at the expense of something else. There is a balance to be struck here. As with product piracy, the grey market problem is about trade-offs and priorities. Potential for these informalities is ever present within formal markets.

The Piracy–Parallel Import Connection

A recent study of piracy in emerging economies led by Joe Karaganis (2011) demonstrates the interconnected nature of legal, grey and pirate markets. Karaganis and his team compared prices for the popular movie *The Dark Knight* in the United States and a range of developing countries (2011: 56–8). Their findings reflect the tight rein that Hollywood keeps on its prices: DVDs cost US$14–15 (in Russia, Brazil, South Africa and India) and US$24–27 (in the United States and Mexico). This is basically a two-tiered system, with a premium price tag for the US domestic market and a discounted (but still relatively high) price for lower-income countries. Mexico is the notable exception to the rule: DVDs were priced at the same level as the United States due, no doubt, to the fear of parallel importation over the US-Mexico border. As Karaganis and his coauthors note, US record and film industries tend not to adjust their prices for local conditions; as a result, 'CDs and DVDs remain luxury items in most middle- and low-income countries' (2011: 58).

Karaganis's next step was to put these prices in context with the economic situation of each country, using the 'comparative purchasing power' method (CPP). This calculation (the second row in table 4.1) estimated the cost of an item as a percentage of GDP: it was designed to suggest how relatively expensive the item would be in US terms. According to this measure, although the nominal cost of the DVD in Russia was $15, for a Russian this would *feel* more like $75

Table 4.1 Comparative prices: *The Dark Knight* DVD, 2008–9

	Legal price	CPP price	Pirate price	Pirate CPP price
United States	$24	–	–	–
Russia	$15	$75	$5	$25
Brazil	$15	$85.50	$3.50	$20
South Africa	$14	$112	$(.4) 2.8	$22.40
India	$14.25	$641	$(.3) 1.2	$54
Mexico	$27	$154	$(.4) .75	$4.25

Source: Karaganis 2011: 57 (CC BY-NC-SA license). Parentheses indicate lowest observed price (generally wholesale).

once you translated that back into the average earnings for that country. Karaganis also measured the average price of the same DVD in local pirate markets, in which prices across all the countries were significantly lower. Here we find CPP prices much closer to US figures. The conclusion? The pirate economy effectively pulls prices down to a level more appropriate to local economic conditions.

This produces a reasonably simple model where high prices correlate with high piracy. When we take the element of parallel imports into account, a triangular dynamic emerges, which binds together three kinds of media markets: authorized legal markets, parallel import (grey) markets and pirate markets. Price structures in any one of those markets inevitably affects what happens in the others. Hollywood movie studios generally opt to price at first world levels, meaning there is less scope for parallel imports compared to other industries. This results in higher levels of piracy. The other option would be to have a much more flexible international pricing structure that reflects local capacity to pay: this would likely result in lower levels of piracy but higher levels of parallel importing. Regardless of pricing, parallel importation that is driven by the availability of a work in one market rather than another will still occur. Media distributors are in the unenviable position of having to juggle these competing market vulnerabilities and find the best solution for their particular needs. But we should not lose sight of the fact that both piracy and parallel importing are, to a significant degree, *produced by* the pricing structures used to regulate international distribution.

The Persistence of Place

This chapter has provided some glimpses into the roles played by secondary markets within the media economy. In particular, we have seen how the grey market is integrally bound up with – rather than separate from – the geographies of formal trade. Grey markets undermine the strategy of market segmentation, but they are also a product of that very strategy; their existence can be best understood as a structural side effect of certain aspects of the organization of the formal media economy. One implication of the preceding discussion is that geography continues to play a vital role in organizing online and offline media markets, and, by extension, in the social distribution of ideas, images, ideologies and capabilities. Despite the promises of a borderless digital world, media market structures forged in the analogue era are remarkably persistent. Digital technologies add layers of complexity without dismantling the old ones: tariffs and import restrictions are superseded but not fully replaced by geoblocking and digital rights management. The tensions that characterize trade at the edges of these market boundaries are not going away; if anything, they are increasing.

There are political dimensions to these border disputes. At least some of the energy fuelling today's cyber-political institutions – from Sweden's Piratbyrån (Pirate Party), some of whose members were founders of the Pirate Bay website, to the vengeful battalions of Anonymous – is fuelled by anger over a perceived exclusion from first-release media citizenship through segmentation strategies like staggered release patterns, or the lack of official subtitling in minor languages. This is one of the more surprising developments in the last decade's digital cultural politics – the idea that market segmentation and digital rights management could help to fertilize a countermovement that, in the case of Piratbyrån at least, has grown into a fully fledged political institution, one 'complete with its own market research, political lobby groups, policy-making associates, public relations work, and with a mainstream market ideology' (Vonderau 2013: 109). In Australia, the level of disquiet has been such that a federal parliamentary inquiry into technology pricing was held in 2012–13; it recommended the lifting of all parallel-import restrictions, the introduction of a digital resale right and removal of anti-circumvention measures from current law, and even suggested government resources be used to educate citizens in how to disable geoblocking (HRSCIC 2013). These extraordinary recommendations are unlikely to be implemented, as they directly conflict with other national trade objectives (such as inclusion in the Trans-Pacific Partnership), yet the recognition of these issues at the highest levels of government reflects the levels of popular concern.

In thinking through these issues, we might remember the other political issue bubbling away in the background of the media geography debates: the relationship between corporate location and taxation. In recent years, journalists have been regularly reporting on the tax affairs of major media corporations and have revealed how they are able to manipulate their global operations to leverage differences in national and state tax law. Google, Microsoft and Adobe are among many companies shuttling profits between a tax haven in Ireland and a notional base in Bermuda, where the tax rate is zero (the infamous Double Irish scheme). Such arrangements reflect an agility that would match the most nimble grey marketers: they leverage the differentials between regulatory systems, operating in the cracks between territories, in a game of globe-hopping that only the biggest businesses can play. Here, as elsewhere, the distinction between formal and informal media business is blurry indeed.

5

Regulation

In their essay 'The Californian ideology', written during the early years of the first dotcom boom, Richard Barbrook and Andy Cameron identified what they saw as a politics of anti-government in the West Coast tech economy. This value system, influenced by political libertarianism, free market economics and 1960s radicalism, was pervasive within computer culture and commerce. It was notable for its hostility to government regulation, which was seen as a repressive force that could only impede innovation:

> Information technologies, so the argument goes, empower the individual, enhance personal freedom, and radically reduce the power of the nation state. Existing social, political and legal power structures will wither away to be replaced by unfettered interactions between autonomous individuals and their software. . . . In place of counterproductive regulations, visionary engineers are inventing the tools needed to create a 'free market' within cyberspace, such as encryption, digital money and verification procedures. Indeed, attempts to interfere with the emergent properties of these technological and economic forces, particularly by the government, merely rebound on those who are foolish enough to defy the primary laws of nature. (Barbrook and Cameron 1995)

Much has changed since the 1990s but Barbrook and Cameron's critique is still relevant because it captures some widely held beliefs about the state's role in technological innovation. Such beliefs – that 'dinosaur laws' fail to keep pace with technology, that the purpose of regulation is to restrict and hamper and that the best thing governments can do is to stay away while markets sort themselves out – still hold sway in Silicon Valley and its analogues elsewhere. The anti-regulation *esprit* finds its apotheosis in the start-up that prefers to 'seek forgiveness' rather than ask permission. From Airbnb, whose users avoid paying tax on accommodation, to online stores that bypass local taxes, many new media businesses are structured in a way that is indifferent – sometimes antagonistic – to formal regulation.

The dinosaurs vs. innovators narrative of technological regulation is commonly reproduced, sometimes persuasive and rarely surprising. Laws in the field of media and communications – including copyright and broadcasting law – have generally been devised with specific media technologies, places and applications in mind, and it is always an ongoing task adapting and revising them as technologies change. But as a line of critique, there are two problems here. First is the risk of circularity, since the deficiency identified in the law is a negative one, a failure to account for the very activity that has arisen outside the current scope of the law. When and if regulatory structures catch up, they remain subject to the same generic criticism. The second problem is that this line of argument sets up a misleading dichotomy between formal control and informal freedom, and downplays both the diversity of existing regulatory structures and their equally diverse effects. Governance certainly prefers the formal; the legal decision-making apparatus depends on well-defined institutions, processes, roles and statuses for key actors. The subtle graduations inherent in the spectrum of informality described in this book rarely translate into the 'bright lines' preferred by legislators, courts and enforcement agencies (Richardson and Goldenfein 2013). However, the law also regularly, and deliberately, leaves room for practices and experimentation beyond the most regulated spaces.

Through three case studies, this chapter explores some counterintuitive aspects of technology regulation. Our starting point is that regulation takes many forms and does not always include top-down control. Carrots may take the place of sticks, and peer pressure may substitute for official rules. We have already discussed some of the control systems at work in the media economy (see Chapter 1), such as authorization, restriction, measurement, codification and promotion. To this list we could add a range of indirect modes of regulatory control – subtle forms of governance that tend to coexist with top-down regulation, and that operate through manners, convention and example; in other words, *informal regulation*. Take, for example, the common workplace complaint that someone has not acted 'professionally'. Think of the bushwalker's ethical injunction to 'Take nothing but photographs; leave nothing but footprints' (sometimes simply abbreviated to LNBF). Such statements invoke tacit expectations and rules, and are intended to address the problems that arise from bad behaviour or poor judgement. Communities of interest, working and professional cultures all develop their own diverse ways of doing things, which are often threaded through everyday working life: the 'rule of thumb' that settles a difficult question; the conventional formulas for dividing resources among a group; the Frequently Asked Questions document that manages debate and discussion productively.

In the stories that follow, we explore the way these bottom-up regulatory mechanisms interact with formal law. The three cases we discuss in this chapter each display a different mix of formal and informal elements, and have had wildly divergent outcomes, ranging from clear regulatory failure to demonstrable success. The conclusion of the chapter reads across the three examples to arrive at some general observations about digital media governance.

Regulating Digital Transport

If you live in a major US city, or have visited one recently, you've probably noticed a new kind of public transport on city streets. Since 2010, cars with pink moustaches have been appearing all over the country, from San Francisco to Tampa and Tucson. The cars come in many different shapes and sizes, from SUVs to sedans, but they all have the same distinct facial hair attached to their fenders. Their

A Lyft car in San Francisco. Image: Alfredo Mendez (CC BY licence, 2013)

drivers wear no uniforms, are impossibly cheerful, and will let you choose the radio station. Where have these strange vehicles come from? Where are they going? And why is everybody inside them doing fist-bumps?

These moustachioed cars – the trademark of San Francisco-based rideshare company Lyft – are part of a high-tech revolution in private transportation that has been sweeping the United States, a revolution that brings together locative and mobile media technologies, on-demand 'sharing economy' service models, and stylized, branded experiences. Lyft's app-based hiring service connects smartphone users with non-professional drivers. Payment is via 'donation', with a minimum amount specified. The app is simple to use: GPS coordinates identify your position, you select a car in the area based on recommendations from previous passengers, and when you reach your destination you use your phone to make a credit card payment. The whole experience is easy and reliable, and fun as well – every Lyft trip begins with a fist-bump between driver and passenger. Company founder John Zimmer compares the experience to a ride from a friend: 'We try to find aspirational, friendly people, and when you take a ride with a person, you think "hey, that could be me"' (in Olanoff 2012).

Uber, Lyft, Allocab, Hailo, Sidecar – these are a few of the app-based transport start-ups that have appeared across the globe in recent years. Some of these new 'transportation network companies' (TNCs) are essentially new-fashioned updates of existing taxi booking and logistics systems. Others are more disruptive. Rideshare apps like Lyft match like-minded ride seekers and drivers. Ridejoy specialized in long-distance ridesharing – a private alternative to Greyhound. Other companies are more ambitious, competing directly with the taxi industry. San Francisco-based Uber is the most well-known example. Its taxi-like black car service has become immensely popular not just in the United States, but across Europe and Asia as well, attracting plenty of media coverage along the way.

The TNCs are bringing Silicon Valley-style innovation to an old, unglamorous industry – and consumers seem to love it. But not everybody is happy. Taxi drivers and taxi associations have been complaining loudly, arguing that the new operators are illegal and ungovernable. 'Illegal taxis and services must be stopped', said a taxi industry representative during a recent, noisy protest in San Francisco. 'We are highly regulated, trained, legally insured, and we drive regularly inspected vehicles – for a reason. . . . Those unlicensed drivers are road bandits. We are the real community drivers' (in Reuters 2013). Taxi associations have gone out of their way to warn the public about the risks of 'uninsured accident claims, fare gouging and other illegal activity' when using the new app-based services (in Jeffries 2013).

Let's take a look at the regulatory issues around Uber, the most controversial of the new operators. Uber began as a premium private car service for San Fran techies. Driven by professional drivers and e-hailed through the proprietary app, Uber town cars were more expensive than a taxi, but cheaper than a limousine; their unique selling point was the 'slick' ride and personalized service. In a *Wall Street Journal* interview, Uber CEO Travis Kalanick explains how he and his business partner came up with the idea:

> 'We were jammin' on ideas,' Mr. Kalanick recalls. 'What's next, what's the next thing, and Garrett [Camp, co-founder] said, "I just want to push a button and get a ride." And I'm like, "That's pretty good." He said "Travis, let's go buy 10 Mercedes S-Classes, let's go hire 20 drivers, let's get parking garages and let's make it so us and a hundred friends could push a button and an S-Class would roll up, for only us, in the city of San Francisco, where you cannot get a ride." ' (In Kessler 2013)

Kalanick is an entrepreneur in the classic Silicon Valley mould, with the CV to suit. A whiz-kid coder who studied computer engineering at UCLA, he dropped out to found a peer-to-peer search engine with college buddies. Rights holders sued, and he declared bankruptcy. Kalanick bounced back with a new venture called Red Swoosh; he later sold this to internet traffic management giant Akamai for US$15 million. Turning his attention to transport, he next secured venture capital backing from Amazon's Jeff Bezos, among others, and founded Uber in 2009. The company commenced operations in San Francisco in 2010. In 2012, Uber launched a lower-cost service (UberX) using private citizen drivers. It now operates at a range of price points and service levels, using private citizen cars, luxury cars and SUVs, and has expanded internationally, starting up everywhere from Guangzhou to Cape Town. Its valuation has risen accordingly. After a recent round of venture funding, the company is said to be worth a jaw-dropping US$18 billion.

Uber operates in a grey area of the law. Legal actions have been brought against the company on all fronts, including public safety, trademark law, consumer fraud and payments processing infringements. Kalanick's attorneys work overtime to defend the company against these actions, and they have mostly been successful – Uber has generally been able to keep its cars on the streets, despite rarely having prior authorization to do so. But there are still a vast number of unresolved legal issues for Uber. At the time of writing, Uber is banned in Las Vegas and Miami; court cases are pending in Chicago and Washington; and taxi drivers have organized large-scale protests in London, Barcelona, Milan and Paris.

For his part, Kalanick enjoys playing the maverick upstart shaking up a tired industry. His media interviews are full of anti-establishment diatribes. A self-declared 'trustbuster', he rails against 'anti-capitalist' protectionism, the taxi industry 'lobbyists [who] try to shut us down' (in Kessler 2013), and the 'propaganda generated by an entrenched incumbent adverse to technology, innovation and progress' (in Jeffries 2013). This heady discourse is straight out of the Californian ideology playbook. According to Kalanick, law is a slow-moving beast outpaced by technology. Truly innovative companies need to act first and let the regulators follow, just like the automobile and aviation pioneers of the early twentieth century who did not wait around for governments to tell them what they could and could not do.

There are some interesting parallels between the new transport companies and new media businesses. Kalanick's approach – which involves setting up operations *before* regulatory approval is granted, then striking deals with the authorities as issues arise – has many media precedents. As we saw in Chapter 1, many cable television operators in the United States operated outside the law in the early years of that industry. Barry Diller's Aereo operation (which rebroadcast free-to-air content on the internet) tried the same thing. Another example is Google Books: Google used the 'act first, negotiate later' approach when it started its massive book-scanning operation in 2004. It was promptly sued by major publishers, to whom it paid a multi-million dollar settlement in 2012. Despite its questionable legality, Google Books is still in operation and has expanded significantly since then. Uber's disruptive strategy is therefore not without precedent, and has clear links to recent media and tech industry history. What we see here is a particular attitude to regulation that now runs through many areas of digital commerce, from transport to creative industries. In *The Net Effect* (2011), Thomas Streeter traces the roots of this laissez-faire futurist discourse back to the early years of the internet. In Streeter's account,

[economic conservatives] set out to show, not just that markets in general were efficient or moral, but more specifically that free markets, unhindered by government regulation, could better handle the most modern of technologies. Radio, television, jet planes, even computers, the underlying argument went, did not need government regulation like the FCC and Federal Aviation Administration, or government-funded research, or protected, regulated monopoly corporations like AT&T; on the contrary, they needed to be freed of the shackles of all these things. (2011: 73–4)

Most of the new transport companies, like many of their sharing economy brethren, use this rhetoric when it suits them. And perhaps they are justified in some of their claims. Apps certainly seem to be more efficient at managing supply/demand dynamics than most existing booking systems, which are characterized by middle-men profiting at the expense of drivers. And the consumer surplus from these new services is very real. But we should not take the claims about overregulation at face value. The spectre of an interventionist state is a convenient fiction, a red herring that allows profit-seeking start-ups to present themselves as countercultural rebels, overstating the degree of state intervention in the service of a heroic innovation narrative. In the case of Uber, the California Public Utilities Commission and other regulatory bodies were actually quite acquiescent and did not need much convincing. The Federal Trade Commission even issued a statement in support of the ridesharing industry (Bilton 2013b). Uber has actually been given a lot of leeway in the name of competition.

Technology journalist Tarun Wadhwa has studied the regulatory issues around these companies. Wadhwa notes a contradiction at the heart of the sharing economy:

> If we keep seeing [start-ups] as the underdog instead of the aggressor, they can get us to fight their regulatory battles for them. Companies like Airbnb want to expand to new markets, but instead of dealing with the legal complications, they pass it on to their customers through the terms of service. Ridesharing services like Lyft and Uber want to have dedicated drivers available at all times, but don't want them considered as employees. By seeing these dozens of companies as a 'movement' instead of individual forces with their own sets of benefits, consequences, and externalities, it becomes much harder to analyze their impacts. (Wadhwa 2013)

Following Wadhwa, we can see how regulatory conflict in the sharing economy is distorted for the purposes of boosterism. The taxi app debate, for example, is really more about *codification* than about a fundamental clash of values between the private sector and the state. Many of the regulatory problems encountered by Uber were technical rather than ideological in nature, stemming from the fact that regulators had no pre-existing language to define Uber. (Was it a transport service or a tech service? A taxi company or a charter carrier? A commercial operation or a neutral infrastructure?) Given Uber's recent dynamic history and multiple 'versions', the fact that regulators might take some time to decide what it was seems more a case of prudence than paralysis. Once California's Public Utilities Commission created the new term 'transportation network company' to describe app-enabled transport services, many of the issues became more manageable. From this point onward an appropriate set of regulations could be built around these companies. The formalizing strategy of describing and categorizing a new practice was necessary before emergent service providers could be treated as an industry. But once in place, this framework has enabled a set of regulatory interventions designed to nurture what is generally seen as a productive new industry.

By the same token, one could reasonably argue that the real regulatory power in this instance lies not with government – whose power over the market may be overstated – but with the apps themselves, which is to say that it operates at the level of code and design. The materiality of the app shapes the way we use the service and, by extension, the social and economic interactions it generates. For example, transport companies' design choices about payment processing will determine who can hail a ride (MasterCard is accepted, cash is not, meaning that the homeless are unlikely to get a ride). User feedback and ratings provide another built-in regulatory system that can function in a more or less automated manner, while being subject to their own kinds of gaming and manipulation. In the new digital transport companies, few of these design choices will attract the level of scrutiny applied to public transport systems. But their social effects will be just as real. In this sense we can speak of a subtle but very real privatization of regulatory capacity, as well as its relocation into code, protocol and software design (Galloway 2004; Gillespie 2009; Lessig 1999).

What does all this mean for media industries? The transport app issue is but one example of a wider collision between technological disruption, entrenched incumbents, informal activity and formal regulation that plays out across different parts of the economy. Compare this situation to other media industry conflicts – such as the digital copyright debate – and similar issues and discourses immediately become visible. Consider the way taxi associations mobilize a particular kind of language against Uber and Lyft: rideshare cars are 'rogue vehicles', a phrase that recalls the rogue websites targeted by rights holders in takedown campaigns. Taxi companies warn of 'felons' driving unlicensed cabs, just as anti-piracy campaigners link copying to organized crime and terrorism. Some discourse frames them as the new gypsy cabs, adding another layer of class and ethnic complexity to what is already a class-based issue (ruling-class geeks vs. largely immigrant and working-class taxi drivers). In their defence, the new transport companies use a different kind of language that has an equally strong connection to recent media policy debates. They claim to be mere intermediaries (in the same way that torrent sites and file-hostage services use the 'safe harbour' defences of US copyright law, which grant certain indemnities). They argue that they are merely providing an infrastructure for individuals to transact privately, and that they should not be held accountable for everything that happens on the network – just as electricity companies are not held accountable for supplying power to criminals.

There are other connections with media industry debates. Some new transport operators, notably Lyft, run a modified version of Radiohead's pay-what-you-want model (although it has since instituted a minimum 'floor' price). There is also a link to be made between the general spirit of sharing-economy businesses and the shift from media ownership to licensing. Why go to the expense of owning and maintaining your own car in a city like New York when you can use the excess capacity of others? This is similar to the argument used by Spotify and other streaming services: why spend your money buying a limited selection of content when you can stream licensed content for a lot less and receive a lot more value in return? The new sharing-economy companies have lifted some songs from the media industry playbook.

Whichever way you look at it, neither the old nor the new taxi industries can claim the moral high ground. In this conflict between formal industries and informal upstarts, the low-tech and the high-tech, everybody is using whatever language is available to shore up their own position. The heroic battle between the dinosaurs and the innovators turns out to be more like a bun fight between different kinds of elites. And the conflict on which the story is based – the three-way game between states, incumbents and emergent businesses – may well turn out to be a sideshow to the main game of private regulation via platform design. Here we can see some of the complexities of technological governance, reminding us that, in digital media, regulatory power is not always where you would expect to find it.

Regulating the Wireless Commons

We now turn to a different site of regulatory conflict, this time located within the publicly managed communications infrastructure that

A customer connects to WiFi at a Starbucks in Kuwait. Image: Pinot Dita
(CC BY-NC licence, 2007)

makes much of our digital consumption possible. This is a story about the wireless internet. More specifically, it is about the long chain of technical, bureaucratic, but politically charged policy decisions that have shaped the way governments allocate radio spectrum, and which have led to the emergence of today's wireless systems. It involves a second kind of regulatory problem: public resource allocation.

In the case of transport apps, questions of incumbency and taxation are central; the regulatory challenges are about how to mediate between different kinds of clashing business interests, while ensuring public safety and preventing tax base erosion. A different regulatory dilemma can be seen in current debates over what economists call 'common-pool' resources: non-excludable but rivalrous public resources (such as forests, fisheries and the airwaves) that need to be managed to avoid detrimental uses. The problems of managing public and common resources may seem somewhat remote, but they are in fact central to contemporary media, especially mobile telephony and its mix of private, public and common-pool infrastructure.

As an example, imagine yourself at a Starbucks café, somewhere in the world, sipping a triple grande latte and playing on your smartphone. After connecting to the complimentary Starbucks WiFi, you spend a few minutes checking your email. Then you receive a text message from an old school friend, and send one in return.

Sufficiently caffeinated, you sign off, exit the store and go on your way. This everyday experience may seem unremarkable, but for our purposes it is interesting because it relies on a series of policy frameworks, principles and settlements concerning government management of radio spectrum. Radio waves are transmitted at different frequencies, and different services operate at different points across the spectrum (from AM radio at the low end to air traffic control at the high other). When you receive a text message, you are using a part of the spectrum reserved for mobile phones. When you connect to the Starbucks WiFi network, however, you use a different part of the spectrum, which in most countries is treated as an 'open' spectrum. This part of the spectrum is usually set aside for general use and local networks, meaning that operators and appliance manufacturers do not need an exclusive licence to transmit on these frequencies. This policy decision has had far-reaching consequences – and some background information is necessary to explain why.

In most countries, the majority of spectrum users require a licence granting them exclusive rights to transmit information over certain designated frequencies at a certain power and in a certain area. The spectrum is generally planned around the interests of such users, ensuring they do not interfere with each others' transmissions. Up until the 1980s and 1990s, spectrum access rights in most developed nations were not sold but were allocated by regulatory authorities on 'public interest' grounds, on the basis of the requirements of the services involved. For example, television broadcasters needed, and therefore received, more spectrum than radio stations. Governments tailored licences to services being offered. In this system, licences were sometimes awarded like prizes by governments to applicants (often incumbent communications businesses) for reasons that were often opaque. Like the spectrum itself in this model, winners were scarce.

The system worked well enough until new technologies – especially mobile telephony – appeared, hungry for the same parts of the spectrum used by television. A reformist argument advanced in 1960 by the distinguished English economist of communications Ronald Coase gained unexpected traction: an alternative, market-driven approach could ensure more productive use of this public resource (Coase 1959). If usable spectrum were a scarce resource limited by the need to avoid interference, the best way to allocate it would be to establish spectrum usage rights as a form of property, and then distribute these to users according to some kind of market mechanism. Like property, the licence involved in such a system would be tradable, and it would not be tied to any particular application: as technology changed, users could use the spectrum for new and unforeseen purposes. These ideas encouraged a wave of microeconomic reforms in spectrum policy across the world, with spectrum auctions in New Zealand (1989), India (1991) and the United States (1994). In one sense, these were privatizations of a public asset: the airwaves themselves were being sold to the highest bidder for private commercial uses. Seen from another angle, they secured a public return for the use of a public resource that was already in commercial hands – and did so in a way that encouraged investment in new and emerging services.

The spectrum auctions of the 1990s changed the political economy of the media in ways we are only just beginning to understand. They generated tens of billions of dollars in revenue for governments. In many countries, the most recent round of these eyebrow-raising dividends has been derived from the sale of spectrum rights formerly reserved for analogue television: the end result of a long process of industry restructuring in which efficient spectrum use was a central policy rationale. The less prescriptive licences involved have had far-reaching effects, encouraging significant investment in the burgeoning mobile telecommunications services of the new millennium. The rollout of third- and fourth-generation mobile networks in particular was a necessary precondition for the uptake of 'second-wave' smart-phones from Apple and Google, and the new kinds of locational media services designed for them. Together with many other analysts, the US Federal Communications Commission now sees the further development of the mobile broadband internet as a vital future source of economic growth (Hazlett et al. 2011).

At the heart of the post-Coasian revolution in communications policy is the idea of the 'property right' in spectrum; the term invokes a real estate metaphor, but effectively means a stronger set of exclusive rights for licence holders. Despite the apparent successes of the property concept, there are alternative models, including a long-running argument for a spectrum commons-based approach (Reed 2002; Lessig 2004); this is a model for managing shared spectrum rather than subdividing it. In most communications policy systems, the notion of a spectrum commons already has a limited existence, particularly when it comes to local, low-powered radio devices, with restricted functionality and little commercial significance. Communications regulators handle things like WiFi routers, garage door openers, cordless phones, Bluetooth devices and wireless medical equipment differently from higher-power services. Instead of making users of these everyday devices acquire spectrum licences, the devices themselves are licensed.

While technical standards are not our focus here, the regulatory frameworks raise many interesting questions for media researchers. There are variations on this theme across jurisdictions, but an Australian example is from the national regulator ACMA (the Australian Communications and Media Authority), which describes its model as a 'public park' – another land-use analogy: 'Users are able to access a small portion of the total resource (the frequency band) and to share that resource in a way that requires minimal regulatory intervention.' The conditions for park use include not interfering with other users, an absence of any protection from interference by others and the right to use the resource without any licence fee (ACMA 2013). The licence for the device is called a 'class licence' – essentially, an open, standing authority for anyone to use the equipment without having to pay a fee or apply for a licence.

As ACMA acknowledges, the problem with a 'class licence' commons is the risk of interference from others, as the numbers of radio transmitters of various kinds grow. But the benefits are substantial, because the costs of compliance are low. Cheap devices mean that wireless devices in the home, at work and at school proliferate, but a network effect applies, with the value of connection increasing as networks grow. So a home wireless network that begins with a laptop and a desktop computer may extend over time to a whole variety of objects: phones, tablets, televisions, games consoles, cameras and media players. Once connected in this way, these devices in turn create new household ecosystems for information and consumption. Outside the home, unpredictable changes occur. In public libraries, galleries and museums, open wireless networks may bring a whole new clientele through the doors. In educational institutions and offices, WiFi networks make possible the 'Bring Your Own Device' approach to managing IT, where institutions concentrate on providing the network infrastructure rather than mandating hardware and software for everyone.

WiFi is now many things: an enormously popular technology, a powerful brand, a set of complex commercial standards managed by a consortium of tech companies, a new communications infrastructure for work and domestic life. It is neither unmanaged nor non-commercial, but its success rests on a crucial element of *relative regulatory informality* under the auspices of the 'public park' model. This approach is about strategically and deliberately shifting the locus of regulation, to encourage uptake and innovation. It is not a hands-off, laissez-faire approach.

The 'public park' only applies to a small sliver of spectrum – most of the rest is given over to commercial, government and military uses.

But its success has encouraged speculation about the merits of extending the spectrum commons. Commons advocates such as David Reed (2002) and Yochai Benkler (2006) argue that the spectrum-as-exclusive-property model reflects the technologies of Coase's age: crude, analogue, high-powered systems dominated by 'dumb receivers'. They and others have pointed to more recent developments in radio transmission, especially the emergence of 'cognitive', or smart, receivers able to manage communications-intensive environments more deftly. Reed argues that the great starting point of twentieth-century spectrum policy – the need to avoid interference between services – rests on a misconception. Interference is not something that happens 'in the ether', as if photon particles were colliding and breaking down in space: it is a technical artefact of receivers that occurs when different transmissions cannot be successfully processed and separated. According to this line of argument, if more sophisticated devices can manage this task better, then spectrum scarcity and the property model of policy that flows from it are not inevitable. As technologies for sharing radio frequencies continue to develop, more innovation will result from extending the 'public park' idea into larger sections of the spectrum, opening up space for new wireless broadband technologies.

Another line of debate and speculation extrapolates from the private space of WiFi (the connected home) to the idea of 'public WiFi' (cities and neighbourhoods connected through ubiquitous WiFi networks). Some councils and city governments provide public access to the internet in this way. Advocates for 'municipal WiFi', as it is sometimes called, argue that broadband should be seen as a twenty-first-century utility, just as necessary as water and electricity. At the same time, private providers are likely to continue to commercialize municipal WiFi, using advertising and other business models. Ian McShane et al. (2014) have analysed the fascinating history of these parallel and competing possibilities, tracing successive waves of enthusiasm and failure over the last decade.

What is interesting here for the broader concerns of this book is not so much the potential of wireless networks, but their practical role in *connecting* formal and informal media and communications systems, as well as the unique nature of their regulatory model – which uses a highly formal regulatory architecture to stimulate informal activity. While Hazlett and other students of communications emphasize the remarkable transformations of the global telecommunications industry over recent years, the emergence and success of mobile broadband would not have been possible without the fixed, place-based, supplementary technology of WiFi. Mobile devices incorporate many network technologies, but they are designed to 'lean towards' WiFi. WiFi connections enable smartphone and tablet users to upload, download and back up apps, data and media over a network connection that is usually cheaper (and faster) than a cellular connection. Some media apps – such as mobile versions of newspapers and magazines – are designed only to download over WiFi connections. WiFi-only mobile devices (iPads and other tablets especially) remain extraordinarily popular because of – amongst other reasons – their pivotal place in mobile and domestic media ecosystems of movies, games, TV shows, newspapers and magazines. Outside the home, commercial WiFi hotspots proliferate, run by telcos, coffee shops and bookstores. WiFi services provided by telcos now supplement cellular coverage in busy areas. At a deep level of system design, new internet protocols are emerging that facilitate switching between networks.

WiFi clearly supports – and is supported by – commercial mobile broadband. It does so not as an element in a static model, but as a kind of building block, demonstrating how a 'space for the informal', sanctioned by a complex public regulatory architecture, is at the heart of the growing mobile ecology. In this way, WiFi exemplifies the interdependence of the formal and the informal; and its history reflects a particular regulatory philosophy, based on strategies of authorization and codification, rather than restriction. From these foundations, an innovative governance system has emerged.

Regulating Copyright Enforcement

If the taxi app battles show the need for regulation in the face of innovation and WiFi reveals the benefits of the controlled 'public park', other conflicts expose different aspects of the regulation issue. One example can be found in the area of digital copyright enforcement. Here, a different kind of regulatory drama has flared up, raising the question *who regulates private enforcers?*

This story has its roots in the file sharing battles of the early 2000s, particularly the Napster case, and the subsequent anti-piracy strategies pursued by rights holders in the music and film industries. It is no secret that these sectors have been through some very difficult times. Digitization has dissolved what were once golden rivers of revenue. Consumer habits have changed rapidly. Thousands of staff have been laid off, especially at the record labels, and companies have been brutally restructured. It is not surprising, then, that media companies in this volatile space are desperate to protect what remains of their revenues. Intellectual property enforcement has once again assumed centre stage.

The resulting 'war on digital piracy' has been the most spectacular, and arguably the most ill-fated, private media regulation effort in recent memory. From one perspective, this war has been about finding regulatory solutions to market problems, from external restriction (criminal prosecution of file sharers) to codification (limiting informal consumption through digital rights management). US record labels and movie studios led the charge, licensing all manner of anti-piracy technologies and creating a small army of technicians, programmers, field investigators, lobbyists and trade negotiators, employed by them to wage the anti-piracy war. In an authoritative report published in 2011, it was argued that anti-piracy activity peaked in the late 2000s, before declining during the global financial crisis: 'Both the number of groups involved and the level of financing of anti-piracy efforts rose significantly in the period'. The authors suggest that the US IP industries' overall budget for anti-piracy enforcement was 'in the low hundreds of millions of dollars per year' (Karaganis 2011: 19).

As a private regulatory effort, the war on piracy makes for a fascinating case study because it brings together two apparently contradictory tendencies. On one hand, it reveals increasing public involvement in private commercial disputes. 'The primary goal of industry activism has been to shift enforcement responsibilities onto public agencies' (Karaganis 2011: 19). US entertainment industry lobbyists have invested enormous political capital in convincing government agencies and lawmakers – from Congress to customs agencies – to wage the war on piracy on their behalf. Increased customs monitoring, tighter trade regulations, anti-circumvention laws: these are some of the official restrictions that have come into force.

At the same time, areas of copyright regulation have become increasingly privatized, leading to the emergence of a whole service sector of companies – employing thousands of people globally – that specialize in enforcing, measuring and monetizing intellectual property infringements. This small army of specialists, lawyers, technicians, data crunchers, media monitors, computer programmers, social media analysts, private investigators, web-lurkers, content protection consultants and security guards work on a contractor or subcontractor basis, at arm's length from the content industries themselves, reflecting what has been described as 'webs of interlocking enforcement efforts and advisory groups that blur lines between public and private power' (Karaganis 2011: 20).

We have tracked some of the companies that do this work as private contractors on behalf of content owners (Lobato and Thomas

2011; Lobato 2012). One area of this burgeoning field is technological prevention of piracy. During the early peer-to-peer (P2P) years, a number of small operators specialized in digital 'spoofing' and 'spoiling'. The aim was to flood P2P servers with defective files in order to annoy would-be pirates and drive them towards legal services like iTunes. Some of the companies involved in this line of business include Anti-Piracy LLC, Overpeer, Nuke Pirates, C-Right and Media Defender. Others specialize in anti-camcording technologies that detect the use of video cameras by audience members in movie theatres. In the case of multiplex screenings, such products and services include digital watermarking and audio fingerprinting technologies (which pinpoint the theatre in which the bootlegs were shot); CCTV systems (which detect the use of camcorders by audience members); and night-vision goggles (used by ushers to spot suspicious activity in theatres). This is a profitable line of business for US-based companies like Sentek, Trakstar, Sarnoff and Cinea. The adoption of these technologies throughout the supply chain has also created commercial opportunities for businesses that wish to use this anti-piracy infrastructure for other purposes. One company, Aralia Systems, has been developing systems to use anti-camcording cameras in movie theatres to record audience reactions to screen content, to sell this data back to advertisers and producers (Torrent-Freak 2010).

Other companies specialize in measurement, developing ways to regulate pirate consumption through ever-finer monitoring. Web analytics companies such as Sandvine and Big Champagne track pirate P2P flows as part of their broader activities. Rights holders recruit major consulting firms to write credible-sounding reports demonstrating the magnitude of revenue leakage (LEK Consulting 2005; IPSOS and Oxford Economics 2011). Companies such as Ipoque and Detica, the latter a subsidiary of BAE Systems with links to the UK defence industry, offer deep-packet inspection of P2P flows (Williams 2009). The anti-piracy research industry also attracts smaller and more explicitly entrepreneurial operators selling made-to-order data. One example is French Solutions Ltd, which advertises the following services:

> Build a portfolio of evidence sufficient enough to present as a handle to lobby for legal and governmental supplements to further protect your business . . . assessments of levels of potential criminal gain in £ or another currency over a set period can be made . . . assessments of likely loss to your turnover in a set period in £ or another currency can be offered. (French Solutions 2008)

Companies like this play a secret but important role in the war on piracy: they provide raw data that fuels the 'numbers game' of lost revenue claims. But they also have their own agenda – namely, to build their own client base by telling appealing stories, through data, to their clients.

At the far edges of this industry we can find yet more companies that specialize in private enforcement and policing. Typically acting as subcontractors for the major rights groups, or as freelance ambulance-chasers, this opaque sub-industry specializes in ground-level investigations and field operations. One older example from the United States is the business model of cable piracy 'stings', which have long been popular among entrepreneurial private investigators. These investigators conduct surveillance on bars and restaurants to detect unauthorized screenings of boxing matches and pay-per-view sports events. They then report these establishments to lawyers who represent cable companies, lodging affidavits that are later used in anti-piracy prosecutions, for a fee of approximately US$250 per venue. Other entrepreneurial strategies for monetizing piracy include 'trash runs' at suspected pirate CD-duplication plants to obtain evidence, such as CD spindles (Thomas 2003). With the global expansion of IP-related trade in the wake of the Agreement on Trade-Related Aspects of Intellectual Property Rights (TRIPS), these enduring business models have gone global, with organized anti-piracy enforcement now reaching into many new markets. China and India are the two biggest IP protection markets for Western multinationals. Here, a flourishing sub-business in field investigations attracts former policemen, heavies, turncoat bootleggers and the like.

Ravi Sundaram (2009) has documented aspects of this industry in Delhi, where anti-piracy field investigators, employed by rights holders, monitor local markets and coordinate police raids. This is poorly paid and unpleasant work. Physical abuse of investigators by vendors is common. Many investigators ultimately switch sides to work with the pirates against the rights holders, finding the conditions better on that side. The boundaries between enforcement and commercial piracy are blurred, to the point of being indistinguishable, as comments from a local MPAA representative indicate:

In India there were some guys who from the beginning were doing the authorized reproduction of cassettes and CDs and were also pirates. So by the time we found them out a good amount of damage was done because they had inroads into us and that began some kind of a competition among the pirates, because one pirate would pay our investigators not to have his premises raided, he would allow a raid maybe once in six months but he would give information about his competitors, the other pirates so that firstly the competitor is harmed and this guy gains his business and guy also grows. We tried to put an end to it, by the time we realized it some of our investigators were also double agents getting money from them also as well as from us. (Sundaram 2009: 133)

From the digital analytics companies to the field investigators, the war on piracy has produced a vast number of private regulatory agents. These examples give a sense of the breadth and depth of what Johns (2009: 498) calls the 'intellectual property defense industry'. Here, regulation mixes with commerce in unusual ways. The work required to enforce copyright protection – and the commercial opportunities that arise from such work – have created a perverse incentive for third-party companies in the piracy wars, who profit from piracy by selling regulatory solutions and knowledge (technological, investigatory, legal) back to rights holders. In other words, the legal regimes designed to contain informal activity have produced their own generative effects: they have become *platforms* for new commercial enterprises, which turn out to have a rather conflicted relationship with the transgressions they are supposed to police.

One consequence of digital copyright policing has been the relocation of energy and investment into solving consumer problems at the margins of this system, in ways that are fundamentally non-productive – which is to say that enormous effort is expended to work around the restrictions. Take the example of region-coded DVDs and Blu Ray discs. Region coding is a content control mechanism (a codification) that deters people from parallel importing discs meant for other markets. Its existence is generative of all kinds of other economic activities. It may encourage you to do a number of things: go to a grey electronics store and buy a region-free DVD player that will play discs from any country; buy from a different kind of mail-order site that sells grey-market and pirate discs (like AliBaba.com); or purchase a DVD player unlocking code from a website (these cost about US$10), through which you can reprogram your player to ignore region codes. A different kind of response to region coding is to skip paid solutions entirely and download the movie from BitTorrent. This would involve visiting a torrent tracking website, which would generate a small amount of revenue for the advertising company which handles the banner ads on the side of the site. To protect your identity from the kinds of anti-piracy companies we discussed earlier, you may also take out a paid subscription to a VPN (virtual private network; also about US$10 per month) or another proxy or anonymizing service, which will conceal your identity from cyber-enforcers. Or perhaps the prospect of being tracked through the open BitTorrent networks means you watch your chosen film another way: you use a linking site to find an online video site in China or the Netherlands or Eastern Europe, where you can stream the film for free, generating ad revenue for both the linking and streaming site in the process. Alternatively, you might use a cyber-locker file-hosting service (used mostly for illegal purposes) through a specialized cyberlocker-specific search engine to locate and download the file, also generating ad revenue. If you are a regular cyber-locker user, you might take out a subscription (US$10 per month) to speed up your downloads and bypass annoying ads. We could go on: the point is that the workarounds become industries in their own right.

These workarounds generate new lines of revenue for parties not involved in content creation, and are all prompted by certain kinds of content control technologies and parallel import restrictions grounded in intellectual property and contract law. In other words, there is a strange economic generativity at work, whereby restrictive regulation triggers a range of second-order activities. In this case, the regulatory strategy of copyright enforcement appears to have had a wide range of unintended consequences, relocating energy and investment into peripheral parts of the media economy.

The increasing automation of IP enforcement, especially copyright and trademark enforcement, has produced its own peculiar side effects. Now, along with all the usual street market surveillance, raids and infringement notices, we also have the phenomenon of automated reporting and takedown, in which bots scour the net for anything that looks vaguely like it might infringe their clients' rights, and then send takedown notices to Google – many thousands per day – to have the content removed from search returns. Bots are a very blunt tool; they cannot easily distinguish between legitimate sites and infringing sites. Much of what they flag as 'piracy' is actually legitimate, non-infringing reportage or fan activity. Google has its own appeal and transparency process – constituting another layer of private regulation – which seeks to temper this automated overreach, but the whole system is taking an increasing amount of effort to administer, diverting useful regulatory capacity into tedious bun fights. At the last count, Google was receiving more than 24 million copyright-related takedown requests a month.

A controversy arose during the 2014 FIFA World Cup. Known for its hard line on IP protection, FIFA, together with its TV partners, employed anti-piracy companies to scour the web and issue takedown notices en masse (TorrentFreak 2014). One such company is the Indian outfit Markscan – a 'consulting boutique dedicated to your IP requirements', according to its website – which has consistently over-reached in its enforcement efforts. Among its more egregious offences was to request takedowns of pages on the websites of *Variety*, the BBC, GigaOm and *Hollywood Reporter* and even FIFA itself, appar-ently because they included 'world cup' and 'streaming' or 'watch' in their content. Google, to its credit, rejected most of these requests. But the time and effort wasted in assessing and contesting indiscrimi-nate takedown requests will only grow as long as the 'takedown spam' business model is viable for companies like Markscan, Detica, Web Sherriff and Mark Monitor. In the anti-piracy industries, as elsewhere, ineffective regulation leads to informal workarounds and formal overreach.

Articulating Formal and Informal Regulation

The three stories recounted here have given us a glimpse of the diver-sity of problems, and consequences, associated with regulating media technologies and industries. The Uber case is essentially about conflict between an emergent technology sector and an established industry; it's about the power of incumbency, and the imperatives of public safety and public services, and what happens when these come uncomfortably into contact with the laissez-faire entrepreneurialism of tech culture. The story of WiFi and spectrum management, in contrast, is about a different kind of public system. It tracks the crea-tion of a relatively informal zone, a narrowly delimited spectrum commons able to solve certain problems of balancing public and private interests, and encouraging innovation within a highly organ-ized regulatory structure. It does so in the context of a dynamic, rapidly changing industry sector that is struggling to deal with the demands of sustained growth. Finally, we examined the rise of the anti-piracy industries. This case shifted the scene to the content indus-tries, where a strong sense of declining demand and endemic business failure has pervaded activity for over a decade. Here, grey areas in the law provide perverse incentives for those in a position to enforce these laws privately. This is a story not so much about bad law as about out-of-kilter incentives and the risks of privatized enforcement.

These three examples do not exhaust the issues that arise in con-temporary media and communications regulation. We have chosen them because they tell contrasting stories about established, emerging and declining industry structures, together with the range of governmental strategies that we introduced earlier in this book (codification, authorization, measurement, restriction, promotion). They show how the 'regulation issue' is not a choice between whether or not to regulate – the prospect of a totally unregulated media landscape is unthinkable – but how best to *combine* formal and informal modes of regulation. Sometimes it is important to authorize and codify new activities in order to affect some kind of settlement between new and established players, as the tale of the new transport services suggests. Sometimes regulatory exceptions and departures are necessary, not in order to 'catch up' with technology but to give emergent ideas room. Effective regulation brings benefits; bad regulation has unintended consequences, which can be destructive or inappropriate: the case of the anti-piracy enterprises reveals how innovation can be diverted into the enforcement of unenforceable laws, and investment into questionable and unproductive new business activities. None of these specific instances negates the general and overriding need for public media regulation to guard against the perils of market or government dominance.

If there is an overarching lesson to be learned here, it is that effective regulatory systems need to be grounded in a rigorous understanding of the dynamics, risks and possibilities of the informal economy and how it shapes, and is shaped by, its formal counterpart. There is little value in seeing informality as 'animal spirits' or 'a force of nature'. As we have argued throughout this book, the informal is always best understood in relation to the formal, and that includes regulatory structures. Informality may often be an unintended consequence of regulation, but you can also regulate for informality. Good regulation opens up spaces where relatively less controlled activity occurs safely and productively. Bad regulation relocates everyday practice into regulatory ghettoes. Linkages between the informal space and the formal are another essential area for investigation. These too can operate both positively and negatively. There is little doubt that the dubious activities of some anti-piracy entrepreneurs have reflected badly on mainstream content producers, unhelpfully reinforcing prejudices, polarizing opinion, tying up resources and hardening rhetoric on all sides. In the case of WiFi, the emergence of a comparatively informal, small-scale technology actually benefited mainstream mobile telecommunications providers by growing markets, and effectively shifting the cost of some of the infrastructure back to consumers. But WiFi has also benefited from the big investments in wireless from the formal industry sector, and from public institutions and universities.

The current wave of interest among policymakers in alternative regulatory models – such as co-regulation, crowdsourcing, decentred regulation, responsive regulation and the like – shows where the debate is heading. Elinor Ostrom and her colleagues, in their groundbreaking work on the management of different kinds of commons, emphasize the need to knit informal regulatory mechanisms into larger mechanisms (Hess and Ostrom 2005). This especially applies to the difficult question of compliance, the prime point of regulatory failure in the case of copyright in the music industries. Governance depends on people following the rules, with a sensible degree of tolerance for minor or exceptional infractions. As Hess and Ostrom suggest, modest sanctions should be the norm for first offenders, with penalties increasing with the severity and number of subsequent offences. In the case of new regulatory structures, systems of informal regulation are particularly important: these must rely to some degree on established and accepted rules, practices and conventions; and on relatively subtle sanctions. The lessons here are clear enough for copyright industries, where regulatory overreach has been counterproductive, and also for many other areas of communications policy that put the cart of formal regulation before the horse of everyday practice. These lessons suggest a different order of priorities. When it comes to solving the problems of media industries in turbulent times, we might be better off starting with the informal.

6

Brands

Like a giant, global photocopier, the informal media economy is constantly producing its own versions of familiar media institutions and objects. In previous chapters we have seen some of the practices, styles and business models that it generates, and how these connect with the established media industries. Chapter 5 considered regulatory structures: the informal norms and expectations that govern the conduct of producers and consumers. This chapter extends that discussion into the area of trademarks. Here we explore what the informal economy does to, and for, brands.

Brands are closely associated with consumer markets and multinational corporations, with the latter among the few institutions capable of creating and sustaining truly global brands. From this perspective, they play a formalizing role, organizing and stabilizing markets. Media industries have a special relationship to brands, because their existence relies on the advertising markets that brand culture helped to create. In the form of trademarks, a legal and administrative structure supports this stabilization. The use of a trademarked brand is controlled through systems of registration and licensing, and this makes the brand itself something that can be bought and sold. Consequently, the value of many major media brands – from Pokémon to Panasonic, Shrek to Shakira, BBC to HBO – is enormous. According to recent industry estimates, Disney's brand is worth US$28 billion, while Apple's brand is valued at a staggering US$98 billion (Interbrand 2013). Given the stakes, it is perhaps unsurprising that the brand has generated a whole industry devoted to its cultivation and protection, including brand consultants, monitoring services, portfolio auditors, market researchers and trade-mark lawyers.

Building on recent critical work foregrounding the brand's socio-economic agency as well as its coercive power (Lury 2004; Arvidsson 2006), we focus on the brand as a site of interconnection between different parts of the economy. Our argument here is that the brand's power is a function of its mobility, and this can include the capacity to move between formal and informal economies. We begin by exca-vating some of the pre-history to current brand culture by showing how the modern trademarked brand has worked to formalize con-sumer and media markets. We then look at the role of brands in contemporary formal media industries, and especially the way in which formal brands seek to connect authorship with commercial control of media goods and services. While brands enable new forms of control and protection, they also expose media brands to new kinds of unauthorized circulation. Finally, we focus on the role of brands in the informal sector, where authenticity, authorship and provenance play out in some surprising ways.

The Trademark and the Brand

A complex governmental technology lies at the centre of contempo-rary media brands: without it, a good deal of the power of brands would evaporate, together with the industries that sustain it. This technology is built around the legal, regulatory and administrative concept of the trademark – a nineteenth-century innovation that gave formal shape and legal solidity to commercial branding practices.

Merchants have used visual symbols for trade and commerce since ancient times. Burn marks, watermarks, monograms and other insig-nia adorned the earliest commodities, including cattle, pottery, swords, porcelain and wine bottles. In this pre-trademark era of the brand, marks were used as visual commercial signalling without the legal architecture that framed such practices in the modern period. This changed when the industrial revolution expanded markets and the reach of producers through advertising. Companies with growing markets wanted to extend and secure control over the marks they used to distinguish their products. They wanted exclusive rights and a legal structure (although the nature of the latter was vigorously debated, particularly the problem of whether this intangible thing constituted a new kind of property – see Bently 2008a, 2008b).

Modern trademark laws took shape between 1860 and 1910. The most important distinguishing element of this new mode of control was not the law as such, but the bureaucratic structures it produced, including nationally organized administrative systems of registration. Registration established an open, publicly accessible source of information on the definitive acceptable form of the mark, and the person who registered it – in England this was known as its 'proprietor'. Registration meant that the mark had been examined and accepted, and also set a condition precedent for litigation. In England, the first huge task for the registrar was to work through many thousands of 'old marks': if a mark was in common use in a certain trade, then it could not be registered, but several firms operating in different local markets could register the same mark (Cornish 2010: 1003). The first registered English trademark was the Bass Red Triangle label, registered in 1876 by Bass Brewery in Burton-upon-Trent. Its distinctive triangle shape is still in use today, even though the brand has since become the property of global drinks giant Interbrew.

Sunlight soap, Wills cigarettes, Cadbury chocolate, Schweppes ginger ale, Peek Frean biscuits – the new system played a vital part in creating what are now recognizably modern markets for the emblematic branded consumer goods of late Victorian England. The markets for these goods were newly national ones, as larger companies gained economies of scale through regional expansion. They depended on (and commercially supported) the press and new printing technologies, such as colour lithography, for what was now a special form of protected communication. The printed communication of the brand was especially vital for companies that sold goods at a distance (Wilkins 1992); and, from this perspective, trademarked brands were well placed in colonial and international trade as the trademark system expanded. The products they sold were in many cases branded versions of familiar, and often even generic, household goods such as soap or tobacco. Some of these products may previously have been produced locally or even within the household. But these markets were socially inclusive, incorporating working- and middle-class populations in provincial and rural settings, as well as wealthier city dwellers. New brands responded not only to new material aspirations, but also to desires and ideas that were deeply culturally rooted; for example, the idea that cleanliness was next to godliness (Church 1999).

What we now call the media brand has a similarly long history, stretching back to early print culture. Brands of one kind or another have always been important for the press. The masthead of a newspaper was its brand: a constant, prominent, highly identifiable signal that functioned to unify both the various contents of any particular issue and the multiple issues that were published over time. In the explosion of unlicensed pamphlets, newssheets, newsbooks and newspapers in England in the mid-seventeenth century, the name of a periodical also had a political function, indicating whether the bundle of textual materials assembled were royalist (such as *Mercurius Aulicus*) or parliamentarian (such as *Mercurius Britannicus*) (Briggs and Burke 2005: 74). In enlightenment France, the brands of some newspapers were so successful that counterfeit circulation became a major problem. Because of the cost of printing and transportation, counterfeiters in remote cities were able to secure lucrative sales. The celebrity editor of the *Annales politiques, civiles et littéraires*, Simon-Nicolas-Henri Linguet, entered into a sophisticated debate with one his German pirates, who responded to Linguet's charge of theft with two well-considered (and now familiar) arguments: his piracy was in the national interest, because it reduced costly imports and increased local production, and it also enabled Linguet's ideas to reach a wider audience (Popkin 1993: 420).

In this brief account of the evolution of branding, two kinds of formalization can be seen. On the one hand, brands have formalized consumer markets, by stabilizing transactions and regularizing consumer experiences. On the other, trademark law has formalized the brand: contemporary brand culture relies on this legal and bureaucratic structure.

Formal Brands: Value, Control, Authorship

The brand has many critics. It is often said that brands dampen competition, erecting barriers to entry around consumer markets. If a company has significant brand power, it is capable of doing things others may find difficult, such as expanding into new and unrelated markets. This often leads to market distortion and oligopoly. Of the thousands of new brands launched each year, 95 per cent of them are reportedly 'extensions of existing brands' (Lury 2008: 214; citing Murphy 1998: 5). Cultural and ideological critiques of branding and brand-based advertising are also common. Every generation since the postwar baby boom has its anti-brand manifesto, from Vance Packard's *The Hidden Persuaders* (1957) to Naomi Klein's *No Logo* (1999), that explains how brands colonize space and turn common culture into private property.

A key theorist of corporate brand culture is the Canadian legal anthropologist Rosemary Coombe. Her influential book *The Cultural Life of Intellectual Properties* offers a powerful critique:

The trademark owner is invested with authorship and paternity; seen to invest 'sweat of the brow' to 'create' value in a mark, he is then legitimately able to 'reap what he has sown.' The imaginations of consumers become the field in which the owner sows his seed . . . – a receptive and nurturing space for parturition – but consumers are not acknowledged as active and generative agents in the procreation of meaning. When positive connotations grow in the promiscuity of social communication, the trademark owner reaps their benefit as goodwill. The generation of new, alternative, or negative connotations are ignored, denied, or prohibited because patrilineal rights of property are recognized as exclusive: no joint custody arrangements will be countenanced. (1998: 71)

Coombe's argument has been widely adopted in critical legal and media studies, and fundamentally concerns the relationship between brand value, control and authorship. Trademarks function to fix and privatize, and to relocate elements of public culture into the sphere of property rights. This terrain is then policed according to the logic of 'no trespassing'. The trademark facilitates a general commodification of meaning: 'figures from our cultural history become private properties that we parody, proliferate or politicize to our peril' (1998: 69). Coombe emphasizes the gendered aspects of this process, in which a particular idea of authorship is mobilized for the legitimation of the trademark's control functions.

Coombe's argument also aptly describes today's technology industries, which reflect a similar conjunction of control, value and authorship. Tech industries are intensively brand-driven, with huge investments in the accumulated value of their successful brands. A recent report by the World Intellectual Property Organization (WIPO 2013: 42) tracks the rise of tech firms within the global top 100 brands, showing that the brand power of these firms has outstripped much older and more powerful companies, including finance and automotive companies. All this is plain in Interbrand's global brand rankings over the last decade (see table 6.1). Interbrand is one of a number of international consultancies that publish such rankings and its estimates are used widely as a general index of perceived brand value. This is of course a branding exercise of sorts for Interbrand itself, which must differentiate itself from competitors like Brand Finance and Millward Brown Optimor.

Note the virtual disappearance of conventional media content companies from Interbrand's list by 2013. Ten years earlier, Disney ranked seventh, but by 2013 it had dropped out of sight completely. GE, with interests in television and movies, slipped just two places over the decade, although by mid-2013 it had completed the sale of

Table 6.1 Interbrand's best global brands rankings, 2003 and 2013

Ranking	2003	2013
1	Coca-Cola	Apple
2	Microsoft	Google
3	IBM	Coca-Cola
4	GE	IBM
5	Intel	Microsoft
6	Nokia	GE
7	Disney	McDonalds
8	McDonalds	Samsung
9	Marlboro	Intel
10	Mercedes	Toyota

NBCUniversal to Comcast. Another vanishing act was the Finnish telecommunications giant Nokia, a venerable conglomerate with a history going back to the 1860s, and one of the first registered trademarks in Europe. Apple and Google, numbers one and two in 2013, can be described as media businesses – but only in part, and in new and different ways. Apple's content operations, primarily built on the iTunes platform, support its hardware lines, while Google relies on advertising. Both are comparatively young companies next to those they have usurped on such lists. Both exhibit the heady mix of value, authorship and control that Coombe describes.

Coombe's account of brand culture foregrounds restrictions and prohibitions: control is one-way, with ownership of the trademark law determining the direction of the traffic, and the public's role in constructing meaning around the brand is appropriated if it is positive, but 'ignored, denied, or prohibited' if it is negative. The issue here may be that Coombe sees the trademark critically but too readily through the eyes of its owners, as another form of intangible property. This is indeed how brands and their attendant trademarks are often understood and described. But brands are also forms of communication. The great nineteenth-century brands succeeded as they became part of the rhythm of everyday culture and consumption: they grew as people ate, worked, cleaned, cooked, smoked and drank. Today, consumers have greater opportunities to communicate back to brands and their owners, both in positive and negative terms. The process of managing a brand is often messier, and riskier, than it may sometimes appear.

How do these problems play out in contemporary media brands? As an example, consider the James Bond franchise – a veritable super-brand that shows no sign of waning in popularity. Bond is still extraordinarily valuable as a media property, generating a series of blockbusters that have now outlived its authors, stars, producers, audiences – and the Cold War that began it all. The Bond brand ties stories, characters, logos and designs together and renders them a solid, protectable and accessible property. It can be licensed and controlled across platforms, technologies and channels. It has also been the subject of a characteristically complicated legal history, involving intense corporate rivalries, and a 40-year old dispute over coauthored film treatments (Poliakoff 2000). Trademark protection is useful in this context because, unlike copyright, the trademark is not defined by particular technologies, texts or the duration of a particular authorial life. In the words of one industry observer, Bond is a 'totally scalable' brand that is 'built on a solid and winning formula that has worked for more than 50 years' (Carbone 2012). But with control comes mess and risk. The Bond brand, despite 007's formidable powers, is not something that can be easily contained within the authorized spaces of the formal media industries, but is forever spilling out into unauthorized spaces and uses, from un-licensed t-shirts and watches to fan fiction and birthday cake designs. Protecting its 'integrity' is a challenging job for MGM and Danjac, the keepers of the Bond brand.

Bond proves a useful point of comparison with another famous English literary property that is just as culturally resonant, just as popular, and has been around for longer, but takes a different legal form – a brand without a trademark. The character of Sherlock Holmes has reportedly been performed on screen by more than 70 actors, and in this sense seems at least as 'scalable' as Bond. The earliest known Holmes film was a 1900 30-second short made for Mutograph machines in New York amusement arcades. Well over a century later, Conan Doyle's attempt to kill the character off remains famously unsuccessful. But there is no Holmes 'franchise' in the Bond sense: no managed, licensed, sequencing of content. There is no single Holmes trademark to match the 007 gun. Rather, there is a palpably alive Holmes character who is animated by a remarkably creative proliferation of content: new stories, fan fiction, games, manga, adap-tations, anthologies and explorations of Holmes in Victorian, con-temporary and speculative settings.

How do Bond and Holmes differ? The answer has much to do with intellectual property. The original Holmes stories and novels were, of course, subject to copyright, but since Conan Doyle's death in 1930, most of these have been in the public domain. Because of the longer duration of copyright in the United States, however, this did not apply to all stories in all places. That discrepancy has given rise to several disputes, with the author's estate actively asserting rights over the character, authorizing (for a fee) various adaptations and litigating rival rights claims. On the basis of a family link with the author – 'Conan Doyle Estate Ltd is owned by the Arthur Conan Doyle family' – the estate's website (conandoyleestate.co.uk) claims that it manages 'the literary, merchandizing, and advertising rights in Sir Arthur Conan Doyle's works and characters, including Sherlock Holmes, Dr Watson and Professor Challenger'. The estate also offers a 'unique seal of approval for new projects', and in recent years the Warner Bros. movies, the BBC *Sherlock* series, the US CBS series *Elementary*, and bestselling author Anthony Horowitz's Holmes novel, *The House of Silk*, have all been authorized in this way.

Elements of the Holmes fan base, however, have taken a different view, with the Free Sherlock blog (free-sherlock.com) claiming that 'Holmes belongs to the world'. A recent case before a lower US Court suggests that the public domain works, including their characters, are indeed freely usable. The estate unsuccessfully argued that such an outcome would be damaging – not only materially, but also to Conan

Sherlock at large: graffiti in London's South Bank. Image: Garry Knight
(CC BY-SA licence, 2012)

Doyle's great achievement, the character of Holmes. According to this view, Sherlock should be seen as a single, complex character, a cumulative creation developed through all of Conan Doyle's Holmes oeuvre, including of course those stories remaining in copyright. The character could not then be divided into a free-to-use 'public domain Holmes' and a licensed 'copyright Holmes', because these would be different figures: vital elements of the characterization appeared in the later, copyright works. The interesting suggestion here was that, ultimately, the character should be the key protectable literary creation, rather than the various stories and novels themselves. If this were not so, the argument went, there would be as many Holmes characters as stories about him: all different, all incomplete, all unstable, as the public domain Holmes over time incorporated additional aspects of the copyright Holmes.

This reading of copyright seems to draw not only on US doctrine protecting the 'durable character', but also on European conceptions of the moral right of authors to the 'integrity' of their work. But the problem of defining the work at issue in these terms remains. A Sherlock Holmes trademark might have made the legal position very different. In contrast, when we think of the many different versions of the licensed Bond characters that have appeared, it is clear that the idea that stronger protection is necessary to protect the integrity of a character is flawed. Popular characters are likely to change as they are adapted and reinterpreted for different times and different ends; their currency depends on a capacity to reappear elsewhere, with enough remaining of their familiar selves to bring their audiences along.

Holmes will never be a brand of the Bond kind, but it is interesting that he – like other public domain characters – seems able to work in brand-like ways. These stories continue to attract producers, networks, studios and actors, despite the lack of exclusive control. The combination of the pipe and the deerstalker remains an evocative and unique visual synecdoche: very much like an unregistered trademark, held in common and coexistent with the strong trademarks of the BBC, Warner Brothers and others. No doubt the fact that so many of Conan Doyle's original stories are in the public domain, combined with an extraordinary legacy of cross-media adaptation, adds to the snowball of demand for retelling.

Informal Activity and Brand Vulnerability

Let us now turn our attention to the more purely informal domain, and the operations of brands in that space. The shift towards the branding of media commodities has worked well for many media companies, allowing them to tie together consumer experiences in increasingly complex media environments, and providing economies of scale for super-brands. But it also has its risks. As we noted earlier, brands are inherently mobile: they circulate across formal and informal markets, and through private and public space. As they move, things happen to them. Nakassis (2013: 110) sees these points of tension as an ideal place for brand analysis. '[T]o study the brand', he writes, 'requires that we situate our analyses in moments when the brand is invoked but called into question, bracketed, refashioned, or negated.'

Illegal copying and reproduction are the most common issues for trademark holders when brands move into the informal economy. Unlicensed businesses, counterfeiters and pirates circulate brands far and wide – on garments, notepads, mobile phone cases, flip-flops, torrents and cigarette lighters. We have seen examples of these informal reproductions already. More recently, the internet and social media have enabled many new kinds of potentially lucrative unauthorized uses of brands, such as cybersquatting, typosquatting, 'black hat' search engine manipulation and misleading paid search ads.

Trademark lawyers and rights holders define these effects in specific ways. A key concept is *dilution*, first coined by Frank Schechter in the 1930s. 'If you allow Rolls-Royce restaurants, and Rolls-Royce cafeterias, and Rolls-Royce pants and Rolls-Royce candy,' he warned, in a famous speech to Congress, 'in ten years you will not have the Rolls-Royce mark anymore.' For Schechter, brand dilution led to devaluation and death. Legal doctrine largely follows this line of thinking, and has generated a wide array of terms to describe the ostensibly deleterious effects of informal reproduction on branded properties: blurring (weakening the link to the brand), tarnishment (besmirching the brand with negative connotations), passing off, and so on.

A famous example is the 1979 case of *Dallas Cowboys Cheerleaders v. Pussycat Cinema*, when the cheerleaders for a major American football team sued a Manhattan porn distributor with mafia connections over trademark violation in the X-rated pornographic film *Debbie Does Dallas* (1978). The film's eponymous protagonist was a cheerleader with the 'Texas Cowgirls' – a thinly veiled reference to the Dallas Cowboys. The cheerleaders' lawyers argued that *Debbie* infringed the team's trademark by, among other things, copying their uniforms. The court ruled in the team's favour, noting that the 'white boots, white shorts, blue blouse, and white star-studded vest' were sufficiently arbitrary to qualify as a trademark; therefore the film's use of the costume infringed the team's trademark rights, leading to dilution and tarnishment of their brand. A settlement was reached with the defendant, film distributor Michael Zaffarano, and scenes featuring the uniforms were cut from the movie.

The kind of conflict seen in the *Pussycat* case, a classic instance of brand protection where wholesome rights owners fend off what they consider unsavoury tarnishment from the underground economy, recurs in internet law disputes today. Take the case of trademark squatters – individuals who register marks in new territories, before the real brand has set up operations there, then try to sell the rights back to the brand for a princely sum. Russian entrepreneur Sergei Zuykov registered 300 global trademarks in Russia in this way, including Starbucks and Audi, and demanded payments of up to US$600,000 to release them (Kramer 2005). A twist on the model is typosquatting, where opportunistic free-riders occupy prime domain names associated with major brands (adobde.com, verizon wirewless.com, fracebok.com).

Given the prevalence of this kind of activity, it is not surprising to see a new focus on policing counterfeit brands in international intellectual property enforcement. In 2011, the United States, Canada, the European Union and a group of developed Asia-Pacific countries signed a new international treaty: the Anti-Counterfeiting Trade Agreement (ACTA). ACTA is thought to have been the result of vigorous lobbying from US movie and music industry organizations, as well as pharmaceutical industry bodies. It contained a series of controversial provisions designed to strengthen the enforcement powers of police and customs agencies and to increase penalties for infringement. Political support for ACTA eroded after 2011 in the face of vigorous opposition, and in July 2012 the European Parliament voted against ratification by 478 votes to 39, throwing the future of the treaty into serious doubt. But if governments have, for the moment at least, stepped back from stronger enforcement in this form, the private sector has stepped up. A flourishing and highly sophisticated branch of the anti-piracy industries we have discussed elsewhere now specialises in what is called 'brand security'. One such business is the Thomson Reuters subsidiary MarkMonitor. Their pitch: 'It costs millions to build global brands – yet they're highly vulnerable to online attacks which can severely undermine marketing investments while putting brand reputation, customer trust and revenues at risk' (Markmonitor.com). MarkMonitor's solution is a software-as-a-service product that uses text searching, photo detection, graphics recognition and scoring devices to scan websites, social media, e-commerce and auction sites constantly. The target: 'brand abuse' in all its forms.

Colourful tales of typosquatters and porn pirates provide ample ammunition for rights holders, lawyers and companies that wish to strengthen trademark protection and increase enforcement activity. Still, such stories do not exhaust the possibilities of what happens to brands in informal economies. Brand circulation in the informal economy is not just about trademark disputes; it is also about the ways that informal actors interact with, extend and reformulate regular trade. To get a handle on these dynamics we can return to our map of formal–informal interactions from Chapter 1, and to the functions, effects and controls we also mapped out there. We argued that the frontier between the formal and the informal is contingent, that it moves over time, and that media goods, including brands, may travel across it. There are a number of control strategies available to police this space, some of which strive to keep certain things on one side or another, others that try to transform the activities by moving them across the border. While dilution is certainly a problem for rights holders, this is only one possible effect. Other things can happen when formal brands come into contact with informal economies.

Consider the counterfeit Louis Vuitton handbag. Sold in a high street store or from the trolley of a crooked air steward in the place of the genuine article, it has a substitution effect – it replaces a regular sale. When sold for a low price at a street market, it may also have a substitution effect if it deters the consumer from purchasing the real thing. However, it is probably more likely in this context to occupy a non-rivalrous parallel market; in other words, the informal economy

Counterfeit handbags on sale in Shanghai. Image: Simon A
(CC BY-NC-ND licence, 2007)

acts as cut-price gap-filler for consumers priced out of formal markets. Some of these aspirational consumers may one day become formal economy participants (though others will stay in the informal holding tank, with no pay-off for the rights holder). In either case, the symbolic value of the brand is likely to be changed in some way by its movement through these informal spaces. A revaluation occurs, not necessarily a simple substitution.

The Brazilian cultural anthropologist Rosana Pinheiro-Machado (2010, 2012) explores these complications. For more than a decade Pinheiro-Machado has been studying the social lives of branded goods in Brazil and China, tracing their commodity routes – beginning in factories in Guangzhou and moving through various intermediaries before ending up in the informal street markets of Porto Alegre and other Brazilian cities. Pinheiro-Machado's work reveals what happens when informal economies and brands come into contact. These interactions are not always predictable. One study about Brazilian youths who operate predominantly in the informal economy shows how they go to extraordinary lengths to purchase (or sometimes steal) legitimate branded commodities (Pinheiro-Machado and Scalco 2012). The study presents a map of competing gang-like brand fanatics – Porto Alegre's competing Nike versus Adidas clans, Rio de Janeiro's well-known Lacoste and Ecko clans (who together 'form the clans of the alligator and the rhinoceros') – who dress uniformly in particular labels, signalling their difference from other clans through brand appropriations. Stories like this suggest that the informal economy can *extend* market opportunities for established brands, by making the brand visible in places where it might not otherwise be seen; and, because their marketability depends on their counterfeit, or perhaps 'replica', status, they draw attention to what they are not – the genuine, or authentic, article. In this light, we can compare the counterfeit branded good with Benjamin's (2008) 'mechanical reproductions' of art works, where what can never be copied is precisely the 'unique existence' of the original. Copies enhance the art work's 'aura' of authenticity.

These ambiguities are part of everyday consumer experience in many parts of the world. They underscore the contingency, but also the persistence, of the boundaries that separate the formal from the informal. Pinheiro-Machado recounts an apocryphal everyday tale of urban life in Brazil that captures this paradox:

> The boss and the maid get into the same elevator of a building, both holding a Louis Vuitton purse. Not knowing the individual histories of these women, it would at first seem sensible to conclude that the

first has a real product and the second a fake one. . . . An outsider would probably assume the maid's purse is not authentic. However, there is a reasonable chance that her purse is a real item, and there are many different places where she could have bought it or received it as a present. In fact, there is a better chance that the boss is wearing the fake item, not because such branded goods are beyond the budget of middle-class citizens, but because a fake product is more likely to be successfully passed off as a real item if worn by a person with high social and symbolic capital. (Pinheiro-Machado 2010: 122)

These stories give us a sense of the complexity of the formal–informal boundary in brand consumption. Formality (like informality) is not always where you would expect to find it.

Pinheiro-Machado's research also considers counterfeit markets in southern China, where informally produced branded goods provide a cut-price invitation to consumption. Perusing the counterfeit stalls of Luohu shopping centre in Shenzhen, Pinheiro-Machado observes the shopping habits of people buying fake Rolex watches. She notes a particular kind of Chinese consumption practice that has the effect of revaluing formal brands within the informal economy by localizing them. The fake Rolex stands in for the real thing with no diminution of quality; in fact, it is considered by some consumers to be even better than the original because it is *made in China*:

> At Luohu shopping center, I daily followed the routine of sales. One of the issues that drew my attention were the differences between Chinese and foreign consumers. [While foreigners] showed their purchases to their friends saying how smart they were because they had acquired a perfect replica of a Rolex watch for a cheap price, Mainland Chinese consumers usually left the store saying 'I bought a Rolex'. An informant, owner of a toy factory, explained to me his point of view about his Rolex watch: 'Western people think this Rolex [he pointed at his wrist] is not a Rolex because is a replica. For us, this is a Rolex, a real one. The difference is the origin, because this was made in China, and for us, it's better to help national industry.' (Pinheiro-Machado 2012: 346–7)

The Rolex fetishism described here is probably brand dilution, but it is something else as well. There is a surplus investment – economic, semiotic and affective. But the work of the brand here is now familiar: it guarantees a certain provenance and authenticity, albeit one that requires an educated consumer to recognize and value correctly.

An object such as a counterfeit handbag or watch illustrates nicely the range of reasons and motivations people have to move a brand into the informal economy. Media content is often more complex than apparel because of its reproducibility, adaptability, and greater semiotic and semantic complexity. But in counterfeit media, authenticity also turns out to be the key. Consider the videogame market in Colombia, where Juan-Diego Sanin (2012) has been studying informal media production. As Sanin has documented, pirate video game circuits in Colombia are producing new kinds of entrepreneurs who – as well as dealing in illegal bootlegs of popular games – are also creating new media commodities based on a deep knowledge of current gaming culture and consumer preferences. One well-known entrepreneur specializes in customized pirate copies of soccer games for Playstation, which have been hacked and modified to include local sports teams so that his customers can play with (or against) their local heroes, or participate in specific Colombian competitions like the Copa Mustang. This trader has become something of a celebrity in the local games scene, and is very proud of his creations. He has created his own website and Facebook page where he warns people against buying pirated versions of his (already hacked and pirated) games. His games sell at a premium to regular bootleg versions, reflecting the customization work that has gone into them. Each game cover is marked prominently with his website URL – his own informal brand.

This suggests another kind of interaction: a formal brand (counterfeited) with an informal brand (original) layered over the top. This is common in pirate and counterfeit circuits, where distributors often leave their own original mark on the product. Pirate books and software CDs sold in street markets regularly feature a 'signature' of some kind. Likewise, torrent files downloaded from the internet are often appended with the brand of the person who did the ripping and encoding. The Axxo brand, for example, has been legendary among movie file sharers for almost a decade, signifying quality, consistency and modest file size.

In this domain, informal brands are as vulnerable as anywhere else. Axxo has been subject to widespread ripping-off, with competitor groups releasing lower-quality rips under the same brand, and using the Axxo brand to direct users to their own commercial pirate sites. This has led to widespread consternation on web forums about 'fake Axxo rip-offs'. As a result, Axxo uploads are appended with the following warning:

All stand-alone DivX Players compatible
BE AWARE OF BOGUS SITES AND LAMERS
DOWNLOAD YOUR aXXo FILES FROM aXXo ACCOUNTS
ENJOY!

This example – involving informal regulation of an informal brand – gives us a sense of the *mise-en-abyme* quality of contemporary brand relations. Pirates develop their own informal brand, which is immediately ripped off by other entrepreneurs, prompting informal education campaigns to teach consumers about the 'authentic' versions. Clearly the brand is of no lesser consequence to key players in the informal media economy, and Axxo's antagonism to copyright does not translate into an open-access approach to its brand. Rosemary Coombe was right: no 'joint custody arrangements' here.

7

Metrics

Game of Thrones is one of the big global TV hits of the decade. Based on George R. R. Martin's popular novel cycle, this fantasy drama from US cable network HBO tells a protracted tale of rivalries among noble families in a climate-challenged, mythical, medieval world. Once described by one of its executive producers as '*The Sopranos* meets Middle Earth', *Game of Thrones* is renowned for the enthusiasm of its fans, manifest in spin-off fiction, social media and, not least, audience numbers. The series has been enormously popular when broadcast, and the DVD box sets and digital downloads have

'Better than an Emmy': Game of Thrones as a torrent phenomenon.
Image: © HBO

been HBO's best selling to date. Unsurprisingly, it was also a massive hit on BitTorrent. The website TorrentFreak (2012, 2013a) named *Game of Thrones* the 'most pirated show' in 2012, and again in 2013. One 2012 episode appeared to have been downloaded 4.3 million times, a figure greater than the programme's estimated US television audience.

In August 2013, an offhand comment by the CEO of HBO's parent company, Time Warner, sparked a media debate about the value of this illegal audience activity. Chief Executive Jeffrey L. Bewkes was on a conference call with financial journalists discussing future cable TV earnings for Time Warner, and at one point mentioned the popularity of *Game of Thrones* on BitTorrent, suggesting that the tag of 'most pirated' show in 2012 could be 'better than an Emmy'. A few months later, *Game of Thrones* writer and episode director David Petrarca also appeared to celebrate its 'most pirated' tag during a panel at the 2013 Perth Writers' Festival. 'That's how they survive', he said, arguing that high-profile premium-cable shows like *Game of Thrones* thrived on this kind of 'cultural buzz' (AAP 2013). 'Our experience is, it [unauthorized viewing] all leads to more penetration, more paying subs and more health for HBO.'

These and other observations by high-profile figures – including the US Ambassador to Australia, who appeared to take some measure of cultural pride in these results while earnestly encouraging Australian pirates to pay up – sparked debate across the media. Partly this was because they appeared to deviate from the TV industries' strong line against piracy. For our purposes, they are interesting for a different reason. At its heart the *Game of Thrones* controversy was about an alternative *metric* for measuring popularity, namely BitTorrent downloads. Bewkes's comments confirmed what many people already suspected: that US TV executives have been monitoring illegal downloads and using this to gauge the popularity of their shows.

BitTorrent downloads appear to have become a kind of informal metric for the industry, sitting alongside the established indexes of audience demand like TV ratings, Hulu streams and iTunes downloads. Like other media metrics, BitTorrent data has instrumental uses. It can be offered to the financial press as proof of a show's success, used to inform strategies for future production and distribution decisions, and deployed internally to convince executives of the viability of particular series. Compared to official media metrics, BitTorrent has a further advantage: it is notable for its transparency. A typical BitTorrent client provides a remarkable amount of public information relating to any given download (see the image below). This information relates not only to a particular user, but also to all those people who are currently sharing that file. It includes people's IP addresses (which can be resolved into host server names), their countries of location, the BitTorrent client software being used, the speed of each download, the progress of each download and exactly what each person is uploading and downloading at any given time. The BitTorrent system also makes it easy to copy the IP addresses of all users, and to log traffic.

Openness serves BitTorrent's main purpose: the efficient and reliable distribution of large files. It also makes the service a valuable source of information for media producers, distributors, analysts and researchers. Anyone who wants to know more about the popularity of certain genres of movies, television shows, music or games, or is considering licensing or producing a particular program, can use BitTorrent as a data source. Netflix and other on-demand services have acknowledged using it for this purpose (Bilton 2013a). Data of this kind is particularly valuable in today's volatile, fragmenting media industries, where conventional measures of success such as TV ratings have lost their grip on fast-moving audience behaviour. It is also important because the emerging formal platforms, such as iTunes, provide very little public data. In Chapter 1, we discussed the ways in which informal consumption can work for the formal sector in

Bit Torrent as a source of public data

taste testing, stimulating and priming markets; here we can begin to
see how important measurement and metrics are for those processes.
It was BitTorrent's design that made it possible for TorrentFreak to
grant *Game of Thrones* the 'most pirated TV show' tag, and then for
the show's producers to promote it with this prized index of popular
demand.

   This example tells us something of the place of informal metrics
– and, indeed, metrics more generally – in current media industries.
It is often assumed that piracy is obscure and surreptitious, occurring
in darkened teenage bedrooms, student dorms, university computer
labs late at night and shady street markets. In fact, as we have seen,
certain practices of downloading and file sharing are sometimes
highly *transparent*, in that they generate considerable quantities of
information and the data involved is widely analysed, understood
and highly valued in the formal media economy. Metrics spark debate
and stimulate new market strategies and tactics. This chapter is about
the business of measuring formal and informal media, the transformation of data into useful and powerful metrics, and the role those
metrics play in defining and shaping media industries.

Why Metrics Matter

Metrics are products of measurement and the statistical sciences of
sampling, collecting, coding and modelling. They are where the epistemological power of particular quantitative methods is made con-
crete. Some metrics (such as GDP, or measures of unemployment)
have an unusually potent role in politics and government. Others are
highly specialized, and are relevant only to small professional
communities.

   Since the 1980s, the history of statistics has emerged as a burgeoning and complex field, increasingly central to our understanding of
modern government (Desrosières 2002; Porter 1996). This body of
research has taught us, among other things, that the creation and
adoption of metrics is historically contingent. Some metrics are taken
up because of their representational power; others come into use
because of historical happenstance, because a powerful stakeholder
is able to set the agenda early on, or by pure accident. The authority
and value of a metric can weather and erode as political environments, technologies and populations change, when new kinds of
metrics emerge and the process of consensus-building starts again. To
take a simple example, measures of poverty were once of foremost
importance. Over the course of the twentieth century, however,

measures of unemployment have come to be seen as more significant because of new understandings of how the economy works and how states act.

The general dynamic is captured well by Timothy Mitchell in his discussion of how electricity measures evolved:

> The forms of technical calculation, distribution and the control of flows, addressing, accounting and billing, and much more helped to constitute the world that would gradually take shape and be identified as 'the economy' . . . Edison was trying to establish a series of what Barry calls 'metrological regimes,' extensive but often fragile zones of measurement that have become relatively standardized. Rival entrepreneurs and corporations were attempting to establish different metrologies. Metrologies create and stabilize objects; the economy is a very large instance of such an object, with rival attempts to define it and to design tools for its measurement and calculation. (2008: 1118)

Here, Mitchell gives us a sense of the amount of the work that goes into establishing consensus around particular metrics. Electricity metrics have proved remarkably durable: a volt means the same thing to engineers in Bangalore and in Budapest. But in the early years of the technology, these metrics appeared fragile and subject to fluctuation. The standardization of more complex metrics – measures of mortality, for instance – remains a huge challenge for national statistical agencies and international organizations.

This example reveals something of the synthetic and variable nature of metrics, which leads to our second point. Metrics helped make societies statistical. Variable, measureable norms replaced essential, determining nature. Ian Hacking's (1990) genealogies of probability illuminate the emergence of metrical techniques in population, health and other domains. He reminds us how these particular knowledge systems have come to shape modern government and modern subjects. When governments began compiling detailed records of certain kinds of incidences and activities – from crime to literacy – they were gathering the resources to govern in more sophisticated ways. The history of modern governance has been characterized by a need to know and to quantify populations in detail: what people do, where they live, how long they live, how they die and how they spend money. Data collection and analysis is now a precondition for governmental action in liberal states. What is involved here is necessarily something that goes beyond enumeration: the population sizes of modern nations require sampling techniques that did not stabilize or find general acceptance until the mid-twentieth century. Desrosières's (2002) parallel histories of institutional evolution and mathematical theory show how sampling was controversial, in part because it involved an alignment of statistical variation with the nation-state itself, a recognition that the multiplicity of local economic and social phenomena could be organized, aggregated and represented at a national level.

Measuring the Informal

The idea of the informal economy is in itself an outcome, an extension and a response to this history of national measurement. A metric such as employment data can become important because it enables governments to frame policy action and administration in a particular way. It also generates new problems. One of the primary characteristics of informal employment, as defined by Keith Hart and others during the 1970s, was its statistical evasiveness: this was the kind of activity *that could not be seen* in labour market enumerations, or in the tax collectors' records. Informality therefore presented a puzzle for social science. What was the best way to measure something elusive and obscure? Economists approached the problem as both a technical and a practical challenge, recognizing that a solution to the problem of measuring the informal might itself involve a certain formalization of activities on the ground. Over the 1970s and 1980s, they experimented with a range of better ways to measure the extent of informal activity. Direct and indirect methods were trialled, from interviewing people about their activities to estimating the extent of off-the-books activity by scrutinizing electricity records and counting cash in circulation. People were surveyed, commodities counted, diaries filled in, marketplaces observed, national accounts and utility bills scrutinized.

Underpinning these measurement efforts was a fundamental debate about different ways of knowing the informal. Economists invented more and better models. Anthropologists took a different view: they emphasized the limitations of quantification itself, the complexity of social life that cannot be captured in statistics, and the in-built politics of particular kinds of metrics (such as employment statistics that ignore women's reproductive and domestic labour). In Hart's account, the ways that many mainstream economists thought about the economy were naive because they relied on data that captured only the most easily observable activities. Hart took economics to task for its reliance on GDP and labour statistics designed for advanced economies, and for the tendency 'to equate significant economic activity with what is measured' (1973: 84).

The techniques of demography may seem removed from the concerns of media studies, but there are lessons here for people who wish to understand media industries. Since the 1930s, the broadcasting and advertising industries have been crucibles for the development of new measurement techniques. Ratings diaries, People Meters, focus groups: media entrepreneurs pioneered these and other technologies. Their history and their effects on media culture have been explored by scholars who have shown us how contentious methods for measuring audience activity (such as broadcast ratings) have come to structure entire media industries at a deep level (Ang 1991; Balnaves et al 2002; Napoli 2003, 2011; Turow 2006; O'Regan et al 2011). Those who control this knowledge wield real industry power. But their power rests not so much on unimpeachably rigorous techniques of measurement as on hard-won agreement to work with the metrics that are derived from inevitably imperfect methods. As Lucas Graves and John Kelly observe: 'It is a long appreciated irony of media measurement that accuracy matters less than consensus' (cited in Ewing 2013).

Measuring New Media

When the internet first emerged as a popular public network of networks, it was entirely outside the formal media and communication industries. There were few tools available to gauge its size or what its users were doing. But as the commercial internet rapidly developed in the mid-1990s, researchers began to measure various aspects of its architecture and uses. Some of the internet's own systems were useful for this purpose because the network itself generated a great deal of information: domains were identifiable and countable, and servers for email or the web logged activity that could be aggregated and analysed. A new industry of web analytics appeared, based largely on automated analysis of the data already produced by internet servers. 'Hits', 'visits', 'page views' and other new metrics entered the language. Many of these metrics were not well defined or understood, and, as web technology developed, many were only briefly relevant. They were devoted to the immediate problem of measuring *traffic*. Attention to what users actually did came later, using more elaborate software embedded in web pages.

As Scott Ewing (2013) has documented, analysts interested in the social and economic aspects of the new communications environment turned naturally to the methods and techniques devised and refined for older media and communications systems. They were interested in problems that had enlivened earlier debates, and asked questions that were framed by those problems. They used data gathering technologies (notably telephone-based sample surveys) that relied on earlier communications systems. The results were metrics that stimulated policy discussion and development, while being framed in the terms of older technologies. Consider three formative, longitudinal US studies of the internet: the *Falling through the Net* surveys (later *A Nation Online*) on internet and broadband adoption, conducted by the National Telecommunications and Information Administration (NTIA) within the US Department of Commerce; the Pew Center's Internet and American Life project; and the World Internet Project, based at the Annenberg Centre, University of Southern California. These projects were not the only significant early surveys of the internet, but they represent alternative possibilities in material and conceptual terms. Their locations and data sources were diverse. The US government funded *Falling through the Net*; universities and research grants funded the World Internet Project; a philanthropic trust paid for the Pew Center work. The starting points were different as well. *Falling through the Net* was the work of a telecommunications and information policy agency, while the Pew internet project evolved out of earlier work by the same body on 'people and the press', and the World Internet Project was an extension of work by television scholars at UCLA.

With these contrasting starting points, it is not surprising that the three projects produced different statistics and ultimately understood the net in very different – but equally influential – ways. The NTIA came at the internet from the telecommunications policy principle of 'universal service', giving rise to the problem of the social and geographical distribution of telecommunications services. The result was a series of reports on what came to be known as the 'digital divide', which influenced government policies supporting and subsidizing take-up around the world. Pew was interested in social and civic life online, well before these became established themes in internet research – its work has turned increasingly to questions of trust and privacy. Ewing (2013) points out that not only did the Pew Center's background in journalism issues frame its interest in the internet as a new public medium, it also shaped its approach to internet research, encouraging a fast-moving, topic-driven approach, rather like a newspaper. It is then not surprising that the Pew research generates more than 1,000 media stories a year, playing a remarkably influential role in shaping media coverage of the internet. The World Internet Project, with its origins in US quantitative social science and television studies, began with a problem left over from early TV: where did the time we spend on TV come from? This has lead the research into an examination of everyday life and internet use, and the relationship between that and other forms of media consumption.

These three studies were always divergent, but it is not an oversimplification (or a criticism of their work) that the metrics they produced described the unknown world of the internet in terms that descended from one of several older and much better known industries: telecommunications, the press or television. The problem with this approach is that consumers do not all see the new media in that way. Research problems and questions need to evolve reasonably quickly to keep up with changing practices. Metrics of the digital divide, for example, are subject to ongoing redefinition, as new technologies (broadband, fast broadband and mobile internet) emerge. Time-use studies of internet users have become difficult, as everyday devices such as smartphones make the distinction between 'online' and 'offline' almost meaningless. Nevertheless, these points of departure provide a certain anchorage for analysis, which has helped to secure the credibility and profile of the work produced. The story of competing internet metrics underscores our fundamental point – that metrics are contingent, necessarily provisional, and always a product of epistemological conflict and of different ways of seeing the world. Consensus is fragile, and trust in any metrics system must be constantly shored up if it is to function effectively.

Transparency and Opacity in Digital Metrics

The stakes have naturally increased in the internet age, as algorithmic metrics become embedded in all aspects of the media supply chain. The astonishing rise of Google, a company described by its former CEO Eric Schmidt as 'founded around the science of measurement' (in Carr 2008), is testament to this. In the political economy of data industries, a small number of metrical commodities (such as Google's ironically named 'natural' or 'organic' page rankings) are now extraordinarily important. Even more than television ratings, these metrics are also entirely opaque. The algorithms that generate them are secret, ranking possibly among the most valuable of all trade secrets. Discovery and exposure would render them valueless.

It is hardly surprising, then, that metrics of this sort have generated a thriving sphere of enterprise. The search engine optimization industry constantly develops, tests and sells new ways for improving rankings. The industry is famously divided between 'white hat' and 'black hat' sectors. The 'white hat' sector works by making websites more

visible to search engine spiders, and through the adept deployment
of popular keywords. Firms design sites that aim to meet the various
guidelines that search engines such as Google outline for webmasters.
These guidelines constitute the regulatory structure designed to
protect and sustain the search engine and its metrics. They consist
mainly of positive recommendations for making websites accessible
and readable. They also include quality guidelines aimed at discour-
aging manipulative or deceptive content. The 'black hat' sector specializes in precisely these deceptions: spam, invisible text, cloaking
and links embedded in widgets.

Google's guidelines provide examples of some standard black hat
strategies. One strategy involves boosting a site's page rank by covertly
linking to the same URL over and over again. Take the following
example of web text: '*There are many wedding rings on the market.*
If you want to have a wedding, you will have to pick the best ring.
You will also need to buy flowers and a wedding dress' (Google
2014). A black hat SEO expert would make all these links point to
the same page, thus boosting its PageRank value. Another sneaky
strategy is to use bots to post generic statements in popular online
forums, using a signature file containing links back to your website.
Here is Google's example:

> *Thanks, that's great info!*
> *– Paul*
> *paul's pizza san diego pizza best pizza san diego*

The white and black are strongly differentiated in Google's guidelines, but the boundaries often blur. Online forums are full of stories
of bloggers and small retailers suffering the consequences of perceived
infringement of Google's rules; in some cases, large companies have
also had the same experience. In 2006, BMW's German website was
delisted from Google search returns because it was found to be using
the classic black hat tactic of a 'doorway' page, heavily populated
with keywords, designed especially for web crawlers, while human
users were redirected to a more user-friendly page.

Adkins and Lury (2011) have written eloquently about the rise of
digital metrics and their increasing centrality to everyday life: Google
is perhaps the paramount example. They argue that the internet
economy is characterized by 'a proliferation of information, data,
calculative and other research instruments, measurements and valu-
ations', which in turn create their own social realities: 'Neither inert
in character nor contained or containable in any straightforward
sense, data increasingly feeds back on itself in informational systems

with unexpected results: it moves, flows, leaks, overflows and circulates beyond the system and events in which it originates' (2011: 6). For Adkins and Lury, this tidal wave of data – and the metrics that have emerged to make sense of it – are reshaping and also expanding the social realm. Given that much of what is being measured is social in nature (interpersonal networks, movements, searches, preferences and online interactions), they conclude that our current big data culture is leading to 'an ongoing expansion of the social by way of techniques of mediation, measurement and valuation' (2011: 5–6).

In our analysis, this expansion of the social is necessarily also an expansion of the communications and media systems that connect people, institutions and industries. Many of these networks and interactions are informal, occurring on social media platforms, through messaging and searching practices that lie well outside the comparatively limited domains of the established media industries, but are increasingly integrated into mainstream internet business. What we observe, then, is a paradoxical dynamic. The sphere of informal media is subject to increasing scrutiny, definition and analysis – and these observations have, as at least one of their consequences, the effect of bringing informal media worlds into closer relation to formal media. But our techniques of measurement and calculation also reveal more as they proceed. Increasingly sophisticated and encompassing, the media worlds they depict are not shrinking but expanding. Our capacity to recognize and measure these informal worlds is the result of another interesting difference: while formal media systems produce important metrics through opaque sources and methods, informal systems appear to rely on transparency. Compare Google's search service with what we have seen about BitTorrent. The reason for this difference no doubt has to do with trust: Google asks for our confidence, and in most cases it has it. The same may not be true of an informal service such as BitTorrent, so in that case transparency is crucial.

It would follow that the more informal a marketplace, the more transparent it should also be. Consider the case of Silk Road, the online marketplace that flourished briefly between 2011 and 2013 before being shut down by the FBI. Silk Road was a 'dark web' site, hidden behind layers of anonymizing software (Tor) designed for secret browsing. Here you could make Bitcoin payments to acquire a range of illicit goods: mostly drugs, but also weapons, pornography, credit card numbers, counterfeit IDs and other illicit commodities. Silk Road did not remain a secret for long. Shortly after its launch in 2011 the word was out that Silk Road was a good place to buy drugs in particular, which could be shipped by mail with little chance of detection (in theory, at least). The site was soon crawling with FBI agents. By September 2013, it had been taken offline. In true internet style, it has been relaunched and imitated many times since.

Although anonymous, the Silk Road marketplace was also transparent in the sense that transactions could be scrutinized. Like Bit-Torrent, it had openness built into its architecture: transactions were recorded and rated in an eBay-like manner. This transparency made it attractive to researchers as well as cops. IT professor Nicolas Christin (2013) from Carnegie Mellon University published a fascinating measurement analysis of Silk Road trade prior to the site's seizure. By tracking transactions over eight months in 2011 and 2012, Christin estimated that the site was generating sales of around US$1.2 million per month. Although some 'stealth mode' transactions were untrackable, Christin was still able to monitor regular transactions with some degree of accuracy, thus determining such information as the country location of vendors (most were in the United States) and the nature of their sales (top four categories: weed, drugs, prescription and Benzos). He could also estimate levels of customer satisfaction (97.8 per cent of buyer feedback was positive), the amount of commission revenue generated for Silk Road operators and a range of other interesting information.

The counterintuitive story of Silk Road, a marketplace that was opaque to law enforcement but highly transparent to statisticians, is not unique. Bitcoin has a similar story to tell. The 'crypto-currency' which has attracted so much attention from the press, and some speculative investment (notably from the Winklevoss twins), has the same paradoxical architecture. Its anonymity means Bitcoin is very difficult to track in terms of connecting real-life individuals with their transactions; its history, credited to pseudonymous inventor 'Satoshi Nakamoto', is obscure, and its uses somewhat questionable. But many other aspects of Bitcoin are open and transparent. One can easily find out how many Bitcoins exist (at the time of writing, 12 million), their total value and their value relative to other currencies. Compared to traditional cash – which can be hidden, lost, counterfeited and defaced – Bitcoin is arguably more formal. Having said that, the currency also has a certain materiality. Unlucky geeks who mined Bitcoins in the early years but who then lost their wallet codes before the currency hit stratospheric levels in 2013 can testify to that.

All these examples illustrate the way metrical transparency can build trust in informal online systems. But the reverse is also true: many systems become *less* transparent once trust has been established. The case of YouTube is interesting in this respect. When YouTube started up in 2006 (and for several years after it was purchased by Google in 2007), it was organized into lists and categories based on easily understood metrics – the newest videos, the most viewed, and so on. The site's structure emulated existing industry metrics, such as bestseller lists and the Top 40. Media researchers who studied YouTube in the mid 2000s, notably Burgess and Green (2009a), were able to use YouTube's transparent metrics to investigate what kinds of videos were most popular, to develop a sample pool of videos, and to do a range of quantitative analyses on this basis. However, this transparency had disappeared by 2008 when YouTube (by then a Google subsidiary) started offering users a more personalized site experience. Localized versions of the site were introduced in an attempt to customize content and enable clearer market segmentation for rights holders and audiences. YouTube eventually abandoned the familiar tables and rankings, replacing them with new features – channels (emulating the medium of television, rather than a random-access database), recommended videos (based on your Google searches) and subscriptions.

This shift from a universal front page, with the site appearing the same to everyone, to a personalized site based on harvested user data, enabled YouTube to leverage advertising more effectively. Since then, YouTube user accounts have converged with Google Plus accounts, enabling a deeper integration with social media and search. But the effect of all these changes has also been to dismantle the transparency of YouTube, meaning that it is increasingly difficult for users to understand the nature of the popularity of certain contributors and content. This retreat into the black box of proprietary data has complicated the idea of a 'YouTube public', notwithstanding the convenience of a pre-selected subset of what is now an impossibly vast archive.

Other digital media platforms are equally reluctant to make their data public. Apple is notoriously guarded about its data on iTunes and App Store consumption, offering little more than a 'top songs' listing. Famous for its advanced data analytics, the music streaming service Spotify is also keeping its data close. Like iTunes, the site features a Top Lists section, with what appear to be the most-played 100 tracks. There is also, however, an array of Spotify-authored lists that provide other pictures of popularity as well. One Spotify Top 10 features the 'hottest' content, another the 'most streamed and shared'; others are organized by genre. The amount of information here is significant, allowing users to easily view what is popular among Spotify users in Denmark, Costa Rica or New Zealand, and inviting us to play with this information. Spotify appears to be experimenting with the chart format in a way that allows it to engineer its own new ideas about novelty, relevance, and audience, and build them into the site architecture. Keeping its metrics opaque also opens up possibilities for pay-for-play partnerships with record companies. Tracks can potentially be bumped up or inserted into lists, creating a mix of 'voted' and 'paid-for' content.

Neither Apple nor Spotify readily give away information about user activity, but they are happy to share the kind of data that leads to favourable press coverage. We know, for example, that Beyoncé's 2013 iTunes-only album sold 828,773 copies in three days – because Apple issued a media release. Likewise, in its 2013 Year in Review page, Spotify divulged a flood of factoids about its performance: the service had clocked up 4,500,000,000 hours of listening, 1 billion playlists, 24 million active users, 20,000 songs added every day, and a record 1.5 million streams in 24 hours (for Daft Punk's *Get Lucky*). Digital media services also use rich, customized data as a selling point in their dealings with record labels and artists, who can access the Spotify and iTunes backend to see who is listening to their content, where, when and how. This inducement is offered as a kind of foil for the more familiar complaints about insufficient revenue return (many artists have publicly attacked Spotify, in particular, for its nugatory royalties). *We can't offer you much money*, these services appear to say, *but we can give you something far more valuable: data*. These selective transparencies and strategic opacities are at the heart of the new digital media economy.

The Piracy Numbers Game

Having considered some of the issues around digital media metrics, we can now revisit *Game of Thrones* and its famous 'most pirated' status. In the wave of publicity and controversy surrounding this distinction, the fact that *Game of Thrones* had won out in the rankings was not the primary source of interest. Rather, it was the reaction to it: from the show, the network and others. The idea that TorrentFreak's recognition was 'better than an Emmy' may have been facetious, but it was also subversive because representations of piracy from large media companies are almost always expressed in terms of losses, rather than gains.

Why did Time Warner embrace the TorrentFreak metric? To answer this we need to delve deeper into the business side of the story. *Game of Thrones*'s circulation followed a distribution pathway well established by HBO, which often sold overseas rights to premium drama cable or satellite channels, and then relied on subsequent physical or digital sales. So when the much-hyped *Game of Thrones* was screened outside the US, it was scheduled on many channels with comparatively small audiences, and delays of a week or so behind US broadcasts also frustrated impatient viewers. Demand effectively overloaded HBO's distribution system.

TorrentFreak reported that there were some notable geographic centres of piracy for the second season. London was the chief pirate city, while Australia was the number one pirate nation. In Australia, a market with a historically low level of cable TV uptake, the series was being aired on the then-premium channel Showtime, a week after US broadcasts. For the third season, changes were made as a clear response to the piracy figures; the delay was reduced to two hours, and episodes were also available on iTunes (an Australian exclusive). The fourth season was exclusive to cable.

Such manoeuvrings reveal something of the complexity of the tactical adjustments of rights holders in a changing environment. A choice must be made between exclusivity and piracy, on the one hand, and broader distribution, on the other; like one of those annoying pay TV bundles, you cannot choose exclusivity *without* piracy. HBO chose exclusivity plus piracy – a rational choice given the kind of content it produces. Long-form drama of the HBO kind now has just as strong a claim on 'quality' as movies do, but the dynamics of demand and distribution are clearly different from most other cinema and TV texts. Writer and director David Petrarca's point about piracy being 'how [these shows] survive' was an observation primarily about the HBO brand and business model, which can rely on healthy post-broadcast DVD sales, downloads and streams. These sales grow as series progress, creating a strong market tail. Unlike movies or books, an HBO series usually has no predetermined end point: new seasons can continue to be made as long as the demand and the talent are there. This explains the particular importance of what Petrarca called 'cultural buzz' for this genre, and it helps us understand CEO Jeffrey Bewkes's willingness (if we understand him correctly) to lose some revenue to piracy early on. It also points to the weakness of international broadcast and pay-TV partners in this particular game. If you license the series, you get a seat at what is a very rich feast. But *Game of Thrones* shows us what can also happen: a moment of weakness or the wrong friends, and you will be very quickly skewered yourself.

To fully grasp the significance of the 'most pirated' metric, we also need to consider the wider political economy of piracy metrics. The TorrentFreak metric, based on aggregated data from torrent trackers, represents a heterodox sortie on the part of a small website into the larger piracy numbers game, a game that is played for high stakes. The 'most pirated' chart was intended to compete in the cut and thrust of other statistical representations of piracy, notably those produced and circulated by media and entertainment industry bodies. Some of the industry metrics have also attracted widespread attention – mainly as 'big numbers' that appear to be constructed for headlines and media grabs. Such numbers figured prominently in US debates over the ultimately unsuccessful Stop Online Piracy Act in 2011. Campaigning for the Bill, the Motion Picture Association of America claimed that 'over $58 billion was lost to the US economy annually due to content theft', together with 373,000 jobs, $16 billion in lost wages, and $3 billion in tax revenue (MPAA 2011). These figures represented something of a retreat from some older and substantially larger estimates, including a famous $200–250 billion estimate of the costs of IP infringement (and 750,000 jobs). Those figures, although widely used even in the 2011 SOPA debate, were eventually shown to derive from a 1993 *Forbes* magazine piece, an unsourced estimate of the entire global market for counterfeit goods (Sanchez 2008).

The most egregious 'big numbers' were based on a paucity of empirical research, an enthusiasm for extrapolation, and a series of questionable assumptions (such as equating every instance of an infringing copy with a lost sale). Just as other early internet research-ers saw the new media through the prism of older technologies, for many years content industry researchers applied a model built around the physical copying of optical disks to the online environment. In this case, there is also an important practical and strategic connection between the metrics and the structures of international intellectual property governance that the United States created in the late 1980s, mainly as a result of vigorous industry lobbying. Joe Karaganis (2011) has noted how industry metrics on piracy, and the research behind them, have been driven by an unusual administrative process: the reporting mechanisms built into Section 301 of the US Trade Act, which require the US Trade Representative to report annually on countries that do not provide 'adequate and effective' protection for US intellectual property. Karaganis points out that the 'Special 301' process has functioned as an avenue for the content industry to com-plain formally and make policy recommendations about deficiencies in international protection. It has provided a formal mechanism for the translation of industry views into official US government trade positions, and a mandate for the creation of an extensive interna-tional network of industry-funded piracy research. Together with other pressures emerging over the last decade, the process has also led to increasingly professional and robust industry research. New methods have become necessary for digital environments, industry sponsors are demanding more sophisticated accounts of consumer practices and inflated claims are now rapidly debunked and debated in what has become a sophisticated and increasingly critical online debate. However, old problems remain. Karaganis writes: 'the basis of credibility in this context is transparency'. So although the industry bodies provide general descriptions of their methods, little is disclosed about 'the assumptions, practices, or data underlying their work' (2011: 6). Every survey is carried out differently; evaluations of the metrics produced are not possible.

On this score at least, invidious comparisons with the Torrent-Freak data are hard to resist. But the instability of these metrics and the debates they arouse – in both these and other areas of new media activity – reflects the volatility and uncertainty of the environment. New metrics are necessary, but they will depend on consensus and trust. With no sign of either, this may be another area where we can learn from the informal.

Conclusion

Much has changed since we started writing this book. In media industries, the continuing rise of social media has brought personal communications into a new commercial domain; online advertising is evolving in leaps and bounds; and mobile media has consolidated around a couple of dominant platforms. All this suggests increasing commercialization and formalization. Yet for all the prominence and dominance of the new digital media giants, the internet has also made the informal sector more visible than ever. A host of hitherto arcane technologies have become well known, from VPNs (virtual private networks) to encrypted email, digital currencies, anonymous search engines and direct messaging. The shutdown of Silk Road and the arrest of its figurehead 'Dread Pirate Roberts' not only illuminated the Dark Web, but also attracted attention to Bitcoin and Tor, the encrypted routing system that aims to protect users from surveillance and traffic analysis. Edward Snowden's revelations about state spying seem only to have reinforced those tendencies, undermining confidence in mainstream systems that we once naively assumed to be safe and secure.

Between them, Dread Pirate Roberts and Edward Snowden underline the need to refresh the critical and conceptual toolkit of media industry research. We hope that *The Informal Media Economy* will be useful in this respect, adding some extra functionality to established media industry theories. Earlier, we likened this book's approach to a browser extension – a small tool that enhances a web browser's capabilities by enabling it to do new things, such as automatically block ads or save video content. Like an extension, the particular way of studying the media industries that we have outlined in this book is intended to subtly enhance the capabilities of existing media studies 'software'. It as an augmentation – not a replacement – for scholarly approaches, including media economics, political economy and regulatory analysis: it pushes the boundaries of these frameworks a little so they can respond to a wider array of media industry phenomena and to the fast-moving actors of the informal economy.

We began this book by emphasizing the economic diversity of media industries. If you have stuck with us all the way to this Conclusion, you will have encountered a very wide array of formal and informal media systems. If nothing else, we hope this book has been useful in its attempt to analytically capture some of this diversity, and in doing so to imagine the media economy as a complex system, including not only firms, producers, institutions and consumers, but also lobbyists, fans, minimum-wage workers, criminals, hackers, pirates, developers, policy wonks, free riders, geeks, street vendors, activists, enthusiasts, technicians and many others. As we have argued, the nature of their interactions is determined not by character or morality, nor by teleology (the informal is not disappearing, nor is it exterminating the formal), but by the institutional contexts produced by the collision of different kinds of economies. We've outlined an analytic language for describing these interactions; we hope it shows one way of thinking through this diversity.

A consequence of seeing the media industries in this way is that the claims of particular stakeholders become relative rather than absolute. Many debates in media regulation are still characterized by absolutist position-taking and overheated rhetoric, becoming unwinnable duels of opposing rights claims. In intellectual property debates especially, for both sides, the apparently solid ground of ethical principle often turns out to be rather thin ice. An understanding of how formal and informal activities are connected may lead to a greater analytical realism and complexity. It may also add some nuance to the ongoing discussions about the future of media industries, because the very idea of industry as a bounded sphere dissolves when viewed in this way.

Of course, our reading of the media economy is not a crystal ball. We have avoided making predictions, other than to suggest that, as media systems grow more complex, they are likely to feature ever-closer interactions between the formal and the informal. Certainly, it would be premature to herald the demise of large-scale institutions and corporations. Here we part ways with some of the more optimistic claims about the death of old media at the hands of social networks and DIY distribution platforms. Kickstarter's Yancey Strickler, among others, has envisaged this kind of media future:

> I think we are at a point where we are asking whether you really need a film industry for a film to be made or a music industry to make music. People can now speak directly to their audiences. . . . And the demands of an audience are very different to the demands of an industry. An industry wants to know about merchandising tie-ins with McDonalds – that's not necessarily what the audience is looking for, or what the artist is concerned with. (In Rushe 2012)

While the film, publishing and broadcast industries may have given us reasons to welcome such a fragmented future, we think that the prospect of a media landscape without formal institutions and companies is remote. Large-scale, formal companies still have an important role to play. Scale brings consistency and long-term investment. Without studios, broadcasters and record labels, we would not have many of the things that are so appealing about popular culture – such as Oscar night, or Eurovision, or the Bollywood star system. We might have other things, but we would not have these things.

Media industry evolution, to the point that it can be predicted, is not going to be about *replacement* of these formal structures with informal ones; it is going to be about interactions of growing complexity. Public institutions and corporations will continue to play a central role in media culture. Just as formal media relies on the informal – a point we have emphasized – so does informal media rely on the formal. Public institutions, from libraries and universities to regulatory agencies and international NGOs, are central to the story we have told here, because they provide many of the skills and stabilities needed to make the informal flourish; and so too are the media corporations whose scale and investment provides the necessary conditions of existence for a great deal of experimentation. No matter how dynamic the informal realm may be, it relies on these solid foundations to give it shape. Kickstarter itself is a good example here. Once the platform of choice for NGOs and indie filmmakers, it is now being used to bankroll Zach Braff movies and university research projects, reflecting a closer integration with the institutions and corporations it ostensibly challenges. Similar things are happening to many other enablers of the informal economy, such as eBay and Airbnb, whose capabilities have been willingly absorbed into the established business models of hotel chains and retail giants. Few things in media are totally, permanently informal. The history and future of media industries will continue to be a story of ongoing rearrangement and recomposition.

It may be worth reiterating that, while we are fascinated by the dynamism of the informal economy, we are not advocates for deformalization. Recent economic history reminds us that the erosion of institutions and regulatory structures has a real human cost. Since 2008, in the wake of the financial crisis in the United States and austerity policies in Europe, informal economic activity has significantly increased in many nations, as laid-off workers turn to off-the-books work to make ends meet. The reality of this situation tempers the enthusiasm for the informal economy that tends to billow during times of economic growth, when informality appears interesting and novel. Indeed, one of the lessons of the crisis has been the importance of sustaining formal governmental mechanisms, including financial regulation and tax collection, even as economies become more open and internationalized, so that such crises may be averted in future. As mundane as they are, these mechanisms play an essential role in shoring up structural stability. Stable structures can productively allow informality to flourish in certain spaces *as exception*; but systemic informality – tax evasion, cronyism, corruption – has the potential to undermine political and social settlements, and to hollow out states from the inside.

With all this in mind, what might a policy agenda for the informal media economy look like? In our view, the most promising approaches allow the 'good' kinds of formality and informality to coexist and cross-pollinate. It is heartening to see a wave of new research appearing in international innovation policy, which stresses the centrality of the informal to cultural and knowledge industries globally (Elahi et al 2013). At a regulatory level too, there is new acceptance of the idea that the informal economy is an ongoing feature of modern life (OECD 2009). Even in the areas of cultural policy and intellectual property, which have been slow to engage with the informal economy, changes are afoot; UNESCO now explicitly addresses informal economies in its cultural policy platforms, such as the latest *Creative Economy* report (UNESCO 2013), and the World Intellectual Property Organization, a UN agency that oversees harmonization of IP regulation worldwide, has commissioned fascinating research into the informal economy's relationship to brands and copyright goods (De Beer et al. 2013).

Perhaps the most important task here will be to understand where we can usefully match innovation and cultural policy priorities with the social *realpolitik* of the informal economy. As we saw in Chapter 3, employment practices in informal economies (including informal media economies) are often poor; the logic of informal production rarely aligns with principles of economic justice. Appreciating the elegance and dynamism of formal–informal interaction in cultural industries at a theoretical level is one thing, but building frameworks to protect and support the people who work in these industries, while

also fostering the kind of cultural dynamism and consumer benefits
that we have explored in this book, is something else again. So there
is a research and development agenda: we need analytic and policy
frameworks that connect cultural and social invention across the
formal and informal economies. This should not be a dialectical
exercise aimed at reconciling differences that will always be recalci-
trant. We would emphasize instead a different kind of task, aimed
at understanding the mobility of practices across geographical, regulatory and commercial boundaries, and the complicated work of
translation that must go on, as media goods are reassembled and
reconstituted in new ways and places.

Informal media is no longer mysterious or obscure. The internet
has not only enabled all kinds of new informal enterprise; it has also
made the informal more visible than ever before. It follows that our
knowledge of this sphere should no longer be a preserved, obscure
specialty of venturous ethnographers or rare breeds of economists.
Informal media are now the topic of mainstream conversation, and
the informal economy is a mainstream policy concern, central to
some of the most difficult problems for both social science and government. So the next challenge on the horizon may be to shift from
'discovery mode' into 'translation mode'. Future research should help
to refine our policy conversation about informal media – less a conversation sometimes, than a bubbling, unpredictable mix of excitement, panic and resentment. The informal media economy can teach
us many things, and one of them could be a more diverse and delib-
erative policy language. Such a language would be more open to
alternative trade and business systems, more attuned to contemporary transnational cultural practices, and more responsive to their
continuing metamorphosis.

References

AAP (2013) Downloads don't matter. *Sydney Morning Herald*, 26 February. Available at: http://www.smh.com.au/entertainment/tv-and-radio/downloads -dont-matter-20130226-2f36r.html

ACMA (2013) Wireless LANs in the 2.4 GHz band FAQ. Australian Communications and Media Authority. Available at: http://www.acma.gov .au/Citizen/Consumer-info/My-connected-home/Wireless-local-area -networks/wireless-lans in the 24-ghz-band-faqs#park

Adkins, L. & Lury, C. (2011) Introduction: special measures. *The Sociological Review* 59: 5–23.

Ang, I. (1991) *Desperately Seeking the Audience*. Routledge, London.

Arvidsson, A. (2006) *Brands: Meaning and Value in Media Culture*. Routledge, London.

Bacon-Smith, C. (1992) *Enterprising Women: Television Fandom and the Creation of Popular Myth*. University of Pennsylvania Press, Philadelphia.

Bakker, P. (2012) Aggregation, content farms and Huffinization: the rise of low-pay and no-pay journalism. *Journalism Practice* 6 (5–6): 627–637.

Balbi, G. & Prario, B. (2010) The history of Fininvest/Mediaset's media strategy: 30 years of politics, the market, technology and Italian society. *Media, Culture & Society* 32 (3): 391–409.

Balnaves, M., O'Regan, T. & Sternberg, J. (2002) *Mobilizing the Audience*. University of Queensland Press, St Lucia.

Banks, M. (2007) *The Politics of Cultural Work*. Palgrave Macmillan, Basingstoke.

Barbrook, R. & Cameron, A. (1995) The Californian ideology. *Imaginary-Futures.net*. Essay. Available at: http://www.imaginaryfutures.net/2007/ 04/17/the-californian-ideology-2/

Barchiesi, F. (2011) *Precarious Liberation: Workers, the State, and Contested Social Citizenship in Postapartheid South Africa*. State University of New York Press, Albany.

Barrington, J. & Tilley, T. (2011) Breaking the rules to get cheaper iTunes. *Hack* 2011, radio broadcast, Triple J (Australia), 19 January. Available at: http://www.abc.net.au/triplej/hack/stories/s3116740.htm

Bell, D. (1973) *Coming of Post-Industrial Society: A Venture in Social Forecasting?* Basic Books, New York.

Benjamin, W. (2008) *The Work of Art in the Age of Its Technological Reproducibility, and Other Writings on Media*, ed. M. W. Jennings, B. Doherty & T. Y. Levin. Belknap Press, Cambridge MA.

Benkler, Y. (2006) *The Wealth of Networks: How Social Production Transforms Markets and Freedom*. Yale University Press, New Haven.

Bently, L. (2008a) From communication to thing: historical aspects of the conceptualisation of trade marks as property. In: G. B. Dinwoodie & M. D. Janis (eds), *Trademark Law and Theory: A Handbook Of Contemporary Research*. Edward Elgar Publishers, Cheltenham, pp. 3–41.

Bently, L. (2008b) The making of modern trade marks law: the construction of the legal concept of trade mark (1860–80). In: L. Bently, J. C. Ginsburg & J. Davis (eds), *Trade Marks and Brands: An Interdisciplinary Critique*. Cambridge University Press, Cambridge, pp. 3–41.

Bilton, N. (2013a) Content creators use piracy to gauge consumer interest. *New York Times – Bits blog*, 17 September. Available at: http://bits.blogs.nytimes.com/2013/09/17/content-creators-use-piracy-to-gauge-consumer-interest

Bilton, N. (2013b) Disruptions: ride-sharing upstarts challenge taxi industry. *New York Times*. 21 July. Available at: http://bits.blogs.nytimes.com/2013/07/21/disruptions-upstarts-challenge-the-taxi-industry

Brendon, P. (1982) *The Life and Death of the Press Barons*. Secker and Warburg, London.

Briggs, A. & Burke, P. (2005) *A Social History of the Media*, 2nd edition. Polity, Cambridge.

Bromley, R. (1979) *The Urban Informal Sector: Critical Perspectives on Employment and Housing Policies*. Pergamon Press, Oxford.

Brunton, F. (2013) *Spam: A Shadow History of the Internet*. The MIT Press, Cambridge.

Brzezinski, M. (2001) *Casino Moscow: A Tale of Greed and Adventure on Capitalism's Wildest Frontier*. Free Press, New York.

Burgess, J. & Green, J. (2009a) *YouTube: Online Video and Participatory Culture*. Polity, Cambridge.

Burgess, J. & Green, J. (2009b) The entrepreneurial vlogger: participatory culture beyond the professional-amateur divide. In: P. Snickars & P. Vonderau (eds), *The YouTube Reader*. National Library of Sweden, Stockholm, pp. 89–107.

Caldwell, J. T. (2008) *Production Culture: Industrial Reflexivity and Critical Practice in Film and Television*. Duke University Press, Durham.

Caldwell, J. (2013) Stress aesthetics and deprivation payroll systems. In: P. Szczepanik & P. Vonderau (eds), *Behind the Screen: Inside European Production Cultures*. Palgrave, Basingstoke, pp. 91–111.

Carbone, K. (2012) 7 ways to build a brand like Bond. *Fast Company*. 5 November. Available at: http://www.fastcompany.com/3002662/7-ways-build-brand-bond

Carney, S. (2006) iPod gray market booms in India. *Wired*. 23 August. Available at: http://archive.wired.com/gadgets/mac/news/2006/08/71639

Carr, N. (2008) Is Google making us stupid? *The Atlantic*. 1 July. Available at: http://www.theatlantic.com/magazine/archive/2008/07/is-google-making-us-stupid/306868/

Castells, M. & Portes, A. (1989) World underneath: the origins, dynamics, and effects of the informal economy. In: A. Portes, M. Castells & L. A. Benton (eds), *The Informal Economy: Studies in Advanced and Less Developed Countries*. Johns Hopkins University Press, Baltimore, pp. 11–40.

Chenoweth, N. (2012) *Murdoch's Pirates*. Allen & Unwin, Sydney.

Choice (2012) Submission to House Standing Committee on Infrastructure and Communications Inquiry into IT Pricing. Available at: http://www.choice.com.au/media-and-news/consumer-news/news/%7E/media/EBC68BC786FA4161AF1E2E966B442DB4.ashx

Chopra, R. (2012) American saints. *The New Inquiry*. 25 September. Available at: http://thenewinquiry.com/essays/american-saints/

Christin, N. (2013). Traveling the Silk Road: a measurement analysis of a large anonymous online marketplace. *Proceedings of the 22nd International Conference on World Wide Web*. Rio de Janeiro, Brazil, pp. 213–224.

Christopherson, S. & Storper M. (1989) The effects of flexible specialization on industrial politics and the labor market: the motion picture industry. *Industrial and Labor Relations Review* 42 (3): 331–47.

Church, R. (1999) New perspectives on the history of products, firms, marketing and consumers in Britain and the United States since the mid-nineteenth century. *Economic History Review* 52: 405–435.

Clarke, I. & Owens, M. (2000) Trademark rights in gray markets. *International Marketing Review* 17 (3): 272–286.

Coase, R. H. (1959) The Federal Communications Commission. *Journal of Law and Economics* 2 (October), 1–40.

Coombe, R. (1998) *The Cultural Life of Intellectual Properties: Authorship, Appropriation, and the Law*. Duke University Press, Durham.

Cornish, W. (2010) Personality rights and intellectual property. In: W. Cornish, J. S. Anderson, R. Cocks, M. Lobban, P. Polden & K. Smith (eds), *The Oxford History of the Laws of England: Volume XIII: 1820–1914: Fields of Development*. Oxford University Press, Oxford.

Cross, J. & Morales, A. (eds) (2007) *Street Entrepreneurs: People, Place and Politics in Local and Global Perspective*. Routledge, London.

Cuneo, C. (2010) He's sold 1.9m CDs, played stadiums but you don't know him. *Daily Telegraph*. 29 January, p. 3.

Cunningham, S. (2013) *Hidden Innovation: Policy, Industry and the Creative Sector*. University of Queensland Press, St Lucia.

Curtin, M. (2003) Media capital: towards the study of spatial flows. *International Journal of Cultural Studies* 6 (2): 202–228.

Dannen, F. (1991) *Hit Men*. Vintage Books, New York.

De Beer, J., Fu, K. & Wunsch-Vincent, S. (2013) The informal economy, innovation and intellectual property – concepts, metrics and policy considerations. WIPO Economic Research Working Paper No. 10. World Intellectual Property Organization, Geneva.

Desrosières, A. (2002) *The Politics of Large Numbers: A History of Statistical Reasoning*. Harvard University Press, Cambridge, MA.

Deuze, M. (2007) *Media Work*. Polity, Cambridge.

Deuze, M. (ed.) (2011) *Managing Media Work*. Sage, Thousand Oaks.

Doctorow, C. (2008) BBC sends legal threat over fan's *Dr Who* knitting patterns. *BoingBoing*. 9 May. Available at: http://boingboing.net/2008/05/09/bbc-sends-legal-thre.html

du Gay, P. (1995) *Consumption and Identity at Work*. Sage, London.

Dwyer, T. (2013) Flapping lips and flubtitles: revaluing screen translation. PhD thesis, School of Culture and Communication, University of Melbourne.

ea_spouse (2004) EA: The human story. blog post. 10 November. Available at: http://ea-spouse.livejournal.com/274.html

Eisenstein, E. (1979) *The Printing Press as an Agent of Change: Communications and Cultural Transformations in Early Modern Europe*. Cambridge University Press, Cambridge.

Elahi, S., De Beer, J., Kowooya, D., Oguamanam, C. & Rizk, N. (2013) *Knowledge & Innovation in Africa: Scenarios for the Future*. University of Cape Town Press/Open AIR Network, Cape Town.

European Commission (2007) *Towards Common Principles of Flexicurity: More and Better Jobs Through Flexibility and Security*. European Commission, Directorate-General for Employment, Social Affairs and Equal Opportunities, Brussels.

Ewing, J. (2002) This ex-hacker's fat is in the fire. *Business Week*. 11 April. Available at: http://www.businessweek.com/bwdaily/dnflash/apr2002/nf20020411_3688.htm

Ewing, S. (2013) Knowing the Australian internet: statistics, public policy and media industry disruption. PhD thesis, Swinburne University of Technology.

Fantone, L. (2007) Precarious changes: gender and generational politics in contemporary Italy. *Feminist Review* 87: 5–20.

Florida, R. (2003) *The Rise of the Creative Class*. Basic Books, New York.

Frank, T. (2010) Bright frenetic mills. *Harper's Magazine*. December, pp. 11–13.

French Solutions (2008) Key performance indicators (KPI). *Frenchsolutions ltd.com*. Available at: http://www.frenchsolutionsltd.com/Attention_Seeker.php

Friedman, T. (2005) *The World Is Flat: A Brief History of the Twenty-first Century*. Farrar, Straus and Giroux, New York.

Fuchs, C. (2013) *Digital Labour and Karl Marx*. Routledge, London.

Fuchs, C. & Sevignani, S. (2013) What is digital labour? What is digital work? What's their difference? And why do these questions matter for understanding social media? *TripleC: Communication, Capitalism & Critique* 11 (2): 237–293.

Galloway, A. (2004) *Protocol: How Control Exists after Decentralization*. The MIT Press, Cambridge.

Gardner, E. (2011) Rapper/mogul Jay-Z decodes his life story in an unusual way. *USA Today*. 16 November. Available at: http://www.usatoday.com/life/music/news/2010-11-16-jayz16_CV_N.htm

Gardner, E. (2012) Meet Alki David: the billionaire Hollywood bad boy being sued by every TV network. *Hollywood Reporter*. 4 October. Available at: http://www.hollywoodreporter.com/news/alki-david-filmon-chris-brown-drake-charlie-sheen-376000

Garnham, N. (1990) *Capitalism and Communication: Global Culture and the Economics of Information*. Sage, London.

Gerry, C. (1987) Developing economies and the informal sector in historical perspective. *Annals of the American Academy of Political and Social Science* 493: 100–119.

Gertz, S. (2007) Advanced Book Exchange (ABE) Changing tunes? *David Brass Rare Books*. 12 July. Available at: http://www.davidbrassrarebooks.com/?p=49

Gibson-Graham, J. K. (2006) *A Postcapitalist Politics*. University of Minnesota Press, Minneapolis.

Gill, R. (2011) 'Life is a pitch': managing the self in new media work. In: M. Deuze (ed.), *Managing Media Work*. Sage Publishing, Thousand Oaks, pp. 249–262.

Gill, R. (2013) Inequalities in media work. In: P. Szczepanik & P. Vonderau (eds), *Behind the Screen: Inside European Production Cultures*. Palgrave, Basingstoke, pp. 189–206.

Gill, R. & Pratt, A. (2008) In the social factory? Immaterial labour, precariousness and cultural work. *Theory, Culture & Society* 25 (7–8): 1–30.

Gillespie, T. (2009) *Wired Shut: Copyright and the Shape of Digital Culture*. The MIT Press, Cambridge.

Gladwell, M. (2011) The tweaker: the real genius of Steve Jobs. *The New Yorker*. 14 November. Available at: http://www.newyorker.com/reporting/2011/11/14/111114fa_fact_gladwell

Glotzbach, M. & Heckmann, O. (2014) Look ahead: creator features coming to YouTube. *Creators: The Official YouTube Partners and Creators Blog*. June 26. Available at: http://youtubecreator.blogspot.com/2014/06/look-ahead-creator-features-coming-to.html

Good, O. (2009) Valve bans gray-market *Modern Warfare 2* keys. *Kotaku.com* Available at: http://kotaku.com/5409642/valve-bans-gray+market-modern-warfare-2-keys

Google (2014) Link schemes. *Google webmaster tools.* Available at: https://support.google.com/webmasters/answer/66356

Greenberg, J. M. (2008) *From Betamax to Blockbuster: Video Stores and the Invention of Movies on Video.* The MIT Press, Cambridge.

Gregg, M. (2011) *Work's Intimacy.* Polity, Cambridge.

Guha-Khasnobis, B., Kanbur, R. & Ostrom, E. (2006) *Linking the Formal and Informal Economy: Concepts and Policies.* Oxford University Press, Oxford.

Gurtoo, A. & Williams, C. C. (2009) Entrepreneurship and the informal sector: some lessons from India. *Entrepreneurship and Innovation* 10 (1): 55–62.

Hacking, I. (1990) *The Taming of Chance.* Cambridge University Press, Cambridge.

Haigh, G. (2010) Untitled Article. *Testmatchsofa.com.* Available at: http://archive.today/FWI6J

Harding, P. & Jenkins, R. (1989) *The Myth of the Hidden Economy: Towards a New Understanding of Informal Economic Activity.* Open University Press, Milton Keynes.

Hardt, M. & Negri, A. (2000) *Empire.* Harvard University Press, Cambridge.

Hardt, M. & Negri, A. (2004) *Multitude: War and Democracy in the Age of Empire.* Penguin, New York.

Hart, K. (1973) Informal income opportunities and urban employment in Ghana. *Journal of Modern African Studies* 11 (1): 61–89.

Hart, K. (2009) On the informal economy: the political history of an ethnographic concept. *CEB Working Paper No. 09/042.* Centre Emile Bernheim, Brussels.

Hazlett, T. W., Munoz, R. E. & Avanzini, D. B. (2011) What really matters in spectrum allocation design. *George Mason Law & Economics Research Paper 11–48.* 27 October. Available at: http://ssrn.com/abstract=1961225

Heller, N. (2013) Bay watched. *The New Yorker.* 14 October. Available at: http://www.newyorker.com/reporting/2013/10/14/131014fa_fact_heller?currentPage=all

Helmke, G. & Levitsky, S. (2012) Informal institutions and comparative politics: a research agenda. In: T. Christiansen & C. Neuhold (eds), *International Handbook on Informal Governance.* Edward Elgar, Cheltenham, pp. 85–113.

Hemmungs Wirtén, E. (2011) *Cosmopolitan Copyright: Law and Language in the Translation Zone.* Uppsala University, Uppsala.

Henry, S. (ed.) (1981) *Can I Have it in Cash?: A Study of Informal Institutions and Unorthodox Ways of Doing Things.* Astragal, London.

Henry, S. (1983) *Private Justice: Towards Integrated Theorising in the Sociology of Law.* Routledge & Kegan Paul, London.

Hesmondhalgh, D. (2011) Assessing media labour in the digital age. Conference paper. *International Communication Association Annual Conference.* Boston.

Hesmondhalgh, D. & Baker, S. (2011) *Creative Labour: Media Work In Three Cultural Industries*. Routledge, Abingdon.

Hess, C. & Ostrom, E. (eds) (2005) *Understanding Knowledge as a Commons: From Theory to Practice*. The MIT Press, Cambridge.

Holt, J. & Perren, A. (2009) *Media Industries: History, Theory, and Method*. Wiley, Malden.

Howkins, J. (2001) *The Creative Economy: How People Make Money from Ideas*. Penguin, London.

HRSCIC (2013) At what cost? IT pricing and the Australia tax. House of Representatives Standing Committee on Infrastructure and Communications. Parliament of the Commonwealth of Australia, Canberra.

Hu, K. (2013) Chinese subtitle groups and the neoliberal work ethic. In: E. B. Ari & N. Otmazgin (eds), *Popular Culture Collaborations and Coproductions in East and Southeast Asia*. Kyoto University Press, Kyoto, pp. 207–232.

Humphrey, C. (2002) *The Unmaking of Soviet Life: Everyday Economies After Socialism*. Cornell University Press, Ithaca.

Hunter, D., Lobato, R., Richardson, M. & Thomas, J. (eds) (2012) *Amateur Media: Social, Cultural and Legal Perspectives*. Taylor and Francis, Hoboken.

Interbrand (2013) Best global brands 2013. Available at: http://www .interbrand.com/en/best-global-brands/2013/Best-Global-Brands-2013 .aspx

International Labour Office (1972) Employment, Incomes and Equality: A Strategy for Increasing Productive Employment in Kenya. Geneva. Available at: http://www.ilo.org/public/libdoc/ilo/1972/72B09_608_engl .pdf

IPSOS and Oxford Economics (2011). Economic consequences of movie piracy. Report commissioned by the Australian Federation Against Copyright Theft. Available at: http://www.mpalibrary.org/assets/IPSOS _Economic_Consequences_of_Movie_Piracy_-_Australia.pdf

Isaacson, W. (2011) *Steve Jobs*. Simon and Schuster, New York.

Ito, M. (2012) Contributors versus leechers: fansubbing ethics and a hybrid public culture. In: M. Ito, D. Okabe & I. Tsuji (eds), *Fandom Unbound: Otaku Culture in a Connected World*. Yale University Press, New Haven, pp. 179–204.

Jeffries, A. (2013) Taxicab association issues fear mongering warning about 'rogue apps' like Uber. *The Verge*. 4 September. Available at: http://www .theverge.com/2012/9/4/3292470/taxicab-limousine-paratransit -association-warning-rogue-apps-uber

Jenkins, H., Ford, S. & Green, J. (2012) *Spreadable Media: Creating Value and Meaning in a Networked Culture*. New York University Press, New York.

Johns, A. (1998) *The Nature of the Book: Print and Knowledge in the Making*. University of Chicago Press, Chicago.

Johns, A. (2009) *Piracy: The Intellectual Property Wars from Gutenberg to Gates*. University of Chicago Press, Chicago.

Kan, M. (2011) Close to half the iPads sold in China are from the gray market. *PC World*. 11 October. Available at: http://www.pcworld.idg .com.au/article/403683/close_half_ipads_sold_china_from_gray_market/

Kandavel, S. (2013) Piracy capital of South Burma Bazaar losing out to online rivals. *The Economic Times*. 20 April. Available at: http://articles .economictimes.indiatimes.com/2013-04-20/news/38693201_1_vcds-and -dvds-piracy-burma-bazaar

Karaganis, J. (ed.) (2011) *Media Piracy in Emerging Economies*. Social Science Research Council, New York.

Kelion, L. (2013) Netflix studies piracy sites to decide what to buy. *BBC News*. 16 September. Available at: http://www.bbc.co.uk/news/ technology-24108673

Kelley, N. (2002) Notes on the political economy of black music. In: N. Kelley (ed.), *Rhythm and Business: The Political Economy of Black Music*. Akashic Books, New York, pp. 6–23.

Kessler, A. (2013) Travis Kalanick: the transportation trustbuster. *Wall Street Journal*. 25 January. Available at: http://online.wsj.com/news/articles/SB1 0001424127887324235104578244231122376480

Klein, N. (1999) *No Space, No Choice, No Jobs, No Logo: Taking Aim at the Brand Bullies*. Picador, New York.

Kramer, A. (2005) Starbucks' move on Moscow market is stymied by a trademark squatter. *International Herald Tribune*, 12 October, F3.

Kravets, D. (2011) Mug-shot industry will dig up your past, charge you to bury it again. *Wired*. 2 August. Available at: http://www.wired.com/ threatlevel/2011/08/mugshots/

Lanier, J. (2013) *Who Owns the Future?* Alfred A. Knopf, New York.

Latour, B. (1991) Technology is society made durable. In: J. Law (ed.), *A Sociology of Monsters: Essays on Power, Technology and Domination*. Routledge, London, pp. 103–131.

Laville, J.-L. (2010) Plural economy. In K. Hart, J.-L. Laville and A. D. Cattani (eds), *The Human Economy*. Polity, Cambridge, pp. 77–83.

Leadbeater, C. & Oakley, K. (1999) *The Independents: Britain's New Cultural Entrepreneurs*. Demos, London.

Lee, D. (2012) The Ethics of insecurity: risk, individualization and value in British independent television production. *Television & New Media* 13 (6): 480–497.

LEK Consulting (2005) The cost of movie piracy: an analysis prepared by LEK for the Motion Picture Association. Available at: http://www.archive .org/stream/MpaaPiracyReort/LeksummarympaRevised_djvu.txt

Leonard, A. (2014) The 1 percent's loathsome libertarian scheme: why we despise the new scalping economy. *Salon*. 11 July. Available at: http://www .salon.com/2014/07/11/the_1_percents_loathsome_libertarian _scheme_why_we_despise_the_new_scalping_economy/

Lessig, L. (1999) *Code and Other Laws of Cyberspace*. Bashowic Books, New York.

Lessig, L. (2001) *The Future of Ideas*. Random House, New York.

Lessig, L. (2004) Coase's first question. *Regulation* 27: 3–4, 38–41.

Lewis, M. (1999) *The New New Thing: A Silicon Valley Story.* WW Norton, London.

Leyshon, A., Lee, R. & Williams, C. C. (2003) *Alternative Economic Spaces.* Sage, London.

Liang, L. (2009) Piracy, creativity and infrastructure: rethinking access to culture. *SSRN eLibrary.* Available at: http://ssrn.com/paper=1436229

Lobato, R. (2012) *Shadow Economies of Cinema: Mapping Informal Film Distribution.* British Film Institute, London.

Lobato, R. & Thomas, J. (2011) The Business of Anti-Piracy: New Zones of Enterprise in the Copyright Wars. *International Journal of Communication* 5: 1–20.

Luckman, S. (2013) Precarious labour then and now: the British Arts and Crafts movement and creative work revisited. In: M. Banks, S. Taylor & R. Gill (eds), *Theorizing Cultural Work: Labour, Continuity and Change in the Creative Industries.* Palgrave, Basingstoke, pp. 19–29.

Lukacs, G. (2013) Dreamwork: cell phone novelists, labor, and politics in contemporary Japan. *Cultural Anthropology* 28 (1): 44–64.

Lury, C. (2004) *Brands: The Logos of the Global Economy.* Routledge, New York.

Lury, C. (2008) Trade mark style as a way of fixing things. In: L. Bently, J. Davis & J. Ginsburg (eds), *Trade Marks and Brands An Interdisciplinary Critique.* Cambridge University Press, Cambridge, pp. 201–222.

Mathews, G. (2011) *Ghetto at the Center of the World: Chungking Mansions, Hong Kong.* Hong Kong University Press, Hong Kong.

Mattioli, D. (2012) On Orbitz, Mac Users Steered to Pricier Hotels. *Wall Street Journal.* 23 August. Available at: http://online.wsj.com/news/articles/SB10001424052702304458604577488822266/325882

Mayer, V. (2011) *Below the Line: Producers and Production Studies in the New Television Economy.* Duke University Press, Durham.

Mayer, V., Banks, M. J. & Caldwell, J. T. (2009) *Production Studies: Cultural Studies of Media Industries.* Routledge, New York.

McBride, S. (2013) Insight: in Silicon Valley start-up world, pedigree counts. *Reuters.com.* 12 September. Available at: http://www.reuters.com/article/2013/09/12/us-usa-startup-connections-insight-idUSBRE98B15U20130912

McChesney, R. (2013) *Digital Disconnect: How Capitalism is Turning the Internet Against Democracy.* The New Press, New York.

McRobbie, A. (2002) Clubs to companies: notes on the decline of political culture in speeded up creative worlds. *Cultural Studies* 16 (4): 516–531.

McRobbie, A. (2011) Reflections on feminism, immaterial labour and the post-Fordist regime. *New Formations* 70: 60–76.

McShane, I., Meredyth, D. & Wilson, C. (2014) Broadband as civic infrastructure – the Australian case. *Media International Australia* 151: 127–136.

Mendes Moreira de Sa, V. (2013) Rethinking 'pirate audiences': an investigation of TV audiences' informal online viewing and distribution practices in Brazil. PhD thesis, University of Western Sydney.

Miller, T. (2010) Culture + Labour = Precariat. *Communication and Critical/ Cultural Studies* 7 (1): 96–99.

Mitchell, T. (2008) Rethinking economy. *Geoforum* 39: 1116–1121.

Moll, Y. (2010) Islamic televangelism: religion, media and visuality in contemporary Egypt. *Arab Media and Society* 10. Available at: http://www.arabmediasociety.com/index.php?article=732&p=0

MPAA (2011) MPAA statement on strong showing of support for Stop Online Piracy Act. Press release. 16 December.

Muise, K. (2011) Freelance writing: how to write a 300 word article in under an hour and avoid the traps of distraction! *Yahoo! Voices*. 30 May. Available at: http://voices.yahoo.com/freelance-writing-write-300-word -article-8559805.html?cat=31

Murphy, J. (1998) What is branding? In Hart, S. & Murphy, J. (eds) *Brands: The New Wealth Creators*. Macmillan, London, pp. 1–12.

Nakassis, C. V. (2013) Brands and their surfeits. *Cultural Anthropology* 28 (1): 111–126.

Napoli, P. (2003). *Audience Economics: Media Institutions and the Audience Marketplace*. New York, Columbia University Press.

Napoli, P. (2011). *Audience Evolution: New Technologies and the Transformation of Media Audiences*. New York, Columbia University Press.

Negus, K. (1999) The music business and rap: between the street and the executive suite. *Cultural Studies* 13 (3): 488–508.

Neilson, B. & Rossiter, N. (2005) From precarity to precariousness and back again: labour, life and unstable networks. *Fibreculture* 5. Available at: http://five.fibreculturejournal.org/fcj-022-from-precarity-to -precariousness-and-back-again-labour-life-and-unstable-networks/

Neilson, B. & Rossiter, N. (2008) Precarity as a political concept, or, Fordism as exception. *Theory, Culture & Society* 25 (7–8): 51–72.

Noam, E. M. (1987) Broadcasting in Italy: an overview. *Columbia Journal of World Business* 22 (3): 19–24.

Nyong'o, T. (2013) Situating precarity between the body and the commons. *Women & Performance: A Journal of Feminist Theory* 23 (2): 157–161.

Oakley, K. (2011) In its own image: New Labour and the cultural workforce. *Cultural Trends* 20 (3–4): 287.

OECD (2009) *Is Informal Normal? Towards More and Better Jobs in Developing Countries*. Organisation for Economic Co-operation and Development, Paris.

Okome, O. (2007) 'The message is reaching a lot of people': proselytizing and the video films of Helen Ukpabio. *Postcolonial Text* 3 (2):1–20. Available at: http://journals.sfu.ca/pocol/index.php/pct/article/view/750/419

Olanoff, D. (2012) Lyft's focus on community and the story behind the pink mustache. *TechCrunch*. 17 September. Available at: http://techcrunch.com/2012/09/17/lyfts-focus-on-community-and-the-story-behind -the-pink-mustache/

O'Regan, T. (1991) From piracy to sovereignty: international VCR trends. *Continuum* 4 (2), 112–135. Available at: http://wwwmcc.murdoch.edu.au/ReadingRoom/4.2/oregan.html

O'Regan, T. (2012) Remembering video: reflections on the first explosion of informal media markets through the VCR. *Television and New Media* 13: 383–398.

O'Regan, T., Balnaves, M. & Goldsmith, B. (2011) *Rating the Audience: The Business of Media*. Bloomsbury Academic, London.

Packard, V. (1957) *The Hidden Persuaders*. Longmans, Green & Co., London.

Page, W. (2011) Economic insight 22: wallet share. PRS for Music, London. Available at: http://www.prsformusic.com/aboutus/policyandresearch/researchandeconomics

Peterson, R. A. & Berger, D. G. (1971) Entrepreneurship in organisations: evidence from the popular music industry. *Administrative Science Quarterly* 16 (1), 97–106.

Picard, R. (2010) Content farms and the exploitation of information. *The Media Business Blog*. Available at: http://themediabusiness.blogspot.com.au/2010/12/content-farms-and-exploitation-of.html

Pinheiro-Machado, R. (2010) The attribution of authenticity to 'real' and 'fake' branded commodities in Brazil and China. In: A. Bevan & D. Wengrow (eds), *Cultures of Commodity Branding*. Left Coast Press, Walnut Creek, pp. 109–129.

Pinheiro-Machado, R. (2012) Copied goods and the informal economy in Brazil and China: outlining a comparison of development models. *Vibrant: Virtual Brazilian Anthropology* 9 (1): 335–359.

Pinheiro-Machado, R. & Scalco, L. M. (2012) Brand clans: consumption and rituals among low-income young people in the city of Porto Alegre. *International Review of Social Research* 2 (1): 107–126.

Polanyi, K. (1944) *The Great Transformation*. Farrar & Rinehart, New York.

Poliakoff, K. (2000) License to copyright: the ongoing dispute over the ownership of James Bond. *Cardozo Arts & Entertainment Law Journal* 18, 387–426.

Popkin, J. D. (1993) The business of political enlightenment in France, 1770–1800. In: J. Brewer & R. Porter (eds), *Consumption and the World of Goods*. Routledge, London, pp. 412–436.

Porter, T. (1996) *Trust in Numbers: The Pursuit of Objectivity in Science and Public Life*. Princeton University Press, Princeton.

Rangaswamy, N. & Smythe, T. (2012) Assembling and aggregating mobile phones: the social ecology of grey mobile phone markets in urban India. *Proceedings of M4D 2012*, 28–29 February. New Delhi, India.

Rankin, J. (2013) Sheryl Sandberg sells $90m of Facebook stock. *Guardian*. 13 August. Available at: http://www.theguardian.com/technology/2013/aug/12/sheryl-sandberg-facebook-stock-sale

Rennie, E., Berkeley, L. & Murphet, B. (2010) Community media and ethical choice. *3CMedia Journal* 6: 11–25.

Reed, D. P. (2002) Comments for FCC Spectrum Policy Task Force on spectrum policy. *Reed.com*. Blog post. Available at: http://www.reed.com/dpr/?sel=OpenSpectrum/FCC02-135Reed.html

Reuters (2013) Flywheel raises $14.8M to help taxi drivers keep up with Lyft, Uber, Sidecar. *Reuters.com*. 31 July. Available at: http://www.reuters.com/article/2013/07/31/idUS357782201520130731

Richardson, M. & Goldenfein, J. (2013) Competing myths of informal economies. In: D. Hunter, R. Lobato, M. Richardson & J. Thomas (eds), *Amateur Media: Social, Cultural and Legal Perspectives*. Routledge, London, pp. 8–26.

Robichaux, M. (2003) *Cable Cowboy: John Malone and the Rise of the Modern Cable Business*. Wiley, Hoboken.

Robinson, T. M. (2011) The many faces of 50. *Black Enterprise*. January, 75–78.

Ross, A. (2003) *No-Collar: The Humane Workplace and Its Hidden Costs*. Basic Books, New York.

Ross, A. (2007) Nice work if you can get it: the mercurial career of creative industries policy. In: G. Lovink & N. Rossiter (eds), *My Creativity Reader: A Critique of Creative Industries*. Institute of Network Cultures, Amsterdam, pp. 108–125. Available at: http://networkcultures.org/_uploads/32.pdf

Ross, A. (2009) *Nice Work If You Can Get It: Life and Labor in Precarious Times*. New York University Press, New York.

Rossiter, N. (2006) *Organised Networks: Media Theory, Creative Labour, New Institutions*. Institute of Network Cultures, Amsterdam.

Rushe, D. (2012) The online copyright war: the day the internet hit back at big media. *Guardian*. 19 April. Available at: http://www.theguardian.com/technology/2012/apr/18/online-copyright-war-internet-hit-back

Sanchez, J. (2008) 750,000 lost jobs? The dodgy digits behind the war on piracy. *Ars Technica*, 8 October. Available at: http://arstechnica.com/tech-policy/2008/10/dodgy-digits-behind-the-war-on-piracy/

Sandberg, S. (2013) *Lean In: Women, Work, and the Will to Lead*. Alfred A. Knopf, New York.

Sanin, J-D. (2012). Informal media economies in Colombia. Unpublished report.

Santos, M. (1979) *The Shared Space: The Circuits of the Urban Economy in Underdeveloped Countries*. Methuen, London.

Sassen, S. (1988) New York City's informal economy. ISSR Working Papers 4 (9). Institute for Social Science Research, UCLA.

Sassen, S. (2008) *Territory, Authority, Rights: From Medieval to Global Assemblages*. Princeton University Press, Princeton.

Schechter, F. I. (1927) The rational basis of trademark protection. *Harvard Law Review* 40 (6): 813–833.

Schumpeter, J. A. (1996/1954) *History of Economic Analysis*. Oxford University Press, New York.

Scott, A. J. (2004a) *On Hollywood: The Place, The Industry*. Princeton University Press, Princeton.

Scott, A. J. (2004b) The Other Hollywood: the Organisational and Geographic Bases of Television-Program Production. *Media, Culture & Society* 26 (2): 183–205.

Shi, Y. (2011) iPhones in China: the contradictory stories of media-ICT globalization in the era of media convergence and corporate synergy. *Journal of Communication Inquiry* 35 (2): 134–156.

Sloan, P. (2013) Spotify's Daniel Ek: I don't worry about Apple, Google. *Cnet.* 12 March. Available at: http://news.cnet.com/8301-14013_3-57573893/spotifys-daniel-ek-i-dont-worry-about-apple-google/

Smith, C. H. (2003) 'I don't like to dream about getting paid': representations of social mobility and the emergence of the hip-hop mogul. *Social Text* 21 (4): 69–97.

Srinivas, S. V. (2003) Hong Kong action film in the Indian B circuit. *Inter-Asia Cultural Studies* 4 (1): 40–62.

Stahl, M. (2013) *Unfree Masters: Recording Artists and the Politics of Work.* Duke University Press, Durham.

Sterne, J. (2012) *MP3: The Meaning of a Format.* Duke University Press, Durham.

Stille, A. (2006) *The Sack of Rome: How a Beautiful European Country with a Fabled History and a Storied Culture Was Taken Over by a Man Named Silvio Berlusconi.* Penguin, New York.

Stone, B. (2009) Amazon faces a fight over its e-books. *New York Times.* 26 July. Available at: http://www.nytimes.com/2009/07/27/technology/companies/27amazon.html?_r=0

Streeter, T. (2011) *The Net Effect: Romanticism, Capitalism, and the Internet.* New York University Press, New York.

Streitfeld, D. (2012) A lawsuit shakes foundation of a man's world of tech. *New York Times,* 3 June, BU1.

Sugden, D. R. (2009) *Gray Markets: Prevention, Detection, and Litigation.* Oxford University Press, Oxford.

Sundaram, R. (2009) *Pirate Modernity: Delhi's Media Urbanism.* Routledge, London.

Swisher, K. (2013) Exclusive: Japan's Rakuten acquires Viki video site for $200 million. *All Things Digital.* 1 September. Available at: http://allthingsd.com/20130901/exclusive-japans-rakuten-acquires-viki-video-site-for-200-million/

Szczepanik, P. & Vonderau, P. (eds) (2013) *Behind the Screen: Inside European Production Cultures.* Palgrave, Basingstoke.

Terranova, T. (2000) Free labor: producing culture for the digital economy. *Social Text* 18 (2): 33–58.

Thomas, R. D. (ed.) (2003). *Secrets of Piracy Investigation for Private Investigators.* Thomas Investigative Publications, Austin.

Thompson, J. B. (2010) *Merchants of Culture: The Publishing Business in the Twenty-First Century.* Polity, Cambridge.

TorrentFreak (2010) Anti-piracy tool for cinemas will recognize emotions. 11 February. Available at: http://torrentfreak.com/anti-piracy-tool-for-cinemas-will-recognize-emotions-101102/

TorrentFreak (2012) 'Game of Thrones' most pirated TV show of 2012. 23 December. Available at: http://torrentfreak.com/game-of-thrones-most-pirated-tv-show-of-2012-121223/

TorrentFreak (2013a) 'Game of Thrones' most pirated TV show of 2013. 25 December. Available at: http://torrentfreak.com/game-of-thrones-most-pirated-tv-show-of-2013-131225/

TorrentFreak (2013b) BBC Thinks TorrentFreak is a *Doctor Who Game of Thrones* pirate. 2 May. Available at: http://torrentfreak.com/bbc-thinks-torrentfreak-is-a-doctor-who-game-of-thrones-pirate-130502/

TorrentFreak (2014) Foul!!! Sony orders Google to censor the World Cup. 22 June. Available at: http://torrentfreak.com/foul-sony-orders-google-to-censor-the-world-cup-140622/

Turow, J. (2006) *Niche Envy: Marketing Discrimination in the Digital Age.* MIT Press, Cambridge, Mass.

UNESCO (2013) *Creative Economy Report 2013 Special Edition: Widening Local Development Pathways.* UNESCO and United Nations Development Programme, Paris and New York.

USTR (2001) WTO dispute with Greece over television piracy resolved. Press Release. Office of the United States Trade Representative, Washington, DC. Available at: http://www.ustr.gov/archive/Document_Library/Press_Releases/2001/March/WTO_Dispute_with_Greece_over_Television_Piracy_Resolved.html

Viebrock, E. & Clasen, J. (2009) Flexicurity – a state-of-the art review. Working Papers on the Reconciliation of Work and Welfare in Europe, Edinburgh. Available at: http://www.socialpolicy.ed.ac.uk/__data/assets/pdf_file/0013/31009/REC-WP_0109_Viebrock_Clasen.pdf

Virno, P. (2004) *A Grammar of the Multitude: For an Analysis of Contemporary Forms of Life.* Semiotext(e), New York.

Vonderau, P. (2009) Writers becoming users: YouTube hype and the writer's strike. In: P. Snickars & P. Vonderau (eds), *The YouTube Reader.* National Library of Sweden, Stockholm, pp. 108–125.

Vonderau, P. (2010) Understanding Orlova: YouTube producers, *Hot For Words*, and some pitfalls of production studies. *Wide Screen* 2, 2. Available at: http://widescreenjournal.org/index.php/journal/article/view/28/35

Vonderau, P. (2013) Beyond piracy: understanding digital markets. In: J. Holt & K. Sanson (eds), *Connected Viewing: Selling, Streaming, & Sharing Media in the Digital Age.* Routledge, London, pp. 99–123.

Wadhwa, T. (2013) The sharing economy fights back against regulators. *Forbes.com.* 16 September. Available at: http://www.forbes.com/sites/tarunwadhwa/2013/09/16/the-sharing-economy-fights-back-against-regulators-with-an-advocacy-group/

Wilkins, M. (1992) The neglected intangible asset: the influence of the trade mark on the rise of the modern corporation. *Business History* 34 (1): 66–95.

Williams, C. C. & Nadin, S. (2010) Entrepreneurship and the informal economy: an overview. *Journal of Developmental Entrepreneurship* 15 (4): 361–378.

Williams, C. J. (2001) Ego-trip through cyberspace yields riches. *Los Angeles Times.* 18 February. Available at: http://articles.latimes.com/2001/feb/18/news/mn-27176

Williams, M. (2009) Virgin Media to trial file sharing monitoring system. *The Register*. 26 November. Available at: http://www.theregister.co .uk/2009/11/26/virgin_media_detica/

WIPO (2013) *World Intellectual Property Report: Brands – Reputation and Image in the Global Marketplace*. World Intellectual Property Organisation Economics & Statistics Series, Geneva.

Zittrain, J. (2008) *The Future of the Internet (and How to Stop It)*. Yale University Press, New Haven.

Index